# The MAILBOX®
## The Idea Magazine For Teachers®
### PRIMARY

# 2003–2004
# YEARBOOK

The Education Center, Inc.
Greensboro, North Carolina

*The Mailbox® 2003–2004 Primary Yearbook*

**Managing Editor, *The Mailbox* Magazine:** Amy Erickson

**Managing Editor, *The Mailbox* Yearbook:** Allison E. Ward

**Editorial Team:** Kimberley Bruck, Karen P. Shelton, Diane Badden, Sharon Murphy, Karen A. Brudnak, Sarah Hamblet, Hope Rodgers, Dorothy C. McKinney

**Production Team:** Lisa K. Pitts, Lois Axeman (COVER ARTIST), Pam Crane, Clevell Harris, Rebecca Saunders, Jennifer Tipton Bennett, Chris Curry, Theresa Lewis Goode, Ivy L. Koonce, Troy Lawrence, Clint Moore, Greg D. Rieves, Barry Slate, Donna K. Teal, Tazmen Carlisle, Amy Kirtley-Hill, Kristy Parton, Debbie Shoffner, Cathy Edwards Simrell, Lynette Dickerson, Mark Rainey, Karen Brewer Grossman

ISBN 1-56234-613-X
ISSN 1088-5544

Printed in the United States of America.

The Education Center, Inc.
P.O. Box 9753
Greensboro, NC 27429-0753

Look for *The Mailbox® 2004–2005 Kindergarten–Grade 1 Yearbook* and *The Mailbox® 2004–2005 Grades 2–3 Yearbook* in the summer of 2005. The Education Center, Inc., is the publisher of *The Mailbox*®, *Teacher's Helper*®, *The Mailbox*® BOOKBAG®, and *Learning*® magazines, as well as other fine products. Look for these wherever quality teacher materials are sold, or call 1-800-714-7991.

# Contents

# ARTS & CRAFTS

# Arts & Crafts

## Crayon Buddy

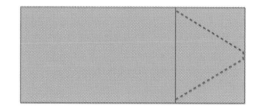

Create a colorful display of student-made crayon buddies! If desired, use the artwork to inspire color-related list poems or to complement the crayon unit that begins on page 264.

**Materials for one crayon buddy:**
6" x 9" construction paper rectangle (for crayon)
two 4½" x 6" construction paper rectangles (for crayon tip, hands, and feet)
two ¾" x 6" black construction paper strips
four 1" x 9" black construction paper strips
pencil
glue
black marker
scissors
stapler

**Steps:**
1. Position one small rectangle horizontally. Draw a crayon tip on it as illustrated and then cut it out.
2. Glue the large rectangle to the tip to resemble a crayon.
3. Make a thin, wavy cut along the long sides of each short black strip. Then glue the strips onto the crayon as shown.
4. Use the marker to draw a face.
5. Accordion-fold the long black strips. Staple them in place to make two arms and two legs.
6. Fold the remaining rectangle in half and then in half again. Unfold it and then cut the rectangle into quarters.
7. Cut an oval from each quarter to make hands and feet. Glue them in place.

Sheila Criqui-Kelley—Gr. 1, Lebo Elementary, Lebo, KS

## Apple Notecards

Whether students use these notecards for open house invitations or to tell their families about a great school week, they'll be a bushel of fun to prepare and deliver! To make one notecard, write a desired message on the lined side of a 4" x 6" index card. Set it aside. Draw an apple on a three-inch square of red construction paper and then cut it out. Cut the apple into narrow vertical strips and set the strips in order on a work surface.

Next, glue the strips in order on the blank side of the index card, leaving a narrow space between them. Color a stem; then make a construction paper leaf and glue it in place. Complete the illustrated side of the index card with a title or the name of the intended recipient(s). After the glue dries, this one-of-a-kind notecard will be ready for hand delivery!

## Sunny Flowers

Cultivate a crop of cheery sunflower blooms! To prepare, cut a few kitchen sponges into approximately 1" x 3" pieces and make several four-inch circle templates for students to share. Pour yellow tempera paint into a shallow container. Also set out paintbrushes and brown and green tempera paint. To make a painting, trace a circle on the upper half of a vertically positioned 12" x 18" sheet of paper. Fill the circle with brown-paint fingerprints to resemble a flower center. Dip a prepared sponge into the yellow paint and then press it onto the paper to make a petal. Continue making petals around the flower center, reloading the paint as necessary. Then paint a green stem and leaves.

For an inspiring extension, tell students that Vincent van Gogh was known for his impressive sunflower paintings. Then share a grade-appropriate book about the famous artist, such as *Camille and the Sunflowers: A Story About Vincent van Gogh* by Laurence Anholt.

Jenna Lea Ott, Mary Jo Burkell, Anne Marie Hallinan, Helen Kelley
Mother Seton School
Emmitsburg, MD

## Twist, Curl, and Bend!

Spark students' imaginations with this three-dimensional art project, and explore action verbs in the process! In advance, prepare a supply of 1" x 9" construction paper strips in a variety of colors. To make a project, a student places a 9" x 12" sheet of tagboard on a work surface. If desired, he cuts chosen strips into shorter lengths. He glues several strips onto the tagboard to create a three-dimensional effect. To do this, he manipulates the strips in a variety of ways, such as folding, bending, twisting, and curling (by wrapping them around a pencil).

After each student completes his project, post a sheet of chart paper and title it "Action Verbs." Have students recall how they manipulated the strips and help them identify the corresponding action verbs. List the words on the paper. Display the list and students' projects on a prepared bulletin board to create an eye-catching word reference!

adapted from an idea by Heather Miller
Auburn, IN

# Arts & Crafts

## Pumpkin Paintings

Use these pumpkin patches to create a seasonal or holiday display! To begin, paint two or more pumpkins on a horizontally positioned 6" x 9" piece of white construction paper. After the paint dries, use crayons to illustrate a nighttime backdrop or a daytime setting. Use provided arts-and-crafts materials to complete the scene. For example, glue on construction paper cutouts to transform the pumpkins into jack-o'-lanterns, add adhesive foil stars to a nighttime sky, or glue on short lengths of raffia to resemble straw. It looks like fall!

adapted from an idea by Alyssa Weller
South School
Glencoe, IL

## 3-D Tree

A watchful owl rests in this three-dimensional tree!

**Materials for one tree project:**
12" x 18" sheet of white construction paper
piece of corrugated paper
4½" x 12" brown construction paper rectangle (tree trunk)
white and colored construction paper scraps (owl, branches, leaves,
    and grass)
scissors
crayons
pencil
glue

**Steps:**
1.  Use the corrugated paper and a black crayon to do a rubbing on the entire sheet of white construction paper.
2.  To form a tree trunk, make a ¾-inch fold along the length of each long side of the brown construction paper rectangle.
3.  To make an owl's perch, carefully use a pencil to poke a hole in the tree trunk. Use scissors to enlarge the hole.
4.  Squeeze a line of glue along each folded edge of the trunk. Position the prepared sheet of paper horizontally; set the trunk in place and gently press the edges to secure it.
5.  Illustrate an owl on a piece of white construction paper. Cut it out and then glue it in its prepared perch.
6.  Cut branches, leaves, and grass from the construction paper scraps. Glue them in place.

Joan M. Macey
Binghamton, NY

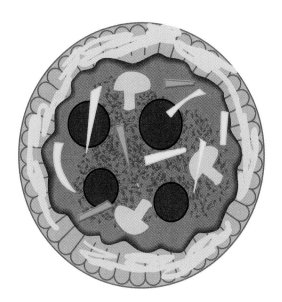

## Pizza With Pizzazz

This October, celebrate National Pizza Month with a multisensory pizza project! To make a pizza, lightly color the rim of a six-inch paper plate brown. Make desired construction paper toppings and then set them aside. Mix red food coloring into white glue so that it resembles the color of tomato sauce. Brush the glue mixture onto the uncolored portion of the paper plate. While the project is wet, sprinkle oregano on top and press the toppings in place.

For a mouthwatering follow-up, have each student respond to a pizza-related prompt such as the ones shown. Display each student's writing and completed pizza on a bulletin board titled "Pizza! Pizza!"

Jodi Bodenheimer—Gr. 2
Vegas Verdes Elementary
Las Vegas, NV

**Writing Prompts**
- What is your favorite type of pizza? Write a paragraph to describe it. Be sure to use words that tell how it looks, smells, and tastes.
- It's National Pizza Month! Write to tell how you think people should celebrate.
- Imagine that you own a pizza shop. What would you do to make your pizza shop the best?

## Tabletop Turkey

No doubt students will be pleased to invite this cute gobbler to join them for Thanksgiving! Before introducing the activity, prepare half of a three-inch foam ball for each student by using a plastic knife to make a slit in it (see the illustration). Also use 3" x 5" tagboard rectangles to prepare turkey templates, similar to the one shown, for students to share.

**Materials for one turkey:**

| | |
|---|---|
| prepared half of a foam ball | paintbrush |
| four wooden ice-cream spoons | scissors |
| 3" x 5" brown poster board rectangle | glue |
| access to a turkey template | colorful broad-tip markers |
| yellow and red construction paper scraps | brown tempera paint |

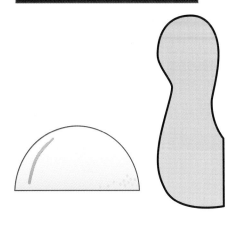

**Steps:**
1. Paint the round side of the ball half. Allow it to dry.
2. Use markers to color both sides of the ice-cream spoons.
3. Trace the template onto the poster board. Cut out the tracing.
4. From the construction paper scraps, make a beak and a wattle. Glue them onto the turkey. Draw eyes.
5. Insert the poster board into the slit as shown.
6. Carefully poke each ice-cream spoon into the turkey so that the spoon resembles a tail feather.

Cheryl Sergi
Greene, NY

# Arts & Crafts

## Peppermint Paintings

Holiday preparations have "scent-sational" possibilities with these red-and-white paintings! Pour red tempera paint into a small container and then mix in a few drops of peppermint extract. Cut a piece of white paper to fit in an empty box or a box lid. Set the paper inside, dribble a small amount of paint on top, and then drop in a marble. Tilt the container to roll the marble through the paint until a desired effect is achieved. Then remove the marble and allow the paint to dry.

Next, remove the painting. Trace the candy cane pattern (page 18) on the back of it a desired number of times. Cut out each tracing. Then use each unique candy cane as desired. For example, hole-punch the top of it and secure a length of string to it as shown to make a gift tag; then address and sign of the back of it. Or to create an ornament, mount the cutout on construction paper and add a hanger. What a treat for the senses!

Sara Humiston, Lawrence, KS

## Old-Time Ornaments

These country-style ornaments are fun to make and oh, "sew" cute!

**Materials for one ornament:**
star or heart pattern (page 18)
brown paper lunch bag
2 cotton balls
1" square of cotton fabric
button
7" length of yarn or jute
scissors
tape
glue
fine-tip marker

**Steps:**
1. Trace the pattern on the unopened bag. Cut out the tracing, cutting through all layers, to make two cutouts. Discard the scraps.
2. On one side of each cutout, use a marker to draw stitches along the edge.
3. Turn one cutout with stitches facedown. To make a hanger, loop a length of yarn or jute and tape the ends to the cutout as shown. Stretch the two cotton balls and set the cotton in the center of the cutout.
4. Squeeze a line of glue along the edge of the cutout. Place the second cutout on top with stitches faceup. Gently press the edges to seal them.
5. Glue on a fabric square and button for decoration.

Rosana Sanchez, Arrey, NM

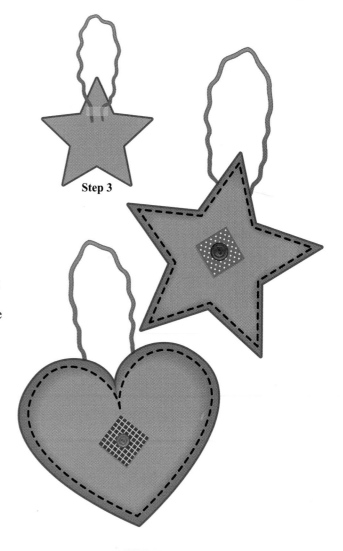

Step 3

## Perfectly Shaped Evergreen

Here's a "tree-mendous" project that pairs geometry and art! To prepare, cut two 1½" x 12" green construction paper strips. Cut each strip into 1½-inch squares. Then cut five squares in half diagonally to make ten triangles.

Next, position a 9" x 12" sheet of construction paper horizontally. Use a ruler to draw a line across the paper near the bottom edge. Then glue four squares side by side on the line, leaving space at either end of the row. Glue three squares in a row centered directly above the first row. Use two squares to make the next row and one square to make a fourth row. Glue one triangle at the top and four triangles on each side to form a tree as shown. If desired, use a hole puncher and construction paper scraps to make a number of small decorations; then glue them onto the tree.

Rita Arnold, Alden Hebron Elementary School, Hebron, IL

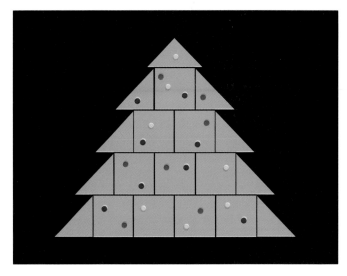

## Supersimple Snowpal

This paper plate snowpal can be made in a twinkling! Make a cut in a nine-inch paper plate from the outer edge just to the inner circle. Then cut along the edge of the circle, stopping approximately one inch from the beginning of the cut as shown. Lift the circle up to make a snowpal head. Tape the back of the project to hold the rim and head in place. Use provided arts-and-crafts materials to add a hat, two eyes, a nose, and a mouth.

To extend the project with alliterative writing, a student uses a template to make a seven-inch white paper circle. He positions his snowpal so that its opening is atop the circle; then he traces the opening. He moves the snowpal aside. Within the tracing, he writes an alliterative sentence about the snowpal. He squeezes a line of glue along the circle, positions the snowpal atop his paper, and then gently presses the project in place. Cool!

Rosemary Contino—Gr. 1
Clara B. Worth Elementary School
Bayville, NJ

The silly snowpal skipped down the icy street.

# Arts & Crafts

## Sweet Cardholders

Candy look-alikes make these valentine holders irresistible! Cut a chocolate kiss shape from each of several six-inch tagboard squares for students to share. To make a cardholder, fold a 12" x 18" sheet of paper in half to 9" x 12". Fold down two inches of the top layer. Turn the project over and then fold down two inches of what is now the top layer. Staple the sides of the project together.

Next, use a template to make a construction paper kiss. Glue the kiss onto the dull side of a piece of aluminum foil. Then trim the excess foil. Snip a triangle from one end of a 1" x 5" white paper strip, as shown, and illustrate the strip with hearts. Glue the other end of the strip to the paper side of the chocolate kiss. Glue the kiss onto the left-hand side of the cardholder and sign your name. Happy Valentine's Day!

adapted from an idea by Deborah Lockhart—Gr. 2
William B. Tecler School
Amsterdam, NY

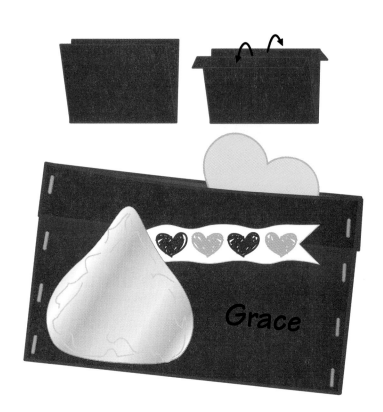

## Bumblebee Valentines

These darling valentines are perfect for declaring, "'Bee' Mine!"

**Materials for one valentine:**

empty toilet tissue tube
4½" x 6" yellow construction paper rectangle
three 4" yellow construction paper squares
three 5" black construction paper squares
3" x 6" black construction paper rectangle

black construction paper scraps
fine-tip marker
clear tape
scissors
glue

**Steps:**

1. Squeeze a line of glue along the edges of the yellow rectangle. Wrap the paper around the toilet tissue tube.
2. Cut the black rectangle into three strips approximately 1" x 6" each. Glue them onto the tube to make stripes.
3. To make three hearts, fold each yellow square in half. Draw half of a heart along each fold as shown; cut it out.
4. Unfold each heart. Draw a face on one.
5. Glue each heart onto a black square. Trim the paper, leaving a border.
6. To make wings, glue together the blank hearts as shown. Tape the wings to the tube.
7. To make a head, cut two antennae from the black paper scraps and glue them onto the back of the illustrated heart. Glue the head to the tube.

Pam Sartory, Palm Beach Gardens, FL

Step 1    Step 2    Step 3    Step 6

12

## Little Lambs

Whether March comes in like a lion or a lamb, these woolly critters will be ready to greet spring. To make a lamb, draw an upside-down pear shape in the center of a white coffee filter to resemble a lamb's head. Trace the shape with a crayon and lightly color it in. Use a crayon to draw two eyes and a mouth. Next, squeeze a small amount of glue in the center of a nine-inch white paper plate. Glue the coffee filter in place, as shown, keeping the edges free. Use construction paper to make two ears, a nose, and two legs. Glue them on. Gently stretch out three or four white cotton balls. Glue the cotton along the edges of the plate. How cute!

Jane Russett—Gr. 1
St. Stanislaus Elementary
Adams, MA

## Colorful Kite

Brighten the classroom with these symmetrical fliers! To begin, fold a nine-inch construction paper square in half diagonally and then fold the resulting triangle in half. Unfold the paper and then position it so that one corner is at the top. In the top two sections, place dabs of tempera paint. Lift up the bottom corner to fold the paper in half diagonally again. Gently rub the top of the folded paper and then unfold it.

After the paint dries, use a permanent marker to trace the fold lines. Position another nine-inch construction paper square so that one corner is at the top. At the bottom, tape on two 18-inch lengths of crepe paper streamers. Glue the painted square on top, aligning the edges. Then hole-punch the top of the resulting kite and add a loop of string for a hanger. Suspend the colorful kite from the ceiling to create a breezy springtime display.

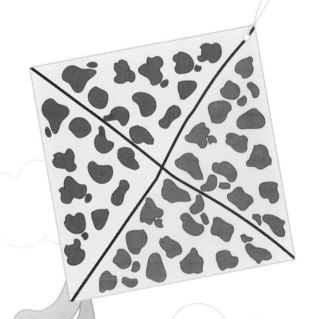

### Did You Know?
Kites were named after a graceful type of bird.

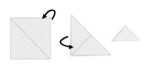

13

# Arts & Crafts

## Bunny Buddy

Celebrate spring or Easter with this adorable bunny project. Hippity, hoppity!

**Materials for one bunny project:**
white construction paper egg approximately 8" x 10"
two 2" x 8" white construction paper rectangles (ears)
2½" x 8" white construction paper rectangle (feet)
two 2½" x 6" white construction paper rectangles (arms)
9" x 12" sheet of colorful construction paper (overalls)
construction paper scraps (bow)
crayons, including pink
fine-tip black marker
scissors
glue

Step 4

**Steps:**
1. Trace the egg onto the sheet of colored construction paper and then cut out the tracing. Draw overalls on the cutout similar to the ones shown.
2. Cut out the overalls. Glue them onto the egg so that the outer edges are aligned.
3. Use the marker and pink crayon to draw a bunny face on the upper portion of the egg.
4. Position the 2½" x 8" rectangle horizontally. Draw a curved line on each end as shown above. Cut along the lines. Add marker details to resemble feet. Glue the feet in place.
5. Trim the 2" x 8" rectangles to resemble bunny ears. Color the inner portion of the ears pink. Glue on the ears.
6. Roll the tip of each ear around a crayon and then unroll it.
7. Round one end of each 2½" x 6" rectangle. Glue the arms in place.
8. Decorate the overalls with a construction paper bow and desired crayon details.

Doris Hautala, Washington Elementary, Ely, MN

## Impressive Paintings

This nifty fingerpainting idea has striking results and no messy cleanup! To begin, draw a simple scribble design with heavy crayon lines on a 9" x 12" sheet of white paper. Use brightly colored crayons to color in the design. Next, place the paper on a newspaper-covered surface and put on a pair of disposable rubber gloves. Squeeze a puddle of liquid tempera paint onto the paper. Mix in a few drops of liquid starch. Spread the mixture over the entire sheet of paper (add more paint if needed). Then use your fingers to make a desired design. After the paint dries, staple the artwork to a larger sheet of construction paper to frame it. Cool!

Janette E. Anderson—K–3 Substitute Teacher
Fremont, CA

## Little Ladybugs

Count on students to go buggy over these handy garden visitors! To begin, glue a three-inch black semicircle (head) to a five-inch black construction paper circle (body) to resemble a ladybug. Cut two antennae from construction paper scraps and glue them on. Turn the ladybug over. Next, fold a 9" x 12" sheet of red construction paper in half to 6" x 9". With fingers either outstretched or together, trace one hand on the folded paper. Carefully cut along the tracing through both thicknesses of the paper. Then position the hand cutouts on the ladybug to resemble wings. Glue them in place. Use black tempera paint to make thumbprints on the wings. Allow the paint to dry; then the spotted critter will be ready for display!

Carol Hargett, Fairborn, OH

## Beautiful Bouquet

A bunch of white lilies is a perfect surprise for a loved one! In advance, prepare tagboard hand templates for students to share. To make one lily, trace a template on white paper. Cut out the tracing. Gently roll up the hand cutout vertically at the base (the fingers will be the petals). Use clear tape to secure the resulting blossom.

Next, cut a four-inch piece from a yellow chenille stem. Loosely fold it in half and then twist one end of a green chenille stem around the center of it as shown. Fold down each yellow tip to resemble the top of a stamen. Carefully poke the free end of the green chenille stem down through the center of the blossom. Adjust the height of the stem so that the stamens are visible. Roll each flower petal outward around a pencil and then unroll it. Make two additional lilies in a similar manner. Use a length of curling ribbon to tie the stems together and then carefully curl the ribbon ends with scissors. How pretty!

Mary Singletary
Summerville, SC

Looking for gift ideas? See the suggestions on page 306.

# Arts & Crafts

## Waterless Aquarium

This unique aquarium gives a clear view of what's under the sea!

**Materials for one aquarium:**
two 9-inch white paper plates
piece of blue plastic wrap that is slightly larger than a paper plate
small amount of green shredded paper
construction paper scraps (for fish)
small amount of sand
glue
crayons
scissors
clear tape
access to a stapler

**Steps:**

1. Squeeze glue onto the lower portion of one paper plate. Sprinkle sand onto the glue. Shake off the excess.
2. Glue on lengths of shredded paper to resemble sea grass.
3. Cut out several fish shapes from construction paper. Add desired crayon details.
4. Glue the fish onto the prepared plate. Allow the glue to dry.
5. Place the prepared plate facedown on the plastic wrap. Tape the plastic wrap to the plate so that it is taut. Then turn the plate faceup.
6. Cut out the inner circle from the undecorated plate to make a ring. Discard the inner portion.
7. Staple the ring to the decorated plate so that the rounded side is facing out.

Mary Beth Knippel, Madison, WI

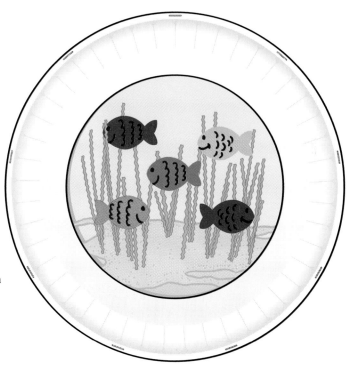

## Somewhere in Space

Send students' imaginations out of this world with a far-out painting project! To begin, a student uses red, orange, and yellow crayons to completely cover a sheet of white construction paper with patches of color. Then he prepares a desired number of tagboard stars and circles (planets). He tacks each cutout to his paper with a loop of tape. Next, he uses black tempera paint and a sponge to paint his entire paper. While the paint is wet, he sprinkles on silver glitter. After the paint dries, he carefully removes the cutouts and shakes off any excess glitter.

For a related writing activity, ask each youngster to pen a brief story inspired by his artwork. Or encourage him to imagine that he discovered a new planet and have him write a description of it.

Tara Hartline—Gr. 2, Allatoona Elementary, Acworth, GA

## Scenic Frame

A vacation photo, student illustration, or summertime poem would look "sand-sational" in this seaside frame. In advance, prepare several frame templates in desired sizes for students to share. To make a frame, a student traces a template on a piece of light blue poster board. She cuts along the outer and inner outlines with adult assistance as needed. Then she cuts from a piece of fine-grained sandpaper a strip that is sized to fit along the bottom of her frame. (See the illustration.) She trims one long edge of the sandpaper with a slightly wavy cut. With the wavy edge up, she glues the sandpaper to her frame. She uses white acrylic paint and a sponge to add clouds. To showcase a photo or piece of work, she attaches it to the back of the frame with clear tape.

Sheila M. Hausbeck, Louisville, CO

## Friendly Fireflies

Students' faces are sure to light up when they make these adorable firefly note holders!

**Materials for one note holder:**

4½-inch-long lightbulb-shaped template (firefly body)
yellow construction paper
brown construction paper scraps
two 1" x 5" waxed paper strips
black marker
2 small wiggle eyes
gold glitter

scissors
glue
tape
paintbrush
spring-type clothespin
magnetic tape

**Steps:**

1. Use the template to make two yellow construction paper bodies.
2. Glue a slightly larger piece of brown paper onto the narrow end of one body. Trim the paper to resemble a firefly head.
3. Round the ends of the waxed paper strips. Stack the strips and then pinch them in the middle. Tape them to the back of the prepared body. Gently fan out the resulting wings.
4. Cut two antennae from brown construction paper. Glue them to the back of the head.
5. Glue the undecorated body to the back of the prepared body.
6. On the front of the project, glue two eyes and draw a mouth.
7. Use a paintbrush to spread glue on the lower part of the body. Sprinkle on glitter and then shake off the excess.
8. After the glue dries, glue a clothespin to the back of the firefly and adhere a strip of magnetic tape to it as shown.

Carol Hargett, Fairborn, OH

**Did You Know?**
Fireflies are beetles, not flies.

# Patterns

Use the candy cane with "Peppermint Paintings" on page 10.
Use the heart and star with "Old-Time Ornaments" on the same page.

# CLASSROOM DISPLAYS

# CLASSROOM DISPLAYS

This cheery display is guaranteed to brighten your classroom and each student's day! Post a jumbo sun and rainbow on a titled bulletin board. Ask each youngster to use a construction paper circle and arts-and-crafts materials to make a self-portrait. Then have him glue his artwork onto a sun cutout. Arrange students' sunny projects on the prepared board.

Jo Fryer—Gr. 1, Kildeer Countryside School, Long Grove, IL

A colorful welcome blooms at this garden entrance! Tack lengths of adding machine tape onto a prepared bulletin board to resemble latticework. Add a door labeled with a desired message. Invite each youngster to personalize a construction paper flowerpot (page 31). Have her pinch tissue paper circles to make blossoms and then glue them in place. Display students' flowerpots and additional blossoms as shown. Beautiful!

Maureen Glennon—Gr. 1, Faller Elementary, Ridgecrest, CA

There's no monkey business here, just plenty of reading motivation! Post a monkey, banana tree, and the title shown on a bulletin board. Place a supply of banana cutouts and blank cards nearby. After a student finishes reading a book he likes, he labels a card with the title and author. He tacks it onto the board along with a signed cutout. Encourage students who are looking for book recommendations to check out the "ap-peel-ing" display!

adapted from an idea by Judi Lesnansky—Title I, New Hope Academy, Youngstown, OH

A can-do attitude is bound to keep students on track! Remind students of *The Little Engine That Could.* Then ask each youngster to create a labeled illustration to represent a chosen school-year goal. Have her staple her paper to a construction paper train car. Showcase students' work on a hallway wall as shown. All aboard for a great year!

Erin Haskins—Gr. 2, Clarksville Elementary School, Clarksville, VA

# CLASSROOM DISPLAYS

## CREEP INTO BOOKS!

Scare up reading motivation with this "spook-tacular" display! Prepare a haunted house; cut along two sides of the door so that it opens. Mount the house on a titled bulletin board or wall area and then add a ghost in the doorway. To share a favorite book, each student prepares a folded ghost cutout. Inside, she writes the title, the author, and a sentence about the book. Display the completed ghosts to treat youngsters to great reading suggestions!

Jill Riedy, Wildwood, MO

Celebrate fall the "write" way! Each student writes "Fall is…" at the top of a provided piece of paper. He pens a fall list poem similar to the one shown and then glues his writing onto a seasonal cutout. Showcase youngsters' eye-catching poetry on a titled bulletin board. Hooray for fall!

Judi Lesnansky—Title I, New Hope Academy, Youngstown, OH

These dapper gobblers are dressed for work, not Thanksgiving! Each student cuts out a construction paper copy of the turkey on page 32. She uses wallpaper, wiggle eyes, and other arts-and-crafts materials to add tail feathers and make the turkey resemble a chosen type of community helper. Then she writes a paragraph that tells about the worker. Display the turkeys and paragraphs as desired. Gobble, gobble!

Maribeth Yerks and Nancy Ketchum—Gr. 3, Georgetown Elementary School, Aurora, IL

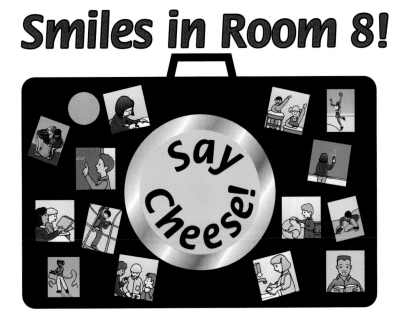

Whether you feature this collection of photos during conferences or throughout the year, it's sure to bring plenty of smiles! Post one or more jumbo camera cutouts. Label the camera(s) as desired and post a title. Then complete the display with snapshots of your students. Smile!

Maureen Glennon—Gr. 1, Faller Elementary, Ridgecrest, CA

# CLASSROOM DISPLAYS

## Deck the Halls!

shining tree lights

colorful gift wrap

very busy shoppers

cookies with red sugar sprinkled on top

gifts with shiny silver bows

sparkling tinsel

Spread holiday cheer with jumbo ornaments! Each student uses a descriptive phrase to label a large construction paper circle with a seasonal sight. She glues on a tagboard ornament topper that she has covered with foil. Then she tapes a chenille stem hanger to the back of it. Display students' resulting decorations on a hallway wall as desired. Fa, la, la, la!

Sharon Rehn—Gr. 2, Sunnyside Elementary, Sobieski, WI

## It's Winter!

Three-dimensional snowpals make this wintry display stand out from the rest! Each student writes a paragraph about winter and then staples it onto a sheet of construction paper. To illustrate his work, he glues on two halves of a small foam ball to resemble a snowpal. He uses a marker to draw eyes, a mouth, and buttons. Then he completes the scene with additional arts-and-crafts materials. Showcase youngsters' work on a titled board. Hooray for winter!

adapted from an idea by Gwyn McGee, Benton Elementary School, Nicholson, GA

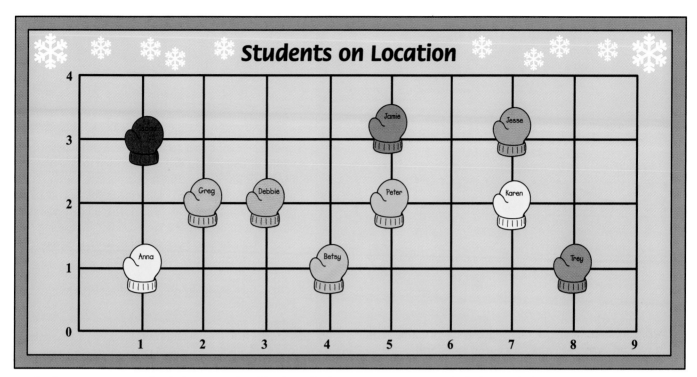

Students are sure to enjoy being spotted at this class display. On a paper-covered bulletin board, draw and label a jumbo grid. Add a desired title. Have each student personalize a seasonal cutout; then tack the cutouts at various locations. Use the coordinates to call on students or to identify classroom helpers. Periodically rearrange the cutouts to keep students' skills sharp. What a creative approach to math!

Patsy Prickett—Gr. 3, Jesse S. Bobo Elementary, Spartanburg, SC

These dapper critters are right at home with chilly temperatures! On a paper ice cube, each student writes an acrostic poem with a winter weather word, such as *chilly* or *freezing,* and then mounts the ice cube on construction paper. She prepares a penguin cutout (pattern on page 33) and glues it atop the ice cube. Display students' frosty work with a snow-covered sign. Brrr!

Judi Lesnansky—Title I, New Hope Academy, Youngstown, OH

# CLASSROOM DISPLAYS

## Straight From the Heart

generous

helpful

kind

My mom was generous when she gave me a huge piece of pie. Jessie

This vocabulary reinforcement comes straight from the heart! Label each of several envelopes with a different word that is often used to describe friends or loved ones. Illustrate a postage stamp on each envelope; then display the envelopes on a titled bulletin board. On a personalized heart cutout, have each student write a sentence with a featured word. Post students' heartwarming work near the appropriate envelopes. "Send-sational"!

adapted from an idea by Amy Barsanti
Plymouth, NC

## Our Writing Is out of This World!

Take writing motivation to new heights! Each student uses desired arts-and-crafts materials to make alien hands and head-and-shoulders cutouts. He describes his character on an irregular-shaped piece of lined paper. He mounts his writing on a sheet of black paper and then glues on his alien to make a paper topper. He completes his project with desired details, such as paint dots or half of a foam ball painted to resemble a planet. Showcase students' projects on a wall with the title shown.

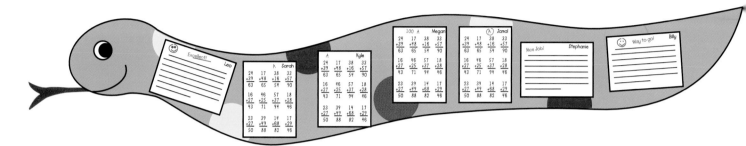

# "Sssuper" Work

"Sssuper" student work makes this reptile a welcome classroom visitor. Cut a long length of bulletin board paper into a snake shape. Illustrate a face and colorful spots or stripes. Display the snake, with a title above it, on a classroom wall. Showcase examples of students' finest work on the snake, adding paper to the length as needed. No doubt each student will be eager to do his part in helping the snake grow!

Lydia Hess, Chambersburg, PA

Create a renewed spirit of cooperation with this student-prepared display. From white paper, cut a class supply of interlocking puzzle pieces sized to fit on a board as shown. Mark a dot on each puzzle piece to identify which side is the top. Have each student sign and color a puzzle piece as desired. Help students assemble the puzzle on a paper-covered board; then add a title.

Sarah Saia
Wilmington, NC

# CLASSROOM DISPLAYS

## Look What Just Hatched!

A. 386 + 421

B.

C.

D. 6 9 + 5

E.

F.

G. 492 + 109

H.

I. 22 31 + 16

J. 511 + 183

E. There are 20 chicks. 8 of them are asleep. How many of them are awake?

12 of the chicks are awake.

Make math "egg-stra" special at this interactive display. To prepare, have each youngster write and solve an original computation or story problem. Check his work, and then ask him to write the approved problem on the front of a folded egg cutout and the answer inside. Letter the eggs for easy reference. Then post them on a titled board along with a chick and a broken eggshell. What a nifty way to hatch renewed interest in math!

adapted from an idea by Stephanie LeDure—Gr. 1
Oak Ridge Elementary School
Oak Ridge, MO

## Happy Earth Day!

Spring

Leafy trees,
Yellow dandelions popping up,
Dragonflies zooming by,
Baby birds hatching.

This Earth Day idea doubles as a tribute to National Poetry Month. Have each student write a nature-related poem on a pastel index card and then staple it to the smooth side of a brown paper lunch bag. Have her use crayons and scraps of colorful paper to illustrate her work. Display students' poetry around a large globe cutout and add a desired title. Happy Earth Day!

Dawn Maucieri—Gr. 3, Signal Hill Elementary School, Dix Hills, NY

Give your budding authors plenty of inspiration with a writing springboard! Post several springtime writing prompts on a board titled as shown. Decorate the display with student-created flowers and insects. When a student needs a writing idea, the springboard will come in handy!

Liana Mahoney—Grs. 1–2 Looping, Beaver River Central School, Beaver Falls, NY

Cultivate good work with this suggestion for showcasing students' best efforts. Display a flowerpot with a few colorful posies on a bulletin board. Add the provided title and student-selected work samples. To keep the display current, periodically invite students to update their work. Students' pride is sure to blossom!

Lydia Hess, Chambersburg, PA

## Memorable Class Picnic

School memories are the talk of this unique picnic! Tack a length of white paper to a hallway wall; then add triangular pieces of red-and-white checkered fabric as shown. Have each student write about a favorite school-related memory on a speech bubble. After he illustrates the memory on a paper plate, ask him to use arts-and-crafts materials and the ant pattern on page 34 to make a six-legged picnic guest. Complete the display with students' work and a title.

Kimberly Parkhurst—Gr. 2, Pershing Elementary, Lincoln, NE

Honor students' accomplishments with this idea, and it will become clear that it's been a hoppin' good year! Ask each youngster to label a lily pad cutout with one of her learning achievements from the school year. Then have her personalize a frog (pattern on page 34) and glue it to her cutout. Showcase students' work on a titled board along with a jumbo frog and lily pad. Ribbit!

Kathy Sherman—Gr. 3, St. Paul Catholic School, Highland, IL

# Turkey Pattern
Use with "Turkeys With Dressing" on page 23.

# Ant and Frog Patterns

Use the ant with "Memorable Class Picnic" on page 30.

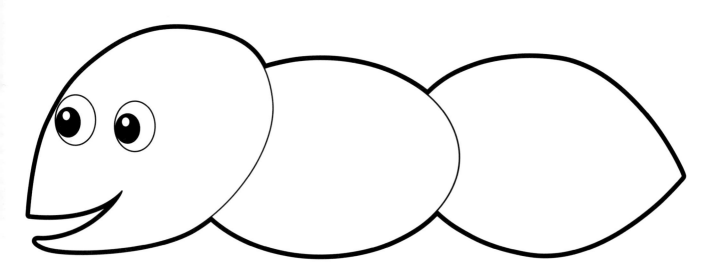

Use the frog with "Learning by Leaps and Bounds" on page 30.

# COMPREHENSION CROSSING

# Comprehension Crossing
## Making Reading Meaningful

### Retelling Tag

What's the secret to the success of this **retelling** activity? Teamwork! After sharing a book with a small group of students, post a list of transition words. Explain that the words can help readers organize their thoughts when retelling stories. Sit with the students in a circle. Begin to retell the story; then stop after a sentence or two and tag a student sitting beside you. This student adds one or more sentences, using transition words as appropriate. Then she tags the next student. The retelling continues around the circle until the story is completely retold and every student has had at least one turn.

Cathie Cuffman—Gr. 3
Jane Romik—Speech/Language
Lebanon City School District
Lebanon, OH

Name _Jay_
#### Chapter Summaries
Title _Charlotte's Web_
Author _E. B. White_

| 1. | 2. | 3. |
|---|---|---|
| 4. | 5. | 6. |
| 7. | 8. | 9. |

### Chapter by Chapter

**Summarizing** skills take shape with this chapter-by-chapter approach. Before beginning a class read-aloud, prepare a graphic organizer similar to the one shown, leaving it unnumbered. Give each student one or more copies so that he has one box per chapter. Instruct each youngster to write his name, the title, and the author. Then have him number the boxes.

After each chapter, compose a one- or two-sentence summary as a class. Ask each youngster to write the summary in the appropriate box. As you continue the book, have volunteers use their sheets to recap the story and bring any previously absent students up-to-date. What a simple way to follow the thread of a story!

Sally Malloy—Gr. 1, Pleasant Hill School, Scarborough, ME

### Question Boxes

Put an intriguing twist on **comprehension questions**! Obtain three boxes that can be used to make a set of nested boxes. To follow up a chosen book, tape a different comprehension question to each box. Inside the smallest box, place an object that represents a significant story detail. Set each box inside the next larger box; then decorate the largest box as desired.

At the book's conclusion, ask a youngster to read aloud the outer question. After one or more students respond, have a volunteer open the box and read the next question. Continue the question-and-answer process until the hidden item is revealed. Then discuss the object's significance with students.

adapted from an idea by Mandy Jones
Oldtown, MD

What is the main problem in the story?

Why do you think the author chose this title?

# Comprehension Crossing
## Making Reading Meaningful

### Puppet Tales

Make **retelling** easier with the help of student-made puppets! After sharing a favorite folktale, guide students to recall the main characters. Have each youngster illustrate each character on an index card half and then tape on a jumbo craft stick to make a handle. Ask him to place his resulting puppets in a resealable plastic bag.

Next, divide students into small groups. For each group, designate a student for each character, assigning a student more than one role if necessary. Have the groups practice retelling the story with their puppets. Then arrange for them to retell the story to students in a lower grade. Plan for each group member to take his puppets home along with a parent note of explanation, and encourage him to give his family an encore presentation.

Rebecca Lance—Gr. 1
Lafayette Central Elementary
Roanoke, IN

**Book News**

We read <u>The Three Little Pigs</u> today. I can use my puppets to tell you the story!

### Character Bags

**Story characters** are the focus of this kid-pleasing project! After a student finishes an independent reading book, he labels a white paper lunch bag with the title and the main character. He decorates the bag with a story-themed illustration. Then, on each of several blank cards, he illustrates an item that represents a character-related detail. For example, after reading *Amelia Bedelia,* he might draw an apron to show that the main character is a maid. On the back of each card, he explains how the item relates to the character. He places the cards in the prepared bag and presents it to the class at a designated time.

adapted from an idea by Valerie Wood Smith
Morgantown, PA

### Lots of Details!

Prompt students to **recall story details** with this toe-tapping approach! Post a sheet of chart paper labeled with the title of a recently completed read-aloud. Sing the song shown below with students; then have a volunteer identify a story detail. Use a marker to write her name and the detail on the poster. Lead the class in another round of the song and invite a different student to contribute. Use a different colored marker to write the information. Continue for several rounds or until each youngster has identified a detail. Each colorful addition is sure to stretch students' thinking!

Lucille Iscaro—Grs. K–1
Public School 257
Bronx, NY

**Storytime Song**
*(sung to the tune of "The Muffin Man")*

Tell us something about the book,
About the book, about the book.
Tell us something about the book;
Please share your thoughts with us.

# Comprehension Crossing
## Making Reading Meaningful

### Packed With Clues

This prereading idea is packed with opportunities to **make predictions.** In advance, conceal a selected read-aloud in a small suitcase or carryall. Also place inside several objects or illustrations that represent story details.

To begin, suggest to students that the suitcase is their ticket to a reading adventure. Explain that it contains a book and several story clues. Next, announce the type of book and subject. Unpack each item, in turn, inviting students to predict how it relates to the story and to explain their reasoning. Then reveal the book with great fanfare. As you read the story, have students check their predictions and revise them as appropriate. No doubt they'll be eager for more reading adventures, so plan to keep your suitcase handy!

Janet Robbins—Title I Reading
Fairview Elementary School
Richmond, IN

### Just the Highlights!

Here's a bright idea for zeroing in on **important details.** Give each student in a small group a highlighter marker and a copy of a multiparagraph nonfiction selection. Read a portion of the selection aloud as students follow along. Then guide the group to identify the important details; ask each youngster to highlight this information with his marker. Next, instruct each student to silently read the remainder of the selection and mark the major points. After students finish, ask volunteers to tell what they highlighted and why. Then, with students' help, use the highlighted details to write a summary.

Stephenie Powell—Gr. 3
Central Elementary, Sand Springs, OK

### Coded Comprehension

What's one way that good readers respond to books? By **asking questions!** Display a chosen book and post a three-column chart that you have labeled as shown. Ask students to share questions they have about the book; list them in the first column. Use the answer code to explain that answers can be found in various ways. Encourage students to keep this in mind as you read the book aloud. After reading, write on the chart any answers that students determined. Use the code to label the answers in the third column and suggest that students research any unanswered questions. For ongoing practice with questioning, have students use individual copies of the chart during independent-reading sessions.

adapted from an idea by Peggy Morin Bruno
  Language Arts Consultant
Squadron Line School
Simsbury, CT

| Question | Answer | How Do We Know? |
|---|---|---|
|  |  |  |
|  |  |  |
|  |  |  |

**Answer Code**
B = The answer was in the <u>book</u>.
I = We used clues in the book and what we knew to make an <u>inference</u>.
R = We did <u>research</u> to find the answer.

# Comprehension Crossing
## Making Reading Meaningful

### Untangling the Details

Invite students to weave a web of **story details**! After reading aloud a chosen storybook or chapter, post a large blank hexagonal web (see the illustration). Use colorful markers to label the center of the web with the book title and an adjoining web section for each of the five Ws and H as shown. Then enlist students' help to write the appropriate story information in each remaining section. For more practice untangling story details, repeat the activity with other class read-alouds or have students independently complete smaller versions of the web for selected books.

Virginia Zeletzki—Grs. 2–5 ESOL
Banyan Creek Elementary School
Delray Beach, FL

### Connecting the Pieces

Piece together **connections** with this display idea. Title a bulletin board "Connecting With Books." Periodically encourage each youngster to contribute to the display when a story reminds him of something or someone. To do this, he visually divides a paper strip into two interlocking puzzle-shaped sections. In one section, he writes the book title and identifies one or more story details that prompted his connection. In the other section, he writes his connection and initials. Then he cuts the two sections apart. Set aside time for each puzzle owner to tell the class about his connection. Then tack his puzzle to the board to assemble it.

*The Chalk Box Kid*
Gregory worries that he won't get used to his new school.

That reminds me of when I moved. I didn't know anyone.
C. N.

Carol A. Felts, Fuquay-Varina, NC

### From the Beginning to the End

These minibooklets are handy **retelling** tools! To make one, cut a sheet of white paper in half lengthwise. Stack the strips vertically and then slide the top strip up about one inch. Fold the stack forward to create four graduated layers and then staple the paper close to the fold. To complete the booklet, a student writes and illustrates a chosen book title on the top flap. Then she sequentially labels a flap with each of the following words: *beginning, middle, end*. On each booklet page, she writes and illustrates the corresponding story events. When she's ready to retell the story, she'll have a perfect reference at her fingertips!

Bette J. Mattox, Jacksonville, FL

# Comprehension Crossing
## Making Reading Meaningful

### In the Reading Zone

If you have students who zip through books without understanding what they read, use this idea to help them **monitor their comprehension.** Display a construction paper traffic signal and post the code shown. Suggest that a good reader pauses periodically and asks himself what he just read; if he can't summarize the main points, he rereads the text more slowly. With the display as a colorful reminder, students will have a direct route to comprehension!

Jennifer Reed—Gr. 3, Rossville Elementary School
Rossville, GA

**Read Carefully!**

**Red:** Stop and ask yourself what you just read.

**Yellow:** If something is hard to understand, read it again more slowly.

**Green:** If the meaning is clear, keep reading!

### Clues to Character

Here's an approach to **character analysis** that's sure to suit youngsters to a T! List the letters *D, F, S,* and *T* on the board. Comment that the letters can help students remember that they can learn about a character from what he does *(D)*, feels *(F)*, says *(S)*, and thinks *(T)*. Then ask each student to label a tagboard strip with a chosen character's name and the corresponding book title. Have her add desired illustrations. Next, using each side of two blank cards, the student writes relevant story details for each listed letter. She uses a hole puncher and lengths of string to suspend the cards from the tagboard strip. She hole-punches the top of her project and attaches a loop of string to prepare her work for display.

Dawn Maucieri—Gr. 3, Signal Hill School, Dix Hills, NY

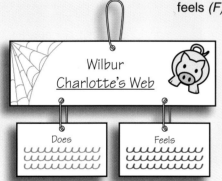

Wilbur
*Charlotte's Web*

Does

Feels

### Inquiring Minds

Promote thoughtful **questioning** with this simple idea. Point out to students that some story-related questions have just one correct answer each, while others have many answers because they are based on readers' ideas. Provide examples such as "Where does the story take place?" and "If you were Goldilocks, what would you have done when the bears returned?" Then, as you share a read-aloud, have each student jot down two questions, encouraging him to write questions that are not answered explicitly in the text. At the conclusion of the reading session, pair students. Have each student use his questions to prompt discussion with his partner. Deeper understanding and a greater interest in stories will result!

Kathleen Thorpe—Gr. 3, Garretson School, Corona, CA

# KEYS TO PROBLEM SOLVING

## Barnyard Solutions
### Strategy: guess and check

When it comes to problem solving, guessing can be a sound strategy! Display the following problem on an overhead projector or distribute individual copies.

> When Farmer Brown buys food for his animals, it costs exactly $10.00 for his horses, $8.00 for his cows, $4.00 for his chickens, and $5.00 for his pigs. On Monday, Farmer Brown spent $13.00. For which two kinds of animals did he buy food? *(cows and pigs)*

Read the problem aloud; then have each child jot down his guess for the answer on provided paper. Instruct him to add the corresponding costs and adjust his guess as needed. After every youngster is satisfied with his answer, discuss the solution as a class. For more barnyard math, modify the problem by changing the day and amount spent.

Susan DeRiso, John W. Horton School, Cranston, RI

## What's on the Menu?
### Strategy: make an organized list

Organized lists are the main course for this challenge! Give each child a copy of a school lunch menu that allows for various combinations of entrées and side dishes. Wonder aloud how many different meals are possible on a selected day. Explain that an organized list can help determine the answer. With students' input, use a code to list on the board each possible meal (an entrée and side dish or another appropriate combination). Then identify the total number.

Later, provide additional modeling with different menus. Then have each child work independently to find all the possible meals for a chosen day, suggesting that she list all of the combinations with one food choice at a time to ensure success. Now that's tempting math!

Amy Barsanti—Gr. 3
Pines Elementary School
Plymouth, NC

| Entrées | Side Dishes |
|---------|-------------|
| P = pizza | A = applesauce |
| N = chicken nuggets | B = beans |
| | C = corn |

| | |
|---------|------|
| P, A | N, A |
| P, B | N, B |
| P, C | N, C |

| Today's Date: September 29 | | | |
|----------|-------|---------|---------|
| Quarters | Dimes | Nickels | Pennies |
| 1 | 0 | 0 | 4 |
| 0 | 2 | 1 | 4 |
| 0 | 2 | 0 | 9 |
| 0 | 1 | 3 | 4 |
| 0 | 0 | 5 | 4 |
| 0 | 0 | 4 | 9 |

## Calendar Cents
### Strategy: make a table

Cash in on this daily approach to the make-a-table strategy! Give each child a resealable plastic bag that contains these imitation coins: one quarter, three dimes, six nickels, and nine pennies. Display a table labeled "Today's Date:" and programmed with the headings shown. Each day write the month and date; challenge students to identify all of the coin combinations that have a value equal to the date. To do this, each student first finds the combination that has the most coins of the greatest value. For example, if the date is the 29th, the child counts out one quarter and four pennies. Write the combination on the table. Guide students to continue systematically until the table is complete. What profitable problem-solving practice!

Heather Leverett, Nashville, TN

# Keys to Problem Solving
## Using Strategies With Success

---

## Lights, Camera, Action!
### Strategy: act it out

Set a stage for the act-it-out strategy! Prepare the following problem for display.
Anthony, Brian, Chris, Denise, and Ele are waiting in line. Brian is second. Anthony is last. Denise is standing right behind Ele. In what order are the friends lined up? *(Chris, Brian, Ele, Denise, Anthony)*
To begin, suggest that the phrase "Lights, camera, action!" can help students solve problems. Explain that "lights" is a reminder to read a problem carefully, "camera" is for focusing on the details, and "action" stands for acting out the problem. Then use the reminders to guide students in acting out and solving the prepared problem. For additional reinforcement, plan to pose other problems for your budding actors to solve.

---

## Gridlock
### Strategy: logical reasoning

This partner game locks in logical-reasoning skills! Give each student pair a file folder, a container of kidney and lima beans, and two 5 x 5 grids labeled as shown. Tell the players to sit facing each other and stand the folder between them so that each player's grid is shielded from his opponent's view. Explain that the object of the game is for one player to determine the location of his opponent's kidney beans. Have the players follow the directions shown.

**Directions:**
1. Player 1 places four kidney beans on his grid to make a 2 x 2 gridlock.
2. Player 2 announces a grid space. Player 1 says "hit" if he has a kidney bean on it or "miss" if he does not.
3. If it is a hit, Player 2 places a kidney bean on his corresponding grid space. If it is a miss, each player marks the space with a lima bean.
4. Play continues with Player 2 strategically asking about grid spaces and placing lima beans on any spaces that he determines the gridlock cannot occupy. When he thinks he knows where the gridlock is, he declares, "Gridlock!" and announces the location. If he is correct, he wins. If he is incorrect or if both players have four lima beans on their grids, Player 1 wins.

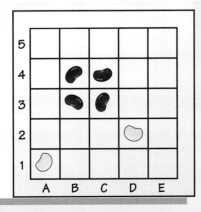

---

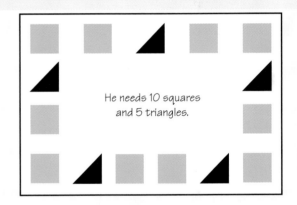

He needs 10 squares and 5 triangles.

## Framed!
### Strategy: use a pattern

Show youngsters that using patterns can be a handy strategy! Give each student a 6" x 9" piece of white paper. Divide students into small groups and give each group access to scissors, glue, and colored paper.

For each group, present a problem about a patterned picture frame, such as "The pattern for a picture frame is square, square, triangle. If Sam uses exactly 15 shapes to decorate the frame, how many squares and triangles does he need?" To solve the problem, each student prepares colored paper shapes. She glues them onto her paper to represent the described frame. She studies the pattern and then writes her answer to the problem in the center of her paper. After students complete their work, invite each group to present its problem and picture-perfect solution to the class.

Kate Gannon—Gr. 3
Korn Elementary School
Durham, CT

# Keys to Problem Solving
## Using Strategies With Success

### Slick Solutions
#### Strategy: guess and check

Students slide into problem solving with this sport-based challenge! Explain to students that *luge* is a winter sport in which one or two people slide down an icy slope on a sled. Next, display the weight information and read the problem aloud. Ask each student to silently guess the answer; then have her complete the appropriate calculations to check her guess. If she is not correct, encourage her to repeat the guess-and-check process. After each student is satisfied with her answer, discuss the solution as a class. Swoosh!

Taylor, Casey, and Jess are luge athletes. When they race during practice, the total weight (body weight and sled weight combined) for each athlete must be the same. Study the weights. Which sled should each athlete use? *(Taylor—Sled C, Casey—Sled A, Jess—Sled B)*

**Body Weights**
Taylor—155 pounds
Casey—165 pounds
Jess—170 pounds

**Sled Weights**
Sled A—35 pounds
Sled B—30 pounds
Sled C—45 pounds

Vicki Dabrowka, Palm Harbor, FL

### Valuable Greeting Cards
#### Strategy: guess and check

Bank on strategic thinking with this greeting card project! Display a variety of card-making materials and a corresponding price list. Designate a spending allowance for each student and explain that he will make a greeting card for a chosen occasion. Next, each youngster refers to the display as he lists desired card-making materials and their prices. To ensure that he stays within his budget, he determines the total cost of his listed materials. He eliminates any items that he cannot afford and makes any desired substitutions or additions. After his work receives teacher approval, he gathers the appropriate materials and prepares a card for later hand delivery.

Suzanne Simpson—Gr. 2
Metrowest Elementary
Orlando, FL

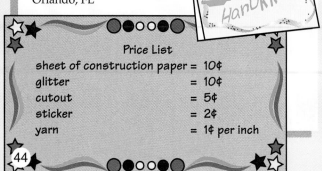

| Price List | |
|---|---|
| sheet of construction paper | = 10¢ |
| glitter | = 10¢ |
| cutout | = 5¢ |
| sticker | = 2¢ |
| yarn | = 1¢ per inch |

| Cups | 🍿 | 1 | 2 | 3 | 4 | 5 | 6 |
|---|---|---|---|---|---|---|---|
| Pieces of Popcorn | 🍿 | 2 | 4 | 6 | 8 | 10 | (12) |
| Cups | 🍿 | 1 | 2 | 3 | 4 | 5 | 6 |
| Pieces of Popcorn | 🍿 | | | | | | |
| Cups | 🍿 | 1 | 2 | 3 | 4 | 5 | 6 |
| Pieces of Popcorn | 🍿 | | | | | | |

### Popcorn Problem
#### Strategy: make a table

Show students that the make-a-table strategy has tasty rewards! Give every two students four small paper cups, a copy of a recording sheet similar to the one shown, and a handful of popcorn in a resealable plastic bag. (Prepare additional popcorn for students to snack on later.) Display a transparency of the form.

To begin, pose this problem to students: If each cup has two pieces of popcorn, how many pieces are in six cups? To determine the answer, guide each twosome to use its popcorn and cups to complete the first four sections of its first table as you add the appropriate information to the transparency. Then have the partners use the resulting pattern to complete the table. Present two more problems for students to solve in a similar manner. What mouthwatering math practice!

Jill Hamilton Lutz—Gr. 1, Schoenecic Elementary, Stevens, PA

# Keys to Problem Solving
## Using Strategies With Success

---

### Stepping Back
**Strategy: working backward**

This backward approach to problem solving leads students straight to the solution! Prepare the following problem for display.

> Kay has a bag of cookies. She gives 2 cookies to her sister and 1 cookie to her mother. She has 3 cookies left. How many cookies did she have to start? *(6 cookies)*

To begin, have each child make ten construction paper cookies to use as manipulatives. Read the problem aloud. Then read it again slowly, allowing time for each student to set aside the indicated quantities of cookies to determine the answer. To check her work, have her act out the scenario with the cookies that she set aside as you reread the problem. (If she has three cookies left, just as Kay did, her answer is correct.) For additional reinforcement, present more cookie-themed problems for students to solve.

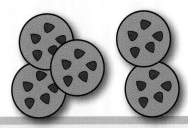

Laura Wagner, Raleigh, NC

---

### Logical Lineup
**Strategy: act it out**

Supply students with this opportunity to practice the act-it-out strategy! Pair students. Have each youngster gather the same four types of school items as his partner and then sit beside him. Instruct partners to stand a folder between themselves and sit so that each youngster's items are hidden from his partner's view.

Next, Partner 1 arranges his items in a row. To determine their sequence, Partner 2 asks strategic yes-or-no questions such as "Is the red crayon after the eraser?" or "Is the pencil first?" After each question-and-answer exchange, Partner 2 adjusts the arrangement of his items, as needed, to reflect Partner 1's response. Then he makes a tally mark on provided paper. When he thinks his items are in the same order as his partner's or he has asked an allotted number of questions, he removes the folder to check his work. Then the partners trade roles and repeat the activity as time allows.

Laura Wagner

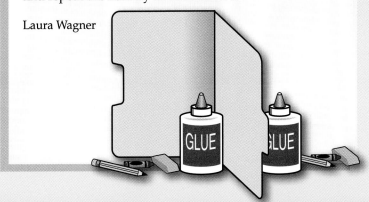

---

### An Everyday Approach
**Strategy: making an appropriate plan**

Here's a way to give problem solving a real-life focus. Periodically present a problem to students that is based on a school activity in your schedule. (See the suggestions on this page.) Guide youngsters to identify the information that is given in the problem and what they need to find out. Then have each student make a plan and use it to determine the solution. Students are sure to agree that knowing how to solve problems comes in handy!

Julie Lewis—Gr. 2, J. O. Davis Elementary
Irving, TX

---

#### Problem-Solving Suggestions
Have students figure out problems such as the following:
- how to fit a special event into the day's schedule
- how many sheets of paper are needed for a project
- how to divide materials equally among group members
- the amount of money needed for a field trip
- how much food to purchase for a class party

## Simply "Marble-ous"!
### Strategy: work backward

Take aim at the work-backward strategy! To begin, tie together the ends of a length of string to make a ring. Set the ring on a flat surface and place several marbles in it. Demonstrate how to use a larger marble to knock marbles out of the ring. Then present the problem shown below. Point out that to determine the answer, it's helpful to start with the known information—the number of marbles that Melvin knocked out of the ring—and then work backward. Have each youngster use this strategy and scrap paper to determine the answer. For additional practice, modify the problem by changing the numbers. Roll on!

Max, Mia, and Melvin played a game of marbles. Max knocked 8 more marbles out of the ring than Mia. Mia knocked 7 more marbles out than Melvin. Melvin knocked 2 marbles out of the ring. How many marbles did Max knock out of the ring? *(17 marbles)*

Valerie Wood Smith—Gr. 1
Robeson Elementary Center
Morgantown, PA

## Number Clues
### Strategy: logical reasoning

Count on this mystery-number activity to boost logical-reasoning skills! Ask four volunteers to stand at the front of the room. Give each volunteer a different number card without revealing the numbers to the seated students. Jot down the cardholders' names and numbers on a piece of scrap paper for your reference. Post a 4 x 4 chart and label it with the numbers and volunteers' names as shown.

Next, announce a clue about a chosen cardholder's number, such as "Nicole's number is three more than Sue's number." Then, with students' input, draw an X in any box that corresponds with a number that the cardholder cannot have and write "yes" in the appropriate box if the clue reveals that the cardholder has a certain number. Continue with additional clues, modeling the process of elimination, until students determine each cardholder's number. Use different volunteers and cards to line up new logical-reasoning challenges!

adapted from an idea by Laura Wagner
Raleigh, NC

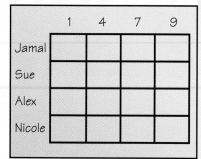

| | 1 | 4 | 7 | 9 |
|---|---|---|---|---|
| Jamal | | | | |
| Sue | | | | |
| Alex | | | | |
| Nicole | | | | |

Michael is practicing for field day. He jumps rope for 3 minutes the first day, 6 minutes the second day, 9 minutes the third day, and so on. If this pattern continues, how many minutes will he jump rope on the fifth day?

| Day | 1 | 2 | 3 | 4 | 5 |
|---|---|---|---|---|---|
| Minutes Jumped | 3 | 6 | 9 | 12 | 15 |

## In Training
### Strategy: make a table

These problems are perfect for building math skills as well as anticipation for an upcoming field day. On each of several days, present a field day–related problem that incorporates a number pattern and can be solved with the make-a-table strategy. For example, announce a problem about a student who runs or throws a Frisbee toy for a greater distance each practice session. Or present a problem featuring a student who jumps rope or hops for a longer time each day. (See the example.) Have each student make a table to solve the problem; then discuss the solution as a class. Your students' problem-solving skills will soon be in tip-top shape!

Valerie Wood Smith

# Keys to Problem Solving
## Using Strategies With Success

### What a Gem!
#### Strategy: make an organized list

Use this dazzling idea to enrich students' list-making skills. Present the following problem to students:

Jim Stone has a jewelry store. He makes rings with blue, green, red, purple, and yellow gems. He uses two different gems for each ring. How many types of rings can he make?

To list the possibilities, each student uses the first letter of each gem color. He pairs each gem with each remaining gem without repeating any combinations. (See the illustration.) When his list is complete, he counts the gem pairs to determine the answer *(10)*. For an easier version of the activity, guide students to illustrate the rings instead of listing them.

Valerie Wood Smith—Gr. 1
Robeson Elementary Center
Morgantown, PA

| BG | GR | RP | PY |
|----|----|----|----|
| BR | GP | RY |    |
| BP | GY |    |    |
| BY |    |    |    |

### Clear Clues
#### Strategy: choose the correct operation

Clue students in on math operations with this simple idea. Have each student label a separate blank card for each grade-appropriate math operation. Suggest that a good problem solver is like a detective because he notices clues in story problems that signal which operations to use. For example, when a problem involves comparing sets, it is a signal that subtraction may be needed.

Next, ask each student to listen for an operation-related clue as you read aloud a chosen story problem. Have him hold up a prepared card to signal the operation he would use to solve the problem. Invite a student with the correct answer to identify the clue. Encourage each youngster to jot down a reminder of the clue on the back of his card. Then determine the solution as a class and continue with additional problems as desired.

Laura Wagner
Raleigh, NC

### Galloping Toward a Solution
#### Strategy: act it out

This hands-on approach to solving problems is a winner! Prepare an overhead transparency of the form on page 48. Use a wipe-off marker to randomly program the first five blanks with the names of the provided riders. In the sixth blank, write the name of the rider that is in the first blank. Have each student color a copy of the patterns (page 48) and then cut them out.

Next, ask each child to imagine that her riders competed in a horse show. To determine the outcome, display the transparency. Then read aloud each clue, pausing for students to sequence their riders as described. After students are satisfied with their work, invite volunteers to share their solutions. Write the answer on the transparency and have students check their work. Wipe off the programming and list the names in a different order to present a new problem. If desired, prepare individual copies of the form to check students' understanding.

Valerie Wood Smith

# Form and Rider Patterns

Use with "Galloping Toward a Solution" on page 47.

## What Are the Results of the Show?

**Clues**

_____ is in fourth place.

_____ finished right ahead of _____.

_____ is not third.

_____ finished behind _____.

**Solution**

1st  _____

2nd  _____

3rd  _____

4th  _____

5th  _____

**Greg**

**Gail**

**Glen**

**Gina**

**Gordon**

# LEARNING CENTERS

# Learning Centers

## Sentence Assembly

Familiar sentences make this **word-order** center a guaranteed success. Write selected sentences from shared writing experiences on sentence strips, or, if appropriate, choose sentence strips that were programmed during the experiences. To prepare each sentence, cut the words apart and number the back of them for self-checking. (For easy management, use a different-colored crayon to number the words for each sentence.) Store each set of words in a separate envelope. Place the envelopes at a center along with writing paper and pencils.

A child removes the words from a selected envelope. She arranges the words to form a sentence and then flips them to check her work. She rearranges the words as needed, writes the sentence on her paper, and then returns the words to the envelope. She repeats the process with the remaining envelopes as time allows.

Michelle Yoko-Rosengrant—Gr. 1, Wingate Elementary School, Wingate, PA

## Sizing Up Snakes

Here's a "sssensational" way to reinforce **linear measurement!** Prepare several construction paper snakes of various lengths. Number the snakes; then make an answer key that lists the length of each snake to the nearest inch (or half inch). Place the snakes and answer key in a decorated container. Place the container at a center along with a ruler, paper, and pencils. A child removes the snakes from the container and numbers his paper. Then he measures each snake to the nearest inch (or half inch) and records its length beside the corresponding number. He uses the answer key to check his work. Measurement skills will be strengthened in short order!

Annie Fitch—Grs. 1–3, Echo Mountain Elementary, Phoenix, AZ

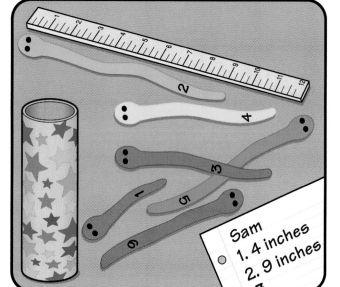

## Stamping Stories

**Writing** earns a stamp of approval at this motivating center! Place at a center several small rubber stamps with decorative images, a washable ink pad, unlined paper, and pencils. A student selects two or three stamps to use in a rebus story. She makes a key for the stamp images at the top of her paper (see the example). Then she writes a brief story, incorporating the stamp impressions as appropriate. What picture-perfect writing inspiration!

Trish Loftus, St. Katherine of Siena School, Philadelphia, PA

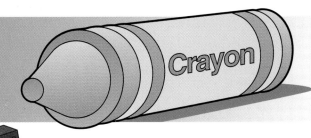

## Alphabet Soup

Serve up "soup-er" practice with **forming words!** At a center, place paper, pencils, a soup ladle, and a small cooking pot containing magnetic letters or lettered tiles. A child uses the ladle to scoop several letters onto her work surface. She forms a word with selected letters and then jots the word on her paper. She rearranges her letters to form additional words. After she writes each word, she returns the letters to the cooking pot. She helps herself to additional scoops and word-building practice as time allows.

Sandy Fader—Gr. 2, Baden Elementary, Brandywine, MD

## Reach for the Stars!

Count on this **addition facts** game to become a class favorite! Place at a center copies of the gameboard on page 59, two different-colored crayons, and two number cubes or dice. Arrange for students to visit the center in pairs. Have the players place one gameboard between them. Each player chooses a crayon and signs his end of the gameboard. To take a turn, a player rolls the cubes or dice. Then he states the corresponding addition fact. He finds the sum on his end of the gameboard. Then, in the corresponding column, he colors the lowest blank space. If a player rolls a sum for which the only available space is a star, he colors the star. If a player rolls a 2, 3, 12, or a sum that has no more available spaces, his turn is over. The first player to color three stars wins!

Josephine Flammer, Adirondack, NY

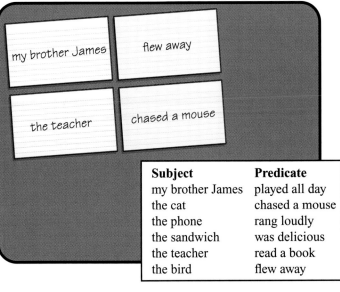

| Subject | Predicate |
|---|---|
| my brother James | played all day |
| the cat | chased a mouse |
| the phone | rang loudly |
| the sandwich | was delicious |
| the teacher | read a book |
| the bird | flew away |

## Sentence Sense

Students brush up on **subjects and predicates** at this easy-to-prepare center. Program an index card for each subject and predicate shown, using a different color of card for each type of phrase. Place the cards at a center along with paper and pencils. A student sorts the subjects and predicates. She arranges pairs of cards to form six sentences that make sense. She writes the sentences on her paper, using correct capitalization and punctuation. Next, she rearranges selected cards to make two silly sentences. She adds these sentences to her paper and draws a smiley face beside each one. Improved sentence-writing skills are sure to be the result!

Mary Beth Maranto—Gr. 3, Tilton School, Haverhill, MA

# Learning Centers

## Fact Wheels

This partner review gets students on a roll with **math facts!** To prepare, make a math-fact wheel by visually dividing a five-inch tagboard circle into eight equal sections. Write a math problem near the outer edge of each section and then punch a hole below each problem. Turn the wheel over; above each hole write the answer to the corresponding problem. Make a desired number of additional wheels; then place the wheels and a pencil at a center.

Partner 1 holds a selected wheel so that his partner can see the back of it. He pokes his pencil tip through a hole and reads the problem aloud. He announces his answer, and Partner 2 confirms or corrects it. The partners continue with the remaining problems. Then they switch roles and repeat the activity with a different wheel. Nifty!

adapted from an idea by Amy Emmons—Gr. 2, Enon Elementary
Franklinton, LA

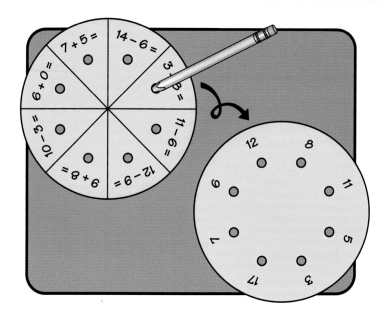

## Fishy Words

Reel in practice with **onsets and rimes.** Cut four fishbowl shapes from construction paper. Cut a large oval from the center of each one and then discard the oval. Label each fishbowl with a rime and each of several fish cutouts with an onset (see the suggested programming). Laminate the fishbowls and fish, leaving intact the laminating film in the center of the fishbowls. Place the fishbowls and fish at a center stocked with paper and pencils.

A student reads the rime on a selected fishbowl. She finds a fish labeled with an onset that can be used with the rime to form a word. She places the fish on the fishbowl and then jots the word on her paper. After she identifies and writes the remaining word possibilities, she removes the fish, selects another fishbowl, and repeats the process.

adapted from an idea by Mary Beth Godbout, Gilford, NH

**Onsets**
b, n, p, r, sp, t

**Rimes**
-ack, -est, -in, -ot

Laticia
back
pack
rack
tack

## Trading Places

**Place-value practice** is in the cards! At a center, place two place-value mats similar to the ones shown and a deck of playing cards (tens, jacks, queens, and jokers removed). Arrange for students to visit the center in pairs.

The players stack the cards facedown. Player 1 takes the top three cards one at a time, placing each card in the first empty column on his mat. If he has a king, he replaces it with another card from the stack and, if possible, rearranges two of his cards to create a larger number (aces represent one); he places the king in a discard pile. Player 2 takes a turn in a similar manner. The player with the greater three-digit number takes all the cards from the mats. Alternate play continues until only four cards remain in the draw pile. The player with more cards wins!

Liana Mahoney—Grs. 1–2 Looping, Beaver River Central School, Beaver Falls, NY

52

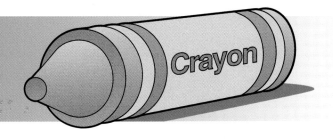

## Compound Worms

These unique earthworms will have students digging into **compound words!** Prepare ten construction paper earthworms and cut each worm into two sections. Program the sections in pairs to form compound words as shown and then make an answer key. Place the prepared sections in a small plastic pail. Set the pail, answer key, paper, and pencils at a center. A student arranges the sections to form ten compound words; she uses the answer key to check her work. Then she chooses five of the compound words and writes a sentence with each one.

Cindy Powell, Erie, PA

## Pocket Change

Bank on improved **coin-counting skills** at this easy-to-adapt center. Mount ten library pockets onto a sheet of poster board. Number the tops of ten vertically positioned index cards 1 to 10. Below each number, stamp a different coin combination that is suitable for students' ability levels. Label an index card half for each total and use a paper clip to attach it to a pocket as shown. Place the prepared poster board, the coin-combination cards, and an answer key at a center.

A student selects a card, counts the coins, and places the card in the corresponding pocket. He repeats the process with the remaining cards and then uses the answer key to check his work. As students' coin-counting skills progress, prepare more challenging cards and label the pockets with the corresponding totals. Priceless!

Anne E. South—Gr. 2, East Oro Public School, Orillia, Ontario, Canada

## Mail Matters

Here's a center that delivers improved **letter-writing skills!** Label a large, empty tissue box "Mail" and remove the plastic from the box opening. Place the resulting mailbox at a center along with a list of suggested in-school mail recipients. Stock the center with letter-writing supplies, such as pencils, stationery, index cards (postcards), and small envelopes or stickers to seal folded letters. Add student references, such as a list of possible letter-writing topics or letter-formatting guidelines.

To use the center, a youngster writes a letter to a chosen student or staff member. She uses established guidelines to edit her writing. She prepares the letter for hand delivery and then drops it in the mailbox for designated student mail carriers to collect. Now that's kid-pleasing letter-writing practice—signed, sealed, and delivered!

adapted from an idea by Janet Robbins—Grs. K–2, Fairview Elementary School Richmond, IN

# Learning Centers

## Chocolaty Place Value

Whet students' appetites for **place value** with this oh-so-tempting partner center. Place 12 red and 12 silver foil-wrapped chocolate Kisses candies in a container. (Set aside additional candy for student snacks.) Place the container, a pair of dice, the provided code, and half sheets of paper at a center.

Each partner divides his paper into fourths. To determine the first addend of a vertical addition problem, Partner 1 rolls the dice and takes this many red candies. He rolls again and takes this many silver candies. He uses the code to identify the corresponding number and then each partner writes it in the first section of his paper. Partner 2 uses the same process to determine the second addend. Each partner finishes setting up his problem and then solves it. The partners return the candies and continue the activity to complete their papers.

Lin Attaya—Gr. 2, Newton Rayzor Elementary, Denton, TX

## Sentences on the Go

Take **sentence writing** on the road! Use the patterns on page 60 to prepare a car and 12 license plates. Store the cutouts in a resealable plastic bag. Place the bag and a supply of writing paper at a center. A student sets the car on a work surface and then places a chosen license plate on it. Next, she reads the license plate letters and writes a noun that begins with the first letter and a verb that begins with the second letter. She pens a sentence with the words and then sets the license plate aside. She repeats the activity as time allows. For a greater challenge, add a letter to each license plate and have students brainstorm adjective-noun-verb combinations for their sentences.

Laura Hess—Grs. 2–3, Providence School, Greencastle, PA

## Letter-Perfect Lists

Line up practice with **ABC order.** Program a supply of seasonal cutouts with words appropriate for your students' alphabetizing skills. Place the cutouts in a decorated gift bag and label the bag with the number of words that you would like students to alphabetize at one time. Place the bag at a center stocked with paper. A student takes the designated number of cutouts at random. He arranges the cutouts in ABC order and then lists the sequenced words on his paper. He returns the cutouts to the bag and scrambles them. Then he takes another selection of cutouts from the bag and uses them to write a second list. Now that's an idea sure to suit students to a T!

adapted from an idea by Jen Ratka—Gr. 2
Hillview Elementary School, Lancaster, NY

## Pasta Punctuation

This **quotation mark** center will be the talk of the classroom! At a center stocked with paper, place a supply of sentence strips, a bowl of uncooked macaroni, permanent markers, and glue. For writing inspiration, cut out various magazine pictures of people. Glue the pictures onto construction paper and place them at the center. A student writes on her paper three sentences of dialogue inspired by one or more pictures, being sure to use quotation marks appropriately. Then she uses a marker to write a selected sentence on a sentence strip, gluing on macaroni noodles in place of the quotation marks.

Natalie Tanner, Houston, TX

## Fishy Measurements

Students size up the day's catch at this **measurement** center. Prepare several fish cutouts in a variety of whole-centimeter lengths. Letter the fish and then place them in a pail. Label the pail with a length that is longer than about half of the fish. To make an answer key, list the fish by letter in groups to show which are shorter than, equal to, or longer than the designated length. Place the pail, the answer key, a metric ruler, and a supply of paper at a center.

A student divides his paper into three columns. He labels the middle column with the designated length and labels the first and third columns as shown. He measures each fish and writes its letter in the correct column. Then he uses the answer key to check his work. What a catch!

adapted from an idea by Linda Stroik—Gr. 2
Bannach Elementary School, Stevens Point, WI

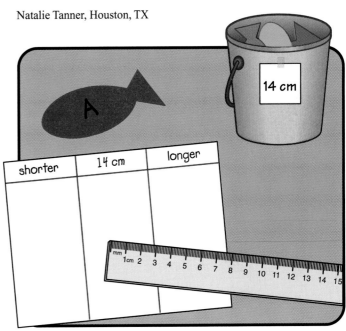

## All Clear!

Strategy and **addition** skills come in to play with this partner game. Divide two sentence strip lengths into 8 sections and then number the sections on each strip. Place the strips, a supply of counters, and a pair of dice at a center. To begin, each player sets one counter in each section of her sentence strip. Player 1 rolls the dice and announces the numbers. She removes the counter from one or both of the corresponding sections on her sentence strip, or she removes the counter from the section that shows the total of her dice. Player 2 takes a turn in a similar manner. As alternate play continues, if a player cannot remove any counters for the numbers rolled, her turn is over. The first player to remove all of her counters wins.

adapted from an idea by Amy B. Barsanti—Gr. 3
Pines Elementary, Plymouth, NC

## Laying Down the Facts

This partner game is well-suited for **addition!** At a center, place a deck of playing cards with the face cards removed. One player deals six cards each to herself and her partner. She stacks the remaining cards facedown. To take a turn, a player studies her cards to determine whether she can represent an addition fact with three of them (jokers stand for zero and aces for one). If she can, she arranges the three cards on the playing surface and states the fact. Then she sets the cards aside and draws three cards (or as many as possible if three cards are not left in the stack). If she cannot represent a fact, she draws one card and her turn ends. Players alternate turns until they cannot represent any more facts. The player who puts aside more cards wins.

Shannon Adams
Waxahachie Faith Family Academy
Waxahachie, TX

## Mouthwatering Opposites

Youngsters get the scoop on **antonyms** at this cool center! Program an ice-cream scoop and cone for each provided antonym pair (see the illustration). Number the backs of the cutouts for self-checking. If desired, laminate the cutouts for durability. Place the cutouts in a sturdy, clean ice-cream container and then set the container at a center. To assemble the ice-cream treats, a child places each scoop on the cone with the corresponding antonym. She flips the cutouts to check her work. Mmm!

Mary Beth Godbout
Gilford, NH

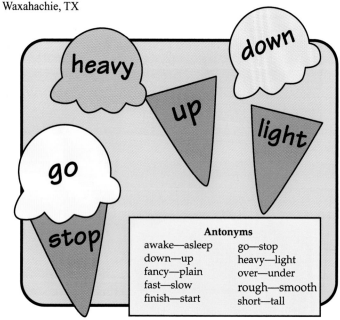

| Antonyms | |
| --- | --- |
| awake—asleep | go—stop |
| down—up | heavy—light |
| fancy—plain | over—under |
| fast—slow | rough—smooth |
| finish—start | short—tall |

## Multiplication Minibooklets

These tiny booklets provide **multiplication** practice in a big way! Stock a center with a stapler, marker, and pencils. Also provide 3" x 12" construction paper strips (booklet covers) and white paper strips approximately 2" x 5½" (booklet pages). A student folds a construction paper strip in half and staples several white paper strips inside. She uses a marker to title and sign her resulting booklet as desired.

Next, she folds back the ends of the pages as a group and then unfolds them. She labels the front of each page with a multiplication fact that she needs to practice, writing the problem to the left of the fold line and the product to the right. She folds back each product so that its page can be turned separately. She reads a problem, identifies the product, and then unfolds the page to check the answer. With each reading, she's sure to recall the facts more quickly!

adapted from an idea by Terri Hamilton, Chariho Schools
Wood River Junction, RI

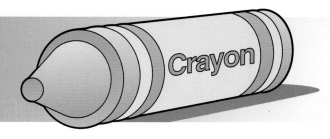

## Lots of Lists!

Reinforce selected skills or topics with this versatile **list-making** idea. On each of several blank cards, identify a different list for students to write, specifying the number of words or items. Place the cards in a labeled container. Set the container at a center stocked with a stapler, 4½" x 12" construction paper strips, and writing paper that has been cut in half lengthwise. A student randomly takes a card and appropriately titles a piece of writing paper. He writes a numbered list and then returns the card to the container. As time allows, he makes additional lists in the same manner. He stacks his completed lists on a construction paper strip and staples the entire stack at the top.

Valerie Wood Smith
Morgantown, PA

## Attractive Fractions

This center attracts plenty of **fraction** practice! Place in each of several disposable cups up to 12 paper clips of two different colors (vary the quantities for each cup). Set the cups and a magnet or magnetic wand at a center stocked with paper and pencils. A student uses the magnet to randomly remove several paper clips from one cup. She sets the paper clips on a work surface and sorts them by color. For each color, she writes the appropriate fractional amount. She returns the paper clips to the cup. Then she repeats the process with the remaining cups.

Karen Fouts—Gr. 3
Honey Creek Elementary School
Conyers, GA

## Clear Endings

Here's a hands-on activity that brings **suffixes** into clear view. For each root word on the answer key shown, label a separate 3" x 5" index card, leaving space after the word. Cut four 3" x 5" rectangles from a blank transparency sheet. Use a permanent marker to write each featured suffix on a different rectangle. Then prepare an answer key. Place the index cards, rectangles, and answer key in a large labeled envelope. Set the envelope at a center with paper and pencils. A student removes the words and suffixes. He positions the suffixes on selected cards to form new words and writes each word on his paper. He adds suffixes to the remaining root words in a similar manner, adding each newly formed word to his paper. Then he checks his work with the answer key.

adapted from an idea by Kish Harris—Gr. 2
Southampton Academy
Courtland, VA

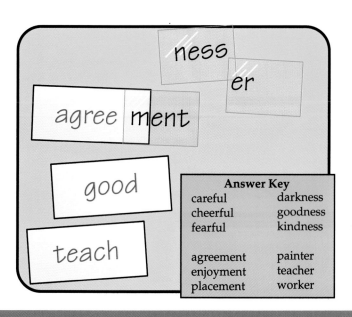

| Answer Key | |
|---|---|
| careful | darkness |
| cheerful | goodness |
| fearful | kindness |
| | |
| agreement | painter |
| enjoyment | teacher |
| placement | worker |

# Learning Centers

## Mouthwatering Words

Dish up refreshing **onset and rime** practice! Label a disposable bowl, as shown, for each listed rime and a Ping-Pong ball (ice cream) for each listed onset. Place the ice cream in a clean, empty ice-cream carton. Set the carton, bowls, an ice-cream scooper, paper, and pencils at a center.

A student divides her paper into fourths and labels each section with a featured rime. She places a scoop of ice cream in a bowl labeled with a rime that forms a word with the onset. Then she writes the word on her paper. In a similar manner, she identifies one more rime that can be used with the onset. Then she repeats the process with the remaining onsets. How tempting!

Laura Hess—Grs. 2–3
Providence School
Waynesboro, PA

## Colorful Packs

Keep **singular and plural** skills sharp! Program a construction paper crayon cutout for each listed word. Seal a letter-size envelope and then cut it in half. With the opening at the top, label one half "singular" and one half "plural." Color each half to resemble a crayon box. Prepare an answer key similar to the one shown and fold it in half. Place the crayons, boxes, and answer key at a center stocked with paper and pencils.

A student sorts the crayons into the appropriate boxes. Then she uses the key to check her work. Finally, she selects one crayon from each box and writes a sentence for each one. **For a more challenging word sort,** label crayon cutouts with singular words and a different box for each plural spelling pattern.

adapted from an idea by Mary Beth Godbout
Gilford, NH

## Chilly Computation

This cool partner game provides a solid review of **basic facts.** Vertically position an empty ice cube tray. Use self-adhesive dots to label the top of each section with a number that is appropriate for addition (or multiplication) practice. Place the tray, two small pom-poms, paper, and pencils at a center.

The players position the tray so that the numbers face Player 2. To play one round, Player 1 closes his eyes and randomly drops each pom-pom into a different section. He turns the tray to view the numbers and then adds (or multiplies) them. He writes his answer and removes the pom-poms. Then Player 2 takes a turn. The player with the greater answer earns one point. (No points are awarded for a tie.) After a total of ten rounds, the top-scoring player is declared the winner.

adapted from an idea by Tracy Abernathy—Gr. 3
Chatsworth Elementary
Chatsworth, GA

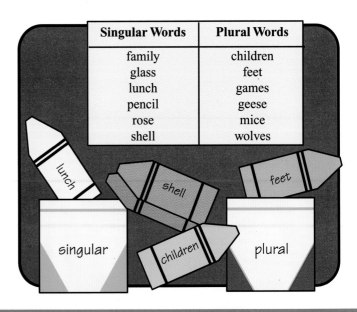

| Singular Words | Plural Words |
|---|---|
| family | children |
| glass | feet |
| lunch | games |
| pencil | geese |
| rose | mice |
| shell | wolves |

| 11 | 10 | 9 | 8 | 7 | 6 | 5 | 4 |
|---|---|---|---|---|---|---|---|
|  |  |  |  |  |  |  |  |
|  |  |  |  |  |  |  |  |
|  |  |  |  |  |  |  |  |
| ★ | ★ | ★ | ★ | ★ | ★ | ★ | ★ |
|  |  |  |  |  |  |  |  |
|  |  |  |  |  |  |  |  |
|  |  |  |  |  |  |  |  |
| 11 | 10 | 9 | 8 | 7 | 6 | 5 | 4 |

# Reach for
# the Stars!

Player 1 _____

©The Education Center, Inc. • *THE MAILBOX® • Primary •* Aug/Sept 2003

**Note to the teacher:** Use with "Reach for the Stars!" on page 51.

59

# Car and License Plate Patterns

Use with "Sentences on the Go" on page 54.

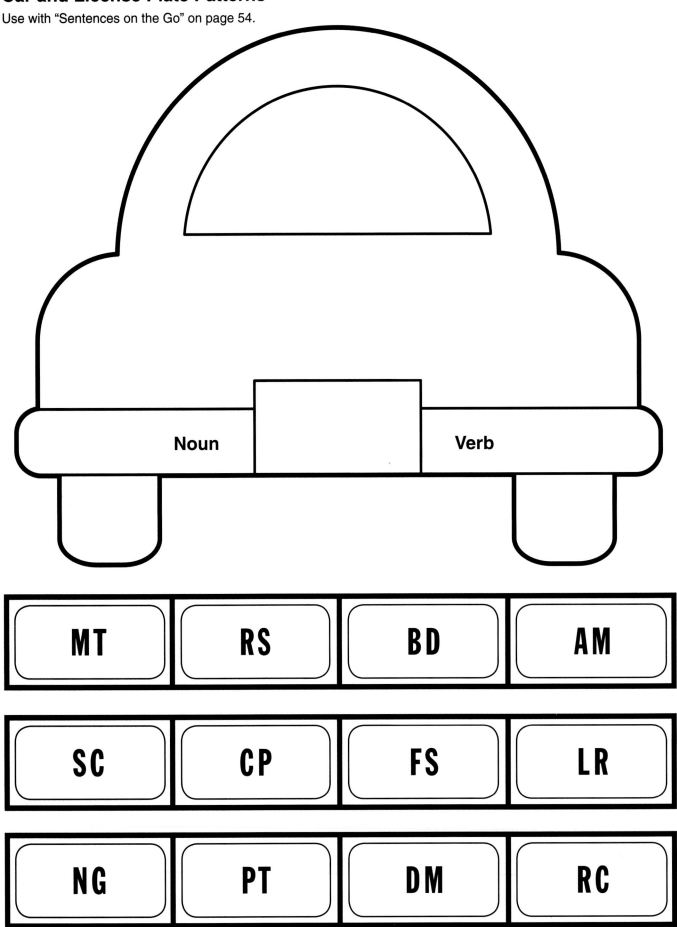

Noun | Verb

| MT | RS | BD | AM |

| SC | CP | FS | LR |

| NG | PT | DM | RC |

# Lifesavers: Management Tips for Teachers

# LIFESAVERS...
## management tips for teachers

## All-in-One Binder

Keep valuable information and forms at your fingertips! Gather important papers, such as a class list, an attendance form, the discipline policy, and the current school lunch menu. Insert each document into a separate top-loading sheet protector and then place the protectors in a binder. Keep the binder in a handy location, updating its contents periodically. Throughout the year, refer any substitutes to this timesaving resource!

Paula Reiner—Gr. 1
Fairview Elementary
Wellsville, OH

## Arrival and Dismissal Wheel

Here's an attendance keeper and dismissal monitor—all rolled into one! Program a multisection tagboard circle with your students' dismissal options. Color it, if desired, and laminate it for durability. Display the circle within students' reach, keeping the border free. Set a container of personalized clothespins nearby. Upon arrival, a child clips her clothespin to the circle to show her dismissal plans. A glance at the clothespin container will reveal any absences. And a quick check of the display will remind you to collect the parent notes for any new dismissal arrangements. Count on dismissal to run like clockwork!

Jennifer Iannuccilli—Gr. 3
Frenchtown School
East Greenwich, RI

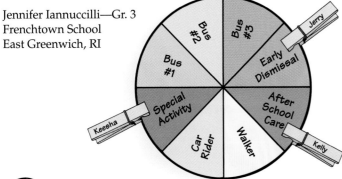

## Absentee Assignments

Keeping track of assignments for absent students just got easier! Label a large manila envelope "Absent? Check here!" and display it in a prominent classroom location. Throughout each day, personalize any assignments you'd like for each absent student to complete and drop them in the envelope. When a child returns to school, he'll know exactly where to find his work!

Judy Copeland—Gr. 3, Start Elementary, Start, LA

## To-Do Lists

You'll refer to this running list of back-to-school tasks year after year! Use a word processing program to prepare a checklist of your anticipated tasks. Print a hard copy of the list. Check off tasks as you accomplish them and jot down any additional tasks as they arise. Before discarding the checklist, modify the document on your computer as needed. Next fall, you'll have a to-do list that's easy to adapt!

Teresa Williams—Gr. 1
Coquihalla Elementary
Hope, British Columbia, Canada

> **Fall To-Do List**
> 1. Prepare desktags.
> 2. Organize library.
> 3. Display welcome poster.
> 4. Post job chart.
> 5. Prepare substitute plans.
> 6. Copy lunch and attendance slips.

## Managing Math Time

Looking for a way to maximize math time? Try this! Prepare several math buckets for students to share. In each one, include pencils, a handheld sharpener, crayons, scissors, and frequently used manipulatives. If desired, add a few laminated sheets of math problems and wipe-off markers for early finishers. Now less time will be spent gathering and returning materials during math lessons. What a great solution!

Dawn Lindboe—Grs. 1–2 Multiage
Five Points Elementary School, Lake City, FL

## Promoting Parent Communication

These refrigerator magnets encourage parents to stay in touch! Use a word processing program to prepare a class supply of address labels with your contact information. Adhere each label to an eye-catching cutout. Laminate the cutout and mount a piece of magnetic tape to the back. Distribute the resulting magnets at a back-to-school event or send them home with a cheerful note. What an attractive way to promote parent-teacher communication!

JoAnn Saunders—Gr. 1
Fort Bend Baptist Academy
Sugar Land, TX

# LIFESAVERS...
## management tips for teachers

### Bottle Buddies

Put a cap on pencil searches with these desktop holders! To make a holder, cut the top off an empty plastic water bottle and discard it. Use adhesive Velcro strips to secure the remaining portion of the bottle to the top of a student's desk. Then have the child stand her pencils in the holder. Time-consuming pencil searches will become a thing of the past!

Tina Schofield—Special Education
Bear Creek Elementary School
Baltimore, MD

### Tuneful Transitions

Smooth transitions after recess are the result of this simple suggestion! As students return to the classroom, dim the lights and play soothing music. Have each child silently select a book and settle into a designated reading area. Then adjust the lights so that students can read easily. At the end of the reading session, turn the music off. At this signal, students silently return their books and turn their attention to you!

Valerie Wittkop—Gr. 2, Coronado Village Elementary
Universal City, TX

### Journal Response Labels

Try this efficient strategy for responding to students' journal entries. Use a word-processing program to prepare blank labels with comments you often use to give students feedback on their writing. After reading a child's journal entry, adhere an appropriate comment to the page and jot down any additional feedback. Students will know that you've checked their journals, plus you'll save precious time!

Ann Marie Stephens
G. C. Round Elementary
Manassas, VA

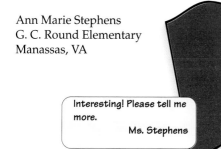

Interesting! Please tell me more.

Ms. Stephens

### Word Wall Filing

If you reuse word wall cards, you won't want to miss this recipe for storage success. Obtain a recipe box that contains lettered tabs. After you remove a card from your word wall, store it in the box behind the appropriate tab. Later you'll know exactly where to find it!

Dana Poore—Gr. 1, Bay View Elementary, North East, MD

### Homework Incentive

Show students that completing homework has its rewards! Each day give an identical paper strip to each youngster who completes all of her homework. Have her sign the strip and place it in a decorated container. After several days, remove a few strips and present each corresponding student with a pass for a desired activity. Help students see the role that probability plays—the more strips a student submits, the greater the chance her name will be chosen.

Joan Holesko—Gr. 3
Ohio Elementary
North Tonawanda, NY

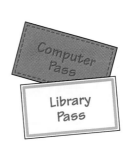

Computer Pass

Library Pass

Brandi

### Attention Getter

Get students' attention with this multilingual approach! With the help of students or colleagues familiar with foreign languages, teach your class to count to three and say, "Ready!" in two or more languages. Post the corresponding words for later reference. When it's time to call the class to attention, count in a chosen language and have students respond, "Ready!" in the same language. Students will be all ears in a jiffy!

Susanne Henton—Gr. 2
St. Charles School
Oakview, MO

63

# LIFESAVERS...
## management tips for teachers

### Classroom Cleanup

Looking for a simple way to maintain a tidy classroom? Try this! Before starting a new activity or lesson, begin whistling a familiar tune. At this signal, have students straighten up their work areas and throw away any trash. To minimize talking, invite youngsters to whistle while they work. You'll have a quiet transition and a classroom that's clean as a whistle!

Mandy Browning
Eastern Elementary
Georgetown, KY

### Pockets of Notes

Parent communication just got easier! For each child, mount a library pocket inside a personalized take-home folder. When you need to relay a message to a parent, jot a note on an index card and then tuck it inside the pocket. Have the parent use the same folder to send any replies. Nifty!

Debby Moon—Gr. 1
Base Primary School
Mountain Home, ID

### Whose Turn?

Everyone has an opportunity to participate when you use this strategy for calling on students. Write each youngster's name on a separate blank card. Hole-punch the cards and use a metal ring to fasten them together. To determine which student to call on first, read the first card on the ring. After the student responds, place a sticky note on his card to mark the beginning of the card ring. Then flip the card to the back to reveal the name of the next student. Continue using the cards in order during various activities until every student has been called on. To vary the calling order, remove the sticky note and cards. Then shuffle the cards and refasten them.

Cindy Ward—Learning Disabilities Grs. K–4
Yellow Branch Elementary, Rustburg, VA

### Schedule in View

Here's a timesaving way to post a daily schedule. Label a colorful tagboard strip for each regularly scheduled activity. Laminate the programmed strips, as well as a few blank ones. (Plan to use a wipe-off marker to label the blank strips with special events.) Adhere a piece of magnetic tape to the back of each strip. Each day, sequence the appropriate strips on a magnetic board and write the anticipated start time beside each activity. The plan for the day will be clear!

Andrea Hetzke
Arlington Heights, IL

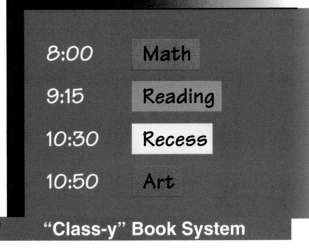

| 8:00 | Math |
| 9:15 | Reading |
| 10:30 | Recess |
| 10:50 | Art |

### "Class-y" Book System

This tip for organizing classroom library books is worth checking out! Use various colors of self-adhesive dots to code selected books by author, series, reading level, or another desired characteristic. Group the books by code in labeled baskets or other suitable containers. Post a color code for student reference. Not only will the code help students find books that suit their interests and needs, but it will also help them return the books with ease!

Julie Lewis—Gr. 2
J. O. Davis Elementary
Irving, TX

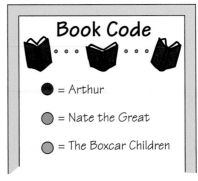

Book Code
● = Arthur
● = Nate the Great
● = The Boxcar Children

# LIFESAVERS...
## management tips for teachers

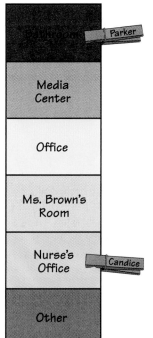

## Destination Display

Keep track of students' comings and goings with this easy-to-prepare display. Divide a tagboard strip into several sections. With the strip vertically positioned, label the sections with various school locations, reserving the last section for "Other." Color the strip if desired. Laminate it for durability, and then post it near the classroom door so that it's within students' reach and the sides are free. Clip personalized clothespins to the rim of an empty shoebox for easy access and then set the shoebox near the display. Before a student leaves the classroom, she clips her clothespin to the appropriate section of the strip. She returns the clothespin to the shoebox when she returns. How handy!

Candice Marshall—Gr. 1
Kensington Parkwood Elementary
  School
Kensington, MD

## Substitute Savvy

Here's a timesaving way to share important information with substitutes. Use a word-processing program to create a pocket-size pamphlet about relevant topics such as classroom procedures and materials. Tuck the pamphlet into a labeled pocket folder and leave the folder in an easy-to-spot location. To prepare for an absence, simply add the day's lesson plans to the folder. You won't need to rewrite routine information, and the pamphlet will be a nifty reference for the sub to keep with her throughout the day!

Tammy Cress
Schaeffer Academy
Rochester, MN

## Team Transitions

If your students sit in small groups, this transition idea is for you! Write on the board a team name or letter for each group. At the completion of a classroom activity, use a designated signal to prompt students to prepare for the next task. Award one point to the first team that is ready, two points to the second team, and so on. At the end of the day (or week), congratulate the team that has the fewest points and reward its members as desired. Go team!

Candi Deal—Gr. 1, Westwood School, Dalton, GA

## Early Finishers

Need a way to help early finishers use their time wisely? Try this tempting suggestion! Cut a supply of cookie shapes from tan construction paper. Program each cookie with a skill-reinforcing task that students can complete independently. Laminate the cookies for durability and then place them in a nonbreakable cookie jar or tin. When a student finishes an assignment early, he randomly takes a cookie and then completes the task. He returns the cookie and selects another task to do if time allows. Periodically prepare fresh batches of cookies to keep student interest high!

adapted from an idea by Stacey Barnett—Gr. 2
Martinez Elementary School
North Las Vegas, NV

## Storing Units for Stories

Organizing materials for literature-based lessons has never been easier! Place a supply of multi-page capacity sheet protectors in a large three-ring binder. For each desired story, insert copies of your favorite teaching ideas and reproducibles into one or more sheet protectors; label each sheet protector with the story's title. When you're ready for a literature unit, you'll have helpful materials at your fingertips. Plus, you can easily remove materials from the binder for photocopying, planning at home, or sharing with a colleague.

Lisa Strieker—Gr. 3, St. Paul Elementary, Highland, IL

65

# LIFESAVERS...
## management tips for teachers

### Buddy Sticks

You'll want to stick with this efficient method for pairing students! Gather a class supply of craft sticks. Adhere a seasonal ministicker to one end of each stick so that each stick is identical to exactly one other. (If you have an odd number of students, prepare an extra stick to make a set of three.) Place the sticks in a decorated container, sticker end down. To pair students, have each youngster randomly select a stick and then find the student who has the identical sticker. If a student has no match because a classmate is absent, invite him to join a twosome of his choice.

Sheila Criqui-Kelley—Gr. 1
Lebo Elementary
Lebo, KS

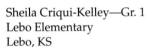
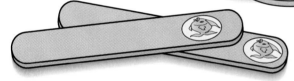

### Who's Next?

Need a way to manage turn-taking for a classroom computer or chosen activity? Try this picture-perfect solution! Insert individual student photographs into the plastic sleeves of a standing flip photo album. To begin, flip to the first photograph and have this student take a turn. When his turn is over, have him flip his photograph and call the following student. Next, please!

Jamie Zidle—Gr. 2
Chattahoochee Elementary School
Duluth, GA

### Sock Solution

If you use individual whiteboards, here's a nifty timesaver for distributing and collecting the materials. For each whiteboard, obtain a clean sock for students to use as an eraser. (Unmatched socks from the laundry are convenient choices.) Place a wipe-off marker inside the sock and store the sock with the whiteboard. When it's time for a student to use a whiteboard, she'll have a writing utensil, an eraser, and marker storage all rolled into one...sock!

Beth Brady
Lake Park Elementary
Lake Park, GA

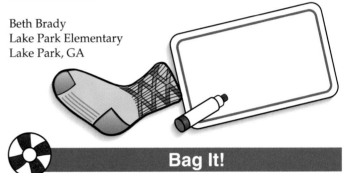

### Bag It!

If time runs short during a student project, use this simple storage idea. Have each youngster use a permanent marker to sign her name on a large resealable plastic bag; then ask her to place all of her materials in the bag. She'll have everything she needs when she returns to the project, and you won't need to keep track of loose pieces. Now that's a clear strategy for keeping things together!

Christine Fischer—Special Education Grs. 1–3
Edward S. Rhodes School
Cranston, RI

### Silent Signals

These colorful signals are perfect for monitoring small-group work. Give each group two disposable plastic cups—one red and one blue. A group member stacks the cups upside down with the blue cup on top. To indicate a need for teacher assistance, a student restacks the cups so that the red cup is on top; then the group continues working. You'll know at a glance who needs your attention. Plus, the students will know that they'll receive help as soon as possible!

adapted from an idea by
Dawn Maucieri—Gr. 3
Signal Hill School
Dix Hills, NY

66

# MATH MAILBAG

# Math Mailbag

## Place-Value Clues
### Skill: interpreting place value

Get students into the rhythm of place value! Display within students' reach the provided chant and a large hundred chart. Secretly choose a number from 1 to 100. To give a clue about the number, recite the chant to students, filling in the blanks with the appropriate digits. Invite a student who correctly guesses the number to point it out on the hundred chart. (If desired, have her also point out the numbers that are ten more and ten less.) Ask the child to secretly select a different number and then use the chant to challenge her classmates to identify it. Plan to repeat the activity often to keep math skills in place!

Ashley Maher—Gr. 2
Forest Park Elementary
Kannapolis, NC

**Chant**
I'm thinking of a number—
Can you guess?
It has [_digit_] tens and [_digit_] ones.
Do your best!

## Graphing ABCs
### Skill: organizing and graphing data

Here's a letter-perfect way to reinforce graphing skills! Prepare a titled and labeled grid like the one shown, leaving it unnumbered. Read aloud *Chicka Chicka Boom Boom* by Bill Martin Jr. and John Archambault, a tale of tree-climbing alphabet letters that topple to the ground in a jumbled heap. Next, tell students that each of them will organize a jumble of letters. Give each child glue, a disposable cup containing Alpha-Bits cereal, and a copy of the prepared grid. Instruct him to number his grid 0 to 10. Have him count out ten unbroken cereal pieces, and confirm that he can distinguish between the vowels and consonants. Then tell him to glue his ten cereal pieces in the appropriate grid spaces. Guide students to discuss and analyze their resulting graphs as they snack on their leftover cereal.

To modify the activity for more advanced students, have each child take 20 cereal pieces, number a prepared grid by twos, and then color it to show the number of cereal pieces in each category.

adapted from an idea by Lisa A. Kelly
Orchard Lake, MI

| Alpha-Bits Cereal Graph | | | | | | | | | | | |
|---|---|---|---|---|---|---|---|---|---|---|---|
| Consonants | B | D | X | T | R | Q | R | | | | |
| Vowels | U | A | O | | | | | | | | |
| | 0 | 1 | 2 | 3 | 4 | 5 | 6 | 7 | 8 | 9 | 10 |

## Number Fans
### Skill: reviewing computation

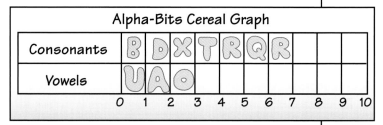

These handy number fans make responding to math problems a breeze! Give each child a brad and twenty 1" x 4" tagboard strips. To make her fan, have each child vertically position her strips. For each number 0 to 9, ask her to label the top of two strips. With adult assistance as needed, she hole-punches the bottom of each strip, stacks the strips from the least to greatest number (pairing identical numbers), and then secures the strips with the brad. To respond to a math problem, she manipulates her fan to show her answer and holds the fan up for teacher verification. Nifty!

Marlene Osman—Gr. 2
Wheelock Primary School
Fredonia, NY

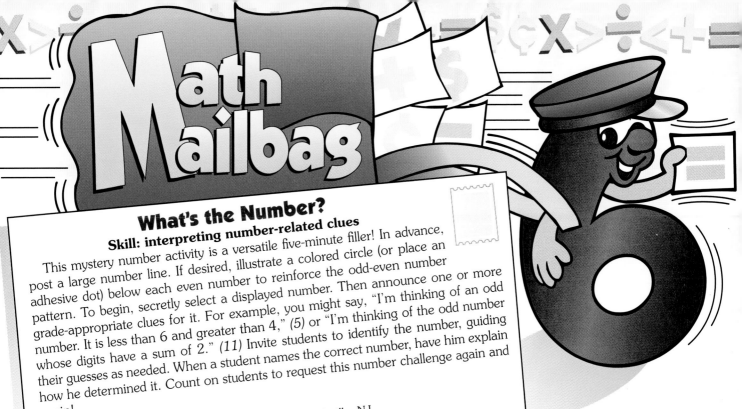

# Math Mailbag

## What's the Number?
### Skill: interpreting number-related clues

This mystery number activity is a versatile five-minute filler! In advance, post a large number line. If desired, illustrate a colored circle (or place an adhesive dot) below each even number to reinforce the odd-even number pattern. To begin, secretly select a displayed number. Then announce one or more grade-appropriate clues for it. For example, you might say, "I'm thinking of an odd number. It is less than 6 and greater than 4," (5) or "I'm thinking of the odd number whose digits have a sum of 2." (11) Invite students to identify the number, guiding their guesses as needed. When a student names the correct number, have him explain how he determined it. Count on students to request this number challenge again and again!

Mary Ellen Burns—Gr. 1, Belleville Public School 7, Belleville, NJ

| Before | | After |
|--------|--------|--------|
| Get dressed. | Ride the bus. | Go to the playground. |
| Eat breakfast. | TOOTHPASTE Brush my teeth. | Put my toothbrush away. |
| Have a snack. | Take my dog for a walk. | Give my dog a treat. |

## Timely Activities
### Skill: understanding concepts of time

The concepts of *before* and *after* become clear with this simple idea. Draw a three-column chart; title the first and last columns as shown. Then give each student a copy. In the first box of the middle column, have her use words and pictures to identify a chosen daily activity. In the appropriate columns of the same row, instruct her to note an earlier and a later activity. Have her complete the rest of her paper in a similar manner. Then ask volunteers to use the words *before* and *after* as they tell the class about the activities in selected rows of their charts.

adapted from an idea by Janet Robbins—Grade 1
Fairview Elementary School
Richmond, IN

## Perfect Polygons
### Skills: forming and identifying polygons

Create a colorful display of student-made shapes! To prepare, list the following shapes on the board: hexagon, pentagon, square, triangle. Confirm that students can identify the number of sides for each shape. Next, divide students into groups of three or four. Give each group 18 craft sticks, glue, and markers. Instruct each group to arrange its craft sticks on a work surface to form each listed shape. After checking a group's work, have the youngsters choose their two favorite shapes. Instruct them to color the craft sticks for these two shapes and then glue the sticks in place. After the glue dries, use string to suspend each figure from the ceiling. What a fun way to shape up geometry skills!

adapted from an idea by Starin Lewis
Phoenix, AZ

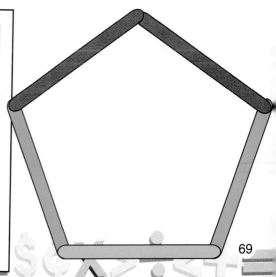

69

# Math Mailbag

## Counting on Estimates
### Skill: making reasonable estimates

This ongoing estimation activity is beyond compare! Collect several clear, unbreakable lidded containers. In each container, place a large quantity of nonperishable items such as buttons, pom-poms, or seashells.

To begin, display one container. Have each child write on scrap paper his estimate of the number of items. Then ask a volunteer to determine the actual count. After students discuss how their estimates compare with this number, the volunteer writes it on the bottom of the lid for your later reference. He uses a sticky note to label the container for students' reference. Periodically add a container to the display until each container has been used. With each addition, repeat the estimating and counting process, encouraging students to use known quantities, the sizes of the containers, and other details to help them make reasonable estimates. Students will gain sharper math skills, and you'll have precounted collections to use for math practice next year!

Kim Hermes—Gr. 1
Furry School
Sandusky, OH

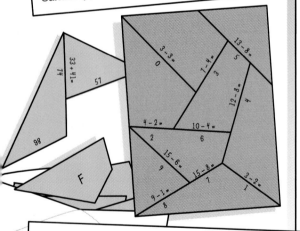

## Problem Puzzles
### Skill: computation

Piece together computation practice! Visually divide a sheet of tagboard into sections of various shapes and sizes (see the illustration). Program the opposite sides of each line with a problem and its answer so that there are no problems that have the same answer. Cut along the lines to make puzzle pieces. For easy management, label an envelope and the back of each puzzle piece with the same chosen letter. Store the puzzle pieces in the envelope. Prepare a desired number of additional puzzles.

A child selects an envelope and removes the puzzle pieces. She solves a selected problem, jotting any calculations on scrap paper. She finds the puzzle piece that has the answer and arranges the two pieces so that the appropriate sides are touching. She continues in this manner until the puzzle is assembled. What a fitting way to practice computation!

Alessa Keener, Reisterstown, MD

## Saving Cents
### Skill: counting coins

Boost coin-counting skills with this bargain of a partner game! Give each twosome several expired or unwanted coupons with cents-off savings, a supply of imitation coins, and a piece of paper for keeping score. To play one round, the players arrange the coupons facedown. Each player randomly selects two coupons. She uses one or more coins to show the value of each coupon. Then she counts her coins to determine her coupons' combined value. The player with the coupons of greater value earns one point. No points are awarded for a tie. The players return the coins and coupons; they continue play for a total of five rounds. The top-scoring player wins.

adapted from an idea by Melanie J. Miller
Nashport, OH

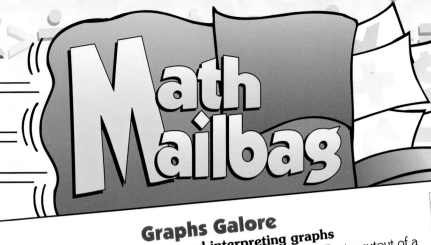

# Math Mailbag

## Graphs Galore
### Skills: making and interpreting graphs

Sharpen graphing skills with the help of a math mascot! Post a cutout of a desired character on the board. Give the character a graph-related name, such as Molly McGraph or Graphing Gus. Each week, draw a speech bubble for the character and label it with a graphing task. For example, ask each youngster to survey friends and family members about their favorite vegetables and graph the results. After he writes two or more sentences about his data, prompt a class discussion about students' results. Then encourage youngsters to check the mascot display the following week for another graphing experience!

adapted from an idea by Madelyn Ferraro—Gr. 1
Immaculate Conception School
Annandale, NJ

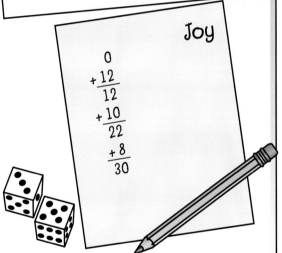

## Number Race
### Skill: computation

This easy-to-adapt partner game gets computation skills on a roll! Give each twosome two sheets of paper and a pair of dice. Have each player write "0" near the top of her paper. To take a turn, a player rolls the dice. She determines the sum (or product) of the numbers and adds it to the last number that she wrote. Players alternate turns until one player has a total of at least 75 or another designated number. This player is declared the winner. To reinforce subtraction skills, each player starts with 100 and subtracts the numbers she rolls. The winner is the first player who rolls a number that is greater than the last number on her paper. Regrouping practice has never been so much fun!

Kate Buschun
Lexington, KY

## Place Cards
### Skill: comparing numbers

Get place-value skills in order with this small-group game. Give each student a place-value mat similar to the one shown and ten squares sized to fit within the columns. Have him label a square for each of the numbers 0–9.

Next, give each group a die and a sheet of paper for keeping score. Each player sets his mat on a work surface and scrambles his squares facedown. To play a round, each player randomly takes four of his squares. Then one player rolls the die and announces the number. If it is four, five, or six, the player who forms the greatest four-digit number will win the round. If it is one, two, or three, the player who forms the smallest number will win. Each player uses his chosen squares to form a four-digit number on his mat. The players compare the numbers, and the winning player earns one point. Then each player clears his mat and scrambles all of his squares. The game continues for a desired number of rounds. The highest-scoring player wins.

Trudy White—Gr. 2
Mayflower Elementary School, Mayflower, AR

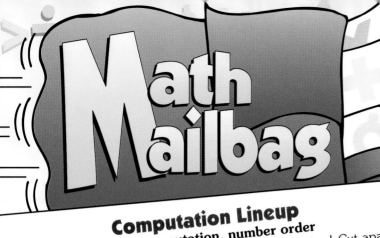

# Math Mailbag

## Computation Lineup
### Skills: computation, number order

Students will be standing in line for this versatile review! Cut apart the problems from one or more computation skillsheets so that there is one problem for each student. Have each youngster write his problem on a blank index card and then solve it. Next, divide students into groups of six or more and ask each youngster to hold his card in clear view. Challenge the students in each group to silently line up in order from least to greatest according to their answers. (Instruct students with identical answers to stand together.) After each group is satisfied with its sequence, have the group members read aloud their problems and answers in order. What a lineup!

Cindy Peterson—Gr. 2
Bluebonnet Elementary
Flower Mound, TX

| Sugar Cookie Menu | |
|---|---|
| Item | Price |
| cookie | 28¢ |
| frosting | 21¢ |
| sprinkles | 14¢ |
| mini candies | 16¢ |
| raisins | 18¢ |

## Snacktime Shopping
### Skills: adding money amounts, counting coins

This "cent-sational" idea is too sweet to pass up! Obtain a class supply of plain sugar cookies, frosting, and toppings. Prepare a grade-appropriate menu that includes prices and make student copies of it. Arrange the food items, plastic knives, and napkins on one or more tables for student access. For easy management, arrange for a volunteer to monitor students when they visit the table(s).

To begin, give each student a price list, a piece of scrap paper, and a resealable plastic bag containing enough imitation coins to give the exact change for each food item. Ask each student to refer to her menu as she calculates how much a sugar cookie and desired decorations cost. Check her work, have her present you with the exact change, and then invite her to prepare her sugar cookie snack. Mmm!

Tamara DeSutter—Gr. 1
Our Lady of Perpetual Help Catholic School
Chattanooga, TN

## Fraction Basketball
### Skill: identifying fractional amounts

Students are bound to give fractions a sporting chance with this partner game! To prepare, a twosome tapes the rim of a 16-ounce disposable cup (basket) to the side of a desk or table in an open area as shown. One player places a strip of masking tape about two feet from the basket to establish a free-throw line. Player 1 attempts to throw a small ball of paper (basketball) into the basket; Player 2 records on provided paper whether or not the throw is successful. After six throws, Player 1 writes the total number of baskets and then determines the fractional amount of baskets that he made. Player 2 takes a turn in a similar manner and Player 1 records the results. The player with the greater fraction wins. For more fraction fun, the players repeat the activity with a different number of total throws.

adapted from an idea by Shannon Hickey—Gr. 2
Our Lady of Consolation School
Philadelphia, PA

# OUR READERS WRITE

## Guess Who!

Celebrate National Grandparents Day with this intriguing display! A student positions a folded piece of paper with the fold at the top. On the outside, he lists three activities that he enjoys with a grandparent or senior friend. On the inside, he signs his name and identifies the adult. He mounts the folded paper and a corresponding illustration onto a sheet of construction paper. Showcase students' work below the title "Guess Who!" Challenge youngsters to identify the owner of each paper, or invite the featured adults to visit and find their pictures!

Molly Copas—Gr. 3, Belle-Aire Elementary, Washington Court House, OH

1. fishing
2. going to the park
3. making chili

## Helping Hands

Here's an easy way to collect inexpensive classroom supplies. Write the name of each needed item on a hand-shaped cutout and a sticky note. Randomly arrange the sticky notes on a bulletin board titled "Lend a Hand!" Tack each cutout atop the matching sticky note. During open house, have each parent who wishes to make a donation remove a selected cutout and sign the corresponding sticky note for your reference.

Lynn Bump—Grs. 2–3, Midway Elementary, Alpharetta, GA

## Birthday Treats

Make students' birthdays a real treat! To prepare a birthday surprise, roll an empty toilet paper tube in colorful tissue paper. Tape the paper along the length of the tube and tie one end with curling ribbon. Place novelty erasers, wrapped candy, or other small treats inside. Tie the second end and personalize the tube. On a student's special day (or a convenient alternate date), present her with the festive surprise!

Victoria Cavanagh—Gr. 1, Troy Hills School, Parsippany, NJ

## Day by Day

What's the catch of the day? Calendar-related vocabulary! Program a fish cutout for each day of the week. Glue the cutouts in sequence on a poster board strip, leaving space above them. Slide a paper clip (fishhook) onto the poster board above each fish. Make a label for each of the following: "Yesterday," "Today," and "Tomorrow." Display the prepared poster board near your classroom calendar. Each morning have a volunteer secure the labels above the appropriate fish as shown. Count on students to fall for this vocabulary practice hook, line, and sinker!

adapted from an idea by Amy Webb—Gr. 1
Sanders Clyde School, Charleston, SC

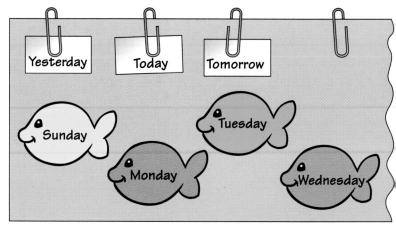

Yesterday   Today   Tomorrow

Sunday   Monday   Tuesday   Wednesday

Today in SSR, look for **adjectives.**

tiny   quiet   smooth   old   funny

## Reading Focus

Use this independent-reading idea, and no doubt students will be eager to get into books! On a laminated poster, use a wipe-off marker to write one or more things for students to look for as they read, such as action verbs, contractions, or a chosen type of sentence. A student marks each find with a sticky note. At the conclusion of the reading session, invite students to announce their findings; write them on the poster. To prepare the poster for another day, wipe it clean and then reprogram it. Read on!

Deborah Patrick—Gr. 2, Park Forest Elementary, State College, PA

## Math in a Flash

This daily dose of math-fact practice is guaranteed to attract student interest. Program an answer card for each flash card in a class set. Then attach a strip of magnetic tape to the back of each flash card and answer card. Display the flash cards on a magnetic surface. Each morning before students arrive, place an answer card on each child's desk. A child's first task of the day is to secure his answer card below a corresponding flash card. After all the cards are in place, use them for a quick review of selected facts.

Sheila Criqui-Kelley—Gr. 1, Lebo Elementary, Lebo, KS

## Word-Wall Practice

Take a colorful approach to reinforcing word-wall words. Give each child a sheet of paper on which you have written selected words in large letters. To practice a word, a child reads it to herself. Then she uses a crayon to trace each letter as she softly spells the word. She repeats this two-step sequence two times, using a different color of crayon each time. What a nifty strategy for learning words!

Teresa Williams—Gr. 1, Coquihalla School, Hope, British Columbia, Canada

are the

## Tech Pals

If your school has Internet access, this is a perfect pen-pal project for you. Contact a local teacher who would like to have pen pals for her students. Throughout the year, have your youngsters exchange electronic mail with her students. Late in the school year, after a number of letters have been exchanged, arrange for the pen pals to meet. Now that's a special delivery of letter-writing and keyboarding practice!

Dorothy Hamilton—Gr. 3, Longfellow School, Oak Park, IL

Cool Books Inside!

## Big-Book Storage

When you use this storage suggestion, you can be sure big books will be among your students' reading choices! Place an open clothes hamper in your classroom library. Stand a selection of big books inside and decorate the outside with a motivating book-themed poster. Not only will this storage option help keep your books in good condition, but it will also entice students to check them out!

Cathy Velardi—Gr. 2, Watsessing School, Bloomfield, NJ

## Key Math Words

This handy reminder unlocks word problems! Prepare two jumbo key cutouts. Label one "Addition" and one "Subtraction." Add the corresponding math signs. Display the keys on a classroom wall and place a supply of blank cards nearby. As students work on word problems, encourage them to look for words that can help them decide which operation to use. When students identify a helpful word or phrase, invite a volunteer to write it on a card and post it near the appropriate key. The resulting reference will be a key to students' math success!

Jessie Chun—Gr. 2, Public School 88, The Seneca School, Ridgewood, NJ

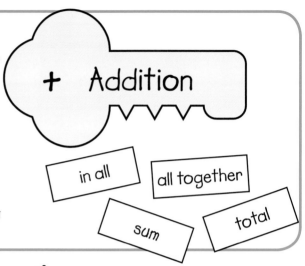

## Conference Collaboration

As you prepare for parent-teacher conferences, why not invite students to lend a hand? Have each youngster look through samples of his work. Then have him write or dictate a letter to his parent(s) that summarizes his progress and notes areas in which he'd like to improve. Present the letter during the conference or arrange for the student to attend and deliver it himself. He'll be pleased to have shared his thoughts, and you'll gain valuable insight!

VaReane Heese, Springfield Elementary, Springfield, NE

## Poppin' Sentence Parts

Subjects and predicates keep popping up during this activity! Have each student write a sentence on provided paper and then draw a line to separate the subject from the predicate. Next, name a student and a sentence part. The named youngster pops up from her chair and says, "Pop, pop!" She reads aloud the indicated part of her sentence and sits down. Keep a quick pace as you call on several more students. If a student's reply is incorrect, immediately call on her again and guide her to a correct response. Periodically stop the activity for students to prepare new sentences. Pop, pop!

Reba Cross—Gr. 3, Alpine Elementary, Alpine, TX

## Take a Guess!

Combine estimating and predicting practice. Here's how! A day or two before beginning a new topic of study or class read-aloud, obtain a supply of small items that relate to the topic or book's plot. For example, use cooked pumpkin seeds for a fall unit or wrapped chocolate candies for *The Chocolate Touch* by Patrick Skene Catling. Place the items in a clear, unbreakable container. Have each youngster estimate the number of items and predict their significance. Then determine the actual count and reveal the upcoming topic or book. Now that's a nifty way to get students thinking!

Nancy King—Gr. 1, McClure School, Yakima, WA

## Progress at a Glance

Track students' writing progress with this simple suggestion. Throughout each month, have each student date his completed writing assignments and store them in a designated folder. At the end of the month, the youngster selects his best work from the folder. He mounts his selection onto a larger sheet of construction paper and takes the rest of his writing home. At the end of the year, he sequences the papers and, if desired, creates an "About the Author" sheet. He uses a hole puncher and string to bind his work between two covers. What a memorable keepsake!

Josephine Flammer, Bay Shore, NY

## Creative Counting

Make skip-counting a regular part of your classroom routine. Each day, pose a real-life question that can be answered with skip-counting, such as "How many days are in five weekends?" or "If everyone raises both hands, how many hands would be raised?" For additional reinforcement, have students skip-count as they line up for recess or head to lunch. With each opportunity to practice, students' number skills will improve. You can count on it!

Kim Caldwell—Gr. 2, McAdenville Elementary, McAdenville, NC

## Listen to This!

Improved listening skills are the result of this motivating idea! Display a stuffed toy parrot or another animal in a prominent classroom location. Occasionally, after giving oral directions, hand the critter to a student. Ask the youngster to use it as a prop as she restates your directions for the class. If she has trouble remembering the directions, enlist the help of other students. The opportunity to show off listening skills means students will be all ears all the time!

Cindy L. Campbell—Gr. 3, Marion Intermediate School, Marion, VA

## Editing With Color

Give editing practice a colorful focus! Evaluate a class writing assignment for a chosen element such as spelling or ending punctuation. Use a colorful highlighter to make a mark at the beginning of each line that has an error. Then return each paper to its owner. Have him find each indicated error and correct it. If a student's work has no errors, suggest that he engage in a free-time writing activity. Improved writing skills are guaranteed!

Mary L. Foess—Gr. 2, Townsend North School, Vassar, MI

## Check Out These Books!

If you have a book display stand, use this creative idea to spark interest in reading. Arrange in the stand a thematic collection of books, such as books that relate to the current season or a topic of study. Use lengths of bulletin board trim to decorate the stand; add a sign with the theme. Periodically change the reading selections and update the display. No doubt students will be eager to read the new offerings!

Sheila Criqui-Kelley—Gr. 1, Lebo Elementary, Lebo, KS

## Celebrate With Buddies

Make special times of the year extra special by sharing them with a buddy class! With a teacher at another grade level, arrange buddy activities such as a wintertime sing-along, seasonal bingo game, or greeting card exchange. Plan to celebrate the end of the year in grand style with a picnic or another kid-pleasing event. Not only will the experiences benefit students socially, but they will also help build a spirit of community!

Kelly A. Lu—Gr. 2, Berlyn School, Ontario, CA

## Season's Readings

The gift of reading makes this cross-generational activity a heartwarming treat. A week before a scheduled visit to a local retirement home, have each student practice reading one or more self-selected books with fluency and expression. Ask him to make a book-related illustration and then sign his artwork. During the visit, arrange for pairs of students to read to individual seniors; then have each pair present the senior with its illustrations. Now that's a gift as much fun to give as it is to receive!

Sue Seipel—Gr. 1, St. Gregory Barbarigo School, Maryville, MO

## Treasured Behavior

Promote a wealth of positive behavior! Use desired arts-and-crafts materials to decorate a foam cooler to resemble a treasure chest. Place the cooler and a supply of yellow construction paper circles (coins) in a central classroom location. When a student observes a classmate's kind deed, she describes the behavior on a coin and then deposits her anonymous note in the treasure chest. Each day, read aloud a few notes and present each one to the child whose deed is described. To ensure that each student is recognized periodically, establish a method of record keeping and deposit additional notes as needed. A bounty of golden behavior is sure to result!

Chrissy Erickson—Substitute Teacher, St. Maria Goretti Catholic School, Westfield, IN

## In the Know

Tracking students' learning is easy with this reusable KWL chart. Draw and label a large KWL chart similar to the one shown. Laminate it for durability. When you begin a topic of study, invite students to label sticky notes with relevant information they already know. Have them read the notes aloud and post them in the first column of the chart. Then ask volunteers to post in the second column things they would like to learn. As students learn desired information, move the appropriate sticky notes from the second column to the third. Use additional sticky notes to record other newly acquired information. Student learning is sure to stick!

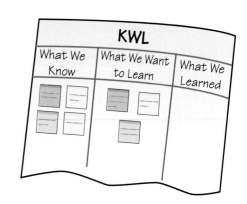

Mandy Jones—Substitute Teacher
Allegany County, MD

## Stories on Display

Increase students' reading motivation, and reduce the time you spend decorating bulletin boards. How? With student-created book displays! Designate a paper-covered bulletin board for this purpose and establish a rotating decorating schedule for small groups. Each group uses provided arts-and-crafts materials to create a story-related display. Then the youngsters refer to the completed bulletin board as they tell the class about the story. Sharing books has never been so much fun!

Susan Johnson, Wausau, WI

## Weather Update

Here's an activity that puts wintry weather in the spotlight! Prompt a class discussion about various winter weather conditions, guiding students to identify potential hazards such as slippery surfaces, cold temperatures, and thin ice on ponds. Help students identify appropriate safety precautions. On each of several days, have a different group of students use desired props to role-play a newscast that features a winter weather scenario. What a creative way to explore weather!

adapted from an idea by Laura Wagner, Raleigh, NC

## Fab Vocab!

Who would own a silo?

Where would you find a mast?

Stretch students' vocabularies (and thinking skills!) with this dictionary activity. Provide pairs of students with grade-appropriate dictionaries. Write an unfamiliar word on the board and pose a related question. Next, each twosome finds the definition of the featured word. The partners use the definition as they quietly determine the answer to the question. Invite volunteers to tell the class their answers and their reasoning. Repeat the process with additional words as time allows. Now that's putting dictionaries to good use!

Karoleigh K. Allison—Remedial Reading, Russell Elementary, Hurtsboro, AL

## Work Space Solution

Give students ample space for showing their math work with this nifty idea. For each student, photocopy a chosen skill sheet on the left-hand side of a horizontally positioned 11" x 17" sheet of paper. Students will have plenty of room to organize and complete their work, and you'll be able to check it with ease!

Dawn Maucieri—Gr. 3, Signal Hill Elementary School, Dix Hills, NY

## Measure Up!

This handy tool makes measuring length a snap! Place a ball of yarn in an empty cylinder-shaped container for disposable wipes. Thread the end of the yarn through the lid and then secure the lid. To measure an item, a student places the yarn along its length, pulling the needed amount of yarn from the container. She snaps the lid flap closed to hold the yarn in place and then uses a ruler or yardstick to measure the loose yarn. No doubt this unique measuring tape will become a favorite math tool!

Jamie Zidle—Gr. 2, Chattahoochee Elementary, Duluth, GA

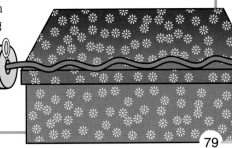

## Red-Hot Readers

Fire up reading enthusiasm! Throughout the month of February, have each student use a reading log to keep track of his independent-reading experiences. When he finishes an especially good book, he writes the title on the front of a folded heart cutout. Then he unfolds the heart and writes why he likes the book. After he signs his heart and adds desired crayon decorations, he deposits it in a designated container. Periodically remove the hearts from the container and add them to a prepared bulletin board. At the end of the month, offer each youngster a few Red Hots candies to enjoy during a class discussion about the featured books.

adapted from an idea by Lisa Blackburn—Gr. 3, Sabal Palm Elementary, Tallahassee, FL

Frog and Toad
Are Friends

I like this book because it's funny. It made me laugh.

Seth

## Quick Skills Check

Students will flip over this fast-paced strategy for math practice. Pair students and give each twosome a mini whiteboard or chalkboard and writing supplies. Present a math problem and have the partners work together to solve it. When the students' work is complete, announce, "One, two, three, flip!" At this signal, one partner in each twosome turns her board and holds it up to reveal her answer. Scan students' work; then confirm the correct answer and follow up with any needed explanation. Have students wipe their boards clean; then continue with additional problems as time allows.

Jennifer Lassalle—Gr. 2, St. Laurence Catholic School, Sugar Land, TX

shamrocks

leprechauns

St. Patrick's Day

green

Ireland

## Party Placemats

If you have holiday or birthday celebrations scheduled, add this suggestion to your party plans. Shortly before the event begins, give each youngster a large sheet of paper to use as a placemat. Invite him to decorate it with illustrations and words related to the celebration. The last few minutes before the festivities will pass by quickly for students, plus the placemats will help keep their desktops clean!

Cathy Belcher—Gr. 1, Ripley Elementary, Ripley, WV

## "Map-nificent" Locations

Use this tip to get geography skills in place. Keep U.S. and world maps on display throughout the year. When locations are introduced during various classroom activities, help students find each one on a map and label it with a sticky note. For example, during a read-aloud, pause to have students mark where the story takes place; or, during a science unit on penguins, point out Antarctica. Now that's taking learning on location!

Pat Hart—Gr. 2, W. S. Freeman Elementary School, Troy, IL

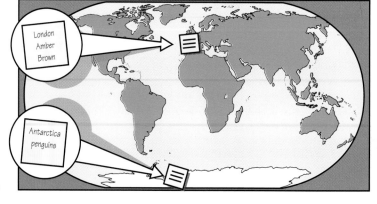

London
Amber
Brown

Antarctica
penguins

## Poetry Party

What better way to celebrate National Poetry Month (April) than with a poetry party for students and their families? Set out a variety of poetry books, and decorate your classroom with balloons and a student-made banner. After the invited guests arrive, have individual students or small groups present chosen poems by Shel Silverstein, Jack Prelutsky, or other favorite poets. Then serve refreshments as the students and guests browse through student-compiled anthologies and displayed poetry books. What fun!

Felicia Arnold—Gr. 3, Rolling Hills Primary School, Vernon, NJ

You're invited to a Poetry Party!
Date: April 16
Time: 9:00
Place: Ms. Arnold's classroom

## Mapping With Attractions

When you visit an attraction such as a zoo or science center, save any brochures that have simple maps. Plan to explore the collected maps with small groups of students. Or display a map in a center along with various skill-based questions, such as "What is east of the gorilla cage?" or "In what direction would you walk to get from the aquarium to the snack bar?" A direct route to improved map skills is guaranteed!

Cheryl Borta, St. Charles, MO

## From Egg to Butterfly

Use this crafty life cycle project with a butterfly unit or as a follow-up to *The Very Hungry Caterpillar* by Eric Carle. Each child visually divides a tagboard strip into fourths and sequentially labels a section with each of the following words: *egg, caterpillar, chrysalis, butterfly*. To illustrate each life cycle stage, he adds crayon illustrations and glues in the appropriate sections a lima bean (egg), green spiral pasta piece (caterpillar), macaroni shell (chrysalis), and bow-tie pasta piece (butterfly). How clever!

Amy Emmons—Gr. 2
Enon Elementary, Franklinton, LA

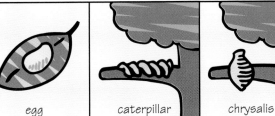

egg | caterpillar | chrysalis | butterfly

## Wild About Reading!

Students will be on the prowl for great books with this jungle-themed reading corner. Tack jungle- or animal-print fabric to the walls in a chosen classroom area. Add plastic vines and fine netting if desired. Set out a few stuffed jungle animals and animal-print pillows, or place a jungle-themed throw rug on the floor. Display independent-reading books as desired. Youngsters are sure to swing by for lots of reading adventures!

Beth Beczak—Gr. 2, Eden Christian Academy, Pittsburgh, PA

## Vote for Books!

Can't decide which read-aloud to share next? Solve the dilemma with title towers! Briefly introduce the book choices to students. Then display each selection on a table and place a class supply of Unifix cubes nearby. To cast a vote, each student sets a Unifix cube by her preferred book, connecting it to any other cubes designated for her book choice. After all of the votes are cast, announce which title has the tallest cube tower. Then let the reading begin!

Sheree McArthur—Gr. 1, Cunningham Creek Elementary, Fruit Cove, FL

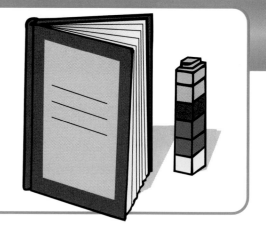

## Tie It Up!

Believe it or not, a balloon can help students write better paragraphs. Show students a deflated balloon and explain that it represents a paragraph topic. To represent the details that fill out a topic, blow up the balloon. Point out the importance of securing the end as you tie it with string. Then suggest that the closing sentence of a paragraph is similar to the string since it ties up the paragraph. Now whenever your students write, this reminder is bound to pop into their minds!

Sharon Ferron—Gr. 3, Willard Model Elementary School, Norfolk, VA

## Mystery Bag

An intriguing unit introduction is in the bag! Decorate a gift bag with question marks. Secretly place inside the bag an item that gives a clue about what students will study next. To guess the item, invite students to ask a predetermined number of yes-or-no questions. After students correctly identify it or when they have exhausted their guessing opportunities, reveal the item with great fanfare and announce the topic.

Sheila Criqui-Kelley—Gr. 1, Lebo Elementary, Lebo, KS

## Memorable Words

This version of Concentration gives ESL students winning vocabulary practice. Make two identical sets of labeled picture cards for a common category such as foods or household objects. To play, students follow the rules for the traditional Concentration game, and they say the name of each picture they reveal during a turn. After a student is familiar with the game, invite him to borrow it for take-home practice with his family.

Alison LaManna, Warrenville, IL

## Sizing Up Measurement

Here's a two-part approach to making measurement meaningful for students. First, ask each youngster to interview his family members about ways that they use measurements in their daily lives. Compile the information into a class list. Then, to identify other real-life examples, have groups of students cut relevant pictures or words from discarded newspapers, advertisements, and magazines. Invite them to contribute their findings to a class measurement scrapbook. A new appreciation for math is sure to result!

James Kellogg—Grs. 1–2, Beaver River Central School, Beaver Falls, NY

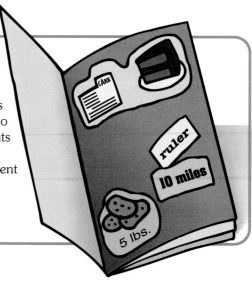

## Treasured Advice

If you'll be saying goodbye to a student teacher, plan to send her off with this thoughtful gift. To prepare, invite each staff member to jot down a few words of advice or a favorite teaching tip on a separate blank index card. Then have her sign the card. Use a blank card to create an illustrated title page similar to the one shown. Insert the prepared cards in a small pocket photo album, adding any desired photos. No doubt the completed album will be a treasured memento!

adapted from an idea by Randi Austin
Gasconade C–4, Falcon, MO

## Invitation to Write

Count on this year-end assignment to spark letter-writing interest! Give each student a letter-size envelope on the last day of school. Have him address it to you and write his home address in the left-hand corner. After he adds a provided postage stamp, instruct him to tuck a folded sheet of paper in the envelope for later use. Ask him to wait at least one week and write a letter to you about his vacation. Promise to answer each letter you receive, and you're sure to get lots of special deliveries!

Julie Kleinberger—Grs. 1–2
George G. Blaisdell Elementary School, Bradford, PA

## Read-Aloud Clubs

Here's a cozy approach to book discussions that gets every student actively involved. At the conclusion of a chosen read-aloud, divide students into small clubs with designated responsibilities, such as the ones shown. Set out several copies of the book for student reference, and have each club complete its task to prepare for a discussion. Then sit with all of the students in a circle and serve cookies. Invite students to enjoy the snack as each group, in turn, shares its work and prompts discussion.

Melanie Spear—Instructional Specialist
Acton Elementary, Granbury, TX

## Club Roles

**Word Finders:** Choose five interesting words from the story. Make a poster to explain what they mean.

**Ready Readers:** Select two passages to read aloud to the class. Be ready to explain why you chose them.

**Question Writers:** Write who, what, when, where, why, and how questions for your classmates to answer.

**Artists:** Illustrate a surprising, funny, or important story event. Write why you chose it.

**Storytellers:** List the main story events. Plan to use the list to retell the story.

## Cool Capacity

Give practice with capacity a colorful twist! Set out two clear containers of colored water (one yellow and one blue), empty containers, and liquid measuring cups. Then use the supplies for various capacity-related tasks. For example, have students estimate how much water one of the empty containers can hold and test their ideas. Or ask students to measure and mix yellow and blue water to make one pint of green water. For a refreshing follow-up, have students use their measurement skills to prepare a class supply of instant lemonade.

Susan Hunter and Margaret Roberts—Gr. 1 Math
Kings Consolidated School District #144, Kings, IL

## Namely, Fractions

Lead students in a few rounds of this catchy song to tune up their fraction vocabularies!

adapted from an idea by Jen Nemeth—Gr. 2
Loomis Elementary, Broomall, PA

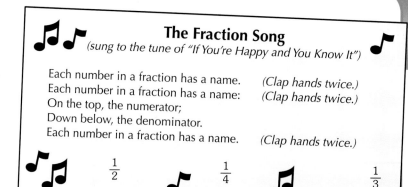

**The Fraction Song**
*(sung to the tune of "If You're Happy and You Know It")*

Each number in a fraction has a name.    (Clap hands twice.)
Each number in a fraction has a name:    (Clap hands twice.)
On the top, the numerator;
Down below, the denominator.
Each number in a fraction has a name.    (Clap hands twice.)

$\frac{1}{2}$     $\frac{1}{4}$     $\frac{1}{3}$

## Pleasing Paint Trays

Trade your easy-to-spill paint cups for convenient paint trays. Collect a supply of clean frozen-dinner trays and use them to dispense paint to students. Since the trays hold more paint than cups do, they're ideal for small groups. Plus, they don't tip when holding paintbrushes.

Pamela Vadas—Gr. 3
Eden Christian Academy, Pittsburgh, PA

## On the Scene

This literature response idea takes readers on location! To prepare, tape a foam ball to one end of a cardboard tube to resemble a microphone; cover the microphone with aluminum foil. When a reading group reaches a preselected point in a book, assign one student the role of a news reporter. Give her the microphone and a press pass similar to the one shown. Ask the remaining group members to take the roles of story characters or bystanders. Then have the news reporter interview them to get the inside scoop on the story.

Susan Johnson, Wausau, WI

## Meaningful Acts

Bring vocabulary to life! For every two or three students, write a different vocabulary word and its meaning on a blank card. Distribute the cards, cautioning students not to reveal their words to other groups. Allow time for each group to plan a brief skit that incorporates its word and gives a hint about the meaning. Then have each group, in turn, announce its word and perform its skit for the class. After each performance, challenge the audience to define the word, asking the actors to provide any needed clarification. Memorable vocabulary connections are guaranteed!

Julie Douglas, St. Louis, MO

## Today's Special

Pique student interest with intriguing daily announcements! Display a small chart tablet near the doorway of your classroom. Each day use colorful markers to title the first blank page "Today's Special." Below the title, advertise one especially kid-pleasing activity or event that you have planned. (Or use a laminated poster and wipe-off markers for this purpose.) Anticipation will be high when students arrive!

Ann Marie Stephens—Gr. 1
G. C. Round Elementary, Manassas, VA

*Today's Special*
We will have a
visitor at 1:30!

# SKILLS FOR
# BEGINNING READERS

# Skills for Beginning Readers

best   nest   rest   pest

## Family of Words
### Word Families

This paper-cutting activity is a family event—a word family event, that is! Each student accordion-folds a 6" x 18" strip of light-colored construction paper into four equal sections. She traces a person-shaped pattern (page 94) on the folded paper as shown. She cuts out the tracing, being careful not to cut where the hands meet the edges. Then she unfolds the paper. She labels each figure with a different word from a designated word family and underlines the rime; she draws a face on each figure. If desired, instruct each student to feature a different word family on the other side of her paper chain. Arrange for each youngster to practice reading her paper chain with a classmate before she uses it for take-home reading practice.

Cindy Barber, Fredonia, WI

## Off the Wall!
### Word Wall Words

Letter patterns and motivating reading practice make this word wall idea a winner! Give each student a minibooklet with construction paper covers and several white pages. Ask him to title and personalize the front cover as desired. Each week, add a word with a chosen letter pattern to your established word wall. Guide students to brainstorm words with this pattern; add the words to the display or write them on the board.

Next, have each student make an entry in his booklet by writing the letter pattern and list of words. Encourage him to review all of the words in his booklet whenever he has spare time. For added reading fun, invite each youngster to make a construction paper worm. Have him draw a mouth and glue on a wiggle eye. Suggest that he use the resulting word worm as a desktop reading buddy. When the youngster knows all of the words in his booklet and has no room for additional entries, have him take his booklet home and present him with a new one.

adapted from an idea by Sue Cox—Grs. K–5 Reading Tutor
Bibich Elementary School, Dyer, IN

# Memorable Word Game
## *Sight Words*

Before beginning work with a small group, warm up students' sight-word skills with this memory game. To prepare, make 16 identical seasonal cutouts and label pairs of them with chosen sight words. Decorate a labeled clasp envelope for later storage. If desired, plan to jot down notes about students' reading accuracy for later reference.

Scramble the cutouts and arrange them facedown on a playing surface. To take a turn, a student flips two cutouts and reads the words aloud. If the cutouts are a match, she uses the word in a sentence and takes the cutouts. If they are not, she turns the cutouts facedown in their original positions. Players alternate turns until no cards remain. Congratulate the students for a job well done; then have each youngster read her cutouts aloud as she puts them in the envelope.

Kim Whorton—Grs. K–3 Special Education, Linda Nolen Learning Center
Alabaster, AL

# Say and Sort
## *Short-Vowel Sounds*

Students tune in to short-vowel sounds with this picture-perfect sorting activity! To prepare for a small-group activity, collect an empty box, a gift bag, and a mug. Label each item *(box, bag, mug)*. Have each student cut out a copy of the cards on page 94. After he initials the back of each card, direct him to place the cards in a resealable plastic bag. Set out the labeled containers and confirm that students can identify the words.

To begin, each student stacks his cards facedown. One student takes his top card. He names the picture and identifies which container has the same vowel sound. After he receives confirmation or redirection from you, he deposits it in the correct container. Students take turns as time allows or until all of their cards are sorted. Then the youngsters empty the containers and return the cards to their owners. Sounds like fun!

Susan Brown—Grs. K–5, Central Elementary, Palmyra, VA

# Stellar Blend
## ST *Blend*

Here's a bright approach to reinforcing the *st* blend! Within student reach, post a large foil-covered star that you have labeled "st." Place a supply of star cutouts and a marker nearby. To introduce the display, have a volunteer identify the featured blend. Write "star" on a cutout and point out that the word begins with the same blend. Display the cutout near the posted star. Then encourage students to be on the lookout for other *st* words whenever they read. When a student sees one that is not already featured, she writes it on a cutout and posts it. Periodically review the displayed words with students. What a stellar way to boost phonics skills!

# Skills for Beginning Readers

## Add a Letter!
### Onsets and Rimes

This letter-perfect twist on tic-tac-toe is guaranteed to attract young readers. To prepare for a group game, draw a large tic-tac-toe grid on a magnetic board. Program each grid space with a letter blank and a different rime as shown. Place in a gift bag a supply of magnetic consonant letters that includes duplicates of commonly used letters. Divide students into two teams and assign each team a symbol (X or O).

To begin, a player from Team 1 takes a letter at random. With the help of his teammates, he determines whether he can use the letter and a displayed rime to form a word. If he can, he places the letter on an appropriate blank and labels the grid space with his team's symbol. If he cannot, he sets the letter aside. Team 2 takes a turn in a similar manner. As alternate play continues, if there is no free space in which a team can form a word, the team members study any spaces that they claimed earlier. If possible, they form a new word by substituting their magnetic letter for one already in place. Play continues until one team claims three spaces in a diagonal, horizontal, or vertical row and is declared the winner, or until every space has been claimed and the game is declared a tie.

Anne Mulrain—Gr. 1, Lake Street School, Spencer, MA

## Team Spirit
### ea, ee

Try this spirited vowel-team activity! Program a blank card for each word shown. Scramble the cards and stack them facedown. Post a large two-column chart; label one column "ea" and one column "ee." To begin, remind students that in words such as *seat* and *bee,* two vowels team up to represent one sound. Have a student take a card, read it aloud, and then tape it in the appropriate column. Continue with different students until each word is displayed.

Next, divide students into two groups—one for each vowel team—and designate a cheerleader for each group. Ask the cheerleaders to stand in front of the class. In turn, have each cheerleader announce, "Let's hear it for the [letter combination] vowel team!" and use a desired type of cheer, such as call and response, to lead her group in reading its words. Hooray for vowel teams!

adapted from an idea by Amy Barsanti, Plymouth, NC

| ea | ee |
|------|-------|
| bean | bee |
| eat | jeep |
| heat | need |
| leaf | seed |
| neat | sheep |
| seat | three |
| tea | tree |

## Impressive Collections
### High-Frequency Words

Here's a pride-boosting strategy for stretching students' reading vocabularies. List several high-frequency words on the board and read them with students. Then have each youngster write the words on separate blank cards. After you check them, he hole-punches each card in the upper left corner. He threads the cards onto a five-inch length of chenille stem and then twists it to make a loop. He stores his resulting word ring in a personalized resealable plastic bag for ongoing reading practice. Periodically, he prepares another word ring for a newly assigned set of words and then adds it to his storage bag. As his collection of words grows, his reading skills will too!

Vivian Sirakis—Grs. K–6 Reading Teacher
New Hyde Park Road School, New Hyde Park, NY

## Blend Clouds
### 1 *Blends*

These clouds don't bring rain; they bring practice with blends! Divide students into small groups and give each group three blank cards. For each group, label both sides of a large tagboard cloud with a chosen *l* blend *(bl, cl, fl, gl, pl, sl)*. To begin, instruct the students in each group to brainstorm words with their assigned blend or search for them in classroom reading materials. Ask them to write a different word on each side of their cards. Have the youngsters use a hole puncher and string to make a hanger and attach the cards to the cloud (see the illustration). After each group reads its words to the class, suspend students' cloudy word references from the ceiling.

Amy Emmons—Gr. 2, Enon Elementary, Franklinton, LA

## Treasured Word Hunt
### Word Families

A bounty of word-family fun is in store with this partner game. Each student pair needs a copy of the gameboard on page 95, two different-colored counters, a small paper clip, and two recording sheets similar to the one shown. Each player sets her counter on a chosen gameboard space. To take a turn, a player uses the paper clip and a pencil to spin. She announces the rime and moves her counter in a clockwise direction to the first unoccupied space that has a word with the rime. She reads the word aloud and uses it in an original sentence. Then, if she has not already listed the word, she writes it in the correct column of her recording sheet. Players alternate turns until one player has written three words in one column and is declared the winner. To unearth more reading practice, reprogram a copy of the gameboard as desired.

adapted from an idea by Michele Daughenbaugh—Gr. 3
Park Forest Elementary, State College, PA

Name _____

| Treasured Word Hunt | | | |
|---|---|---|---|
| -ail | -ide | -ine | -ate |
| 1. | 1. | 1. | 1. |
| 2. | 2. | 2. | 3. |
| 3. | 3. | 3. | 3. |

# Skills for Beginning Readers

## Catch!
### Word Wall Words

This word wall review is sure to catch on! In advance, use a permanent marker to write chosen words on a beach ball. To begin, stand with students in a circle. Then call a student's name and gently toss the ball to him. After he catches the ball, he reads the word that is closest to his right thumb. (If he needs help reading the word, he seeks assistance from a neighboring student.) Next, he calls the name of a classmate who has not yet had a turn and tosses the ball to her. This student reads a word and passes the ball in a similar manner. The activity continues until each student has had at least one turn reading a word. There's no doubt about it—students will have a ball reading!

Jeana Patterson—Gr. 2
Jones Elementary School
Gainesville, GA

## Digraph Lineup
### Consonant Digraphs

Digraphs form the winning lineup of this partner game. Give each youngster a 4 x 4 grid. Have her draw a smiley face in a chosen grid space and randomly label five grid spaces for each of the following: *ch, sh, th*. Ask each twosome to cut out a copy of the game cards on page 96. (If desired, label a copy of page 96 with the appropriate digraphs and give each twosome a copy to use as an answer key.) Give each student pair a supply of counters.

To play one round, the players scramble the cards and stack them facedown. Each player places a counter on her smiley face. Player 1 takes the top card, identifies the picture, and names the digraph with her partner's help, as needed. She places a counter on a corresponding grid space and then places the card in a discard pile. If an appropriate grid space is not available, she discards the card and her turn is over. Player 2 takes a turn in the same manner. Alternate play continues until one player marks four grid spaces in a horizontal, vertical, or diagonal line and is declared the winner. To play another round, the players clear their grids and reshuffle the cards.

adapted from an idea by MaryLouise Alu Curto—Language Arts
Newgrange School, Hamilton, NJ

# Phonics From Home
## *Review*

Give show-and-tell a phonics twist! To prepare, choose three or more familiar blends, digraphs, and/or vowel sounds. Label a section of a bulletin board for each one. Have each youngster list the phonics elements on a paper lunch bag. Then ask him to use the bag to bring from home an item whose name includes one of the elements.

When the youngster returns his bag, have him write the name of his item on a blank card and underline the phonics element. Invite him to share his item and word card with the class. Then help him post his card in the appropriate section of the display. The result will be a phonics reference with personal meaning for students!

Vicki Joshpe—Gr. 2
Stamford Central School, Stamford, NY

# Colossal Cones
## *Sight Words*

Put a cool spin on sight word collections! Give each youngster a few construction paper ice-cream cones and a personalized resealable plastic bag for storage. (Plan to provide additional cones after she accumulates a certain number of sight words.) When the student acquires a sight word, she uses a provided template to make a construction paper ice-cream scoop. She writes the word on her scoop and adds it to her bag. To practice reading her words to you, she sets out her cones and takes a scoop at random. If she reads the word correctly, she positions it on a cone or a previously placed ice-cream scoop. If she does not, she returns it to the bag to try again later. She continues with the remaining words in the same manner. Her appetite for reading is sure to grow, scoop by scoop!

adapted from an idea by Jamie Coppola
Indian Hollow School, Commack, NY

# Who Can Make a Word?
## *Onsets and Rimes*

Try this kid-pleasing idea to strengthen word-building skills throughout the day. Prepare a list of rimes so that there is one rime per student; then program a blank card for each rime. Give each student a card to keep on his desk. (If desired, secure a library pocket to his desktop for this purpose.) When it's time to choose a youngster for a particular task or privilege, announce an onset that can be used to form a word with a listed rime. If a student has an appropriate rime, he raises his hand. Call on a student and ask him to say the word. Then write his word on the board and award him with the task or privilege. At the day's end, collect the rimes and plan to reuse them on another day.

Kristi Ballash—Gr. 3 Title I Reading
South Harnett Elementary School, Bunnlevel, NC

# Skills for Beginning Readers

## Family Trees
### Word Families

"Tree-rific" word families are the focus of this activity. Divide students into small groups. Each group prepares a large construction paper tree and then labels the treetop with an assigned rime. On each of several strips of paper, the group members write a different word that has the rime. Then they glue the words in a column on their tree trunk.

After each group completes its work, invite the students to "climb" their tree by reading the words from bottom to top. Display each group's tree on a classroom wall. (If adequate space is not available, display the trees individually for a few days at a time.) Periodically ask individual students or small groups to "climb" up and down the trees to help their reading vocabularies grow.

adapted from an idea by Alessa Giampaolo Keener
Reisterstown, MD

## Roll and Read
### Word Wall Words

Your word wall and several dice are the perfect tools for a reading review! Divide students into small groups. Give each group a die and one sheet of paper. Explain that each number represented on the die stands for the number of letters in a word. (If your word wall does not have at least one word for each number, reprogram the die with masking tape, repeating numbers as needed.)

In each group, one student divides and labels the paper to make one column for each number. Another student rolls the die and announces the number to her group. She reads aloud a corresponding word, writes it in the appropriate column, and then passes the die and paper to the next student. The students continue taking turns in this manner, writing each word only once. If a student rolls a number for which all of the words have been written, she reads aloud a previously chosen word and makes a check mark beside it. What a fun way to encourage students to look closely at words!

Julia F. Simmons—Title I Reading K–2
Aberdeen Elementary School
Hampton, VA

| 3 | 4 | 5 | 6 |
|---|---|---|---|
| was | have | there | always |
| | only | would | little |
| | with | | |

# Flipping Over Words
## Sight Words

Cook up sight word practice with this partner activity! Prepare 12 or more construction paper hamburger patties. Laminate the patties and use a wipe-off marker to label each one with a different sight word. Set out the patties, a large cookie sheet, and a spatula. One student arranges the patties word side down in a single layer on the cookie sheet, setting aside any that do not fit. To take a turn, a student flips a chosen patty with the spatula. He reads aloud the word and uses it in an original sentence. Then he flips the patty back over. The partners alternate turns, pausing after several turns to replace selected patties with any that were set aside.

Robbye Losada—Grs. K–1 Special Education
Lindeneau Elementary, Edison, NJ

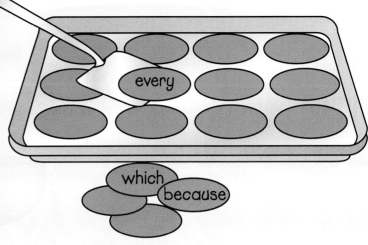

# Puzzling!
## Word Families

Here's a word-family review that students piece together. Each youngster visually divides a 5" x 8" card into four jigsaw-style pieces. She labels each puzzle piece with a different word from an assigned word family. She cuts out the pieces and then places them in a resealable plastic bag.

Next, collect students' puzzles and divide youngsters into small groups. Give each group one puzzle per group member. In each group, one student scrambles all of the puzzle pieces. Then the group members work together to assemble each puzzle. After each group reads its puzzles to the class, the students bag each set of puzzle pieces for later center use.

Mary Towles—Gr. 2, Wellington Elementary, Louisville, KY

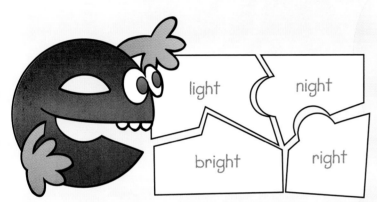

# Sticky Diphthong
## ow

This game tunes students in to the *ow* diphthong! To prepare for a group of two or three students, program a blank card for each word shown and then place the word cards in a small gift bag. On each of ten additional blank cards, adhere an adhesive bandage and write "Ow!" Stack the resulting Ow! cards.

Each player divides a half sheet of paper into two columns. At the top of one column, he draws a bandage to symbolize the vowel sound in *Ow!* At the top of the other column, he draws a snowflake to represent the long *o* sound. To take a turn, a player shakes the bag. He removes a card at random and reads the word aloud. If it has the vowel sound in Ow!, he takes an Ow! card. He writes the word in the correct column (he may write a word more than once) and then returns the card to the bag. The players alternate turns until one player collects four Ow! cards and is declared the winner.

adapted from an idea by Sara E. Adams—Gr. 2
West View Elementary, Knoxville, TN

# Pattern and Picture Cards

Use the pattern with "Family of Words" on page 86 and the picture cards with "Say and Sort" on page 87.

# Treasured Word Hunt

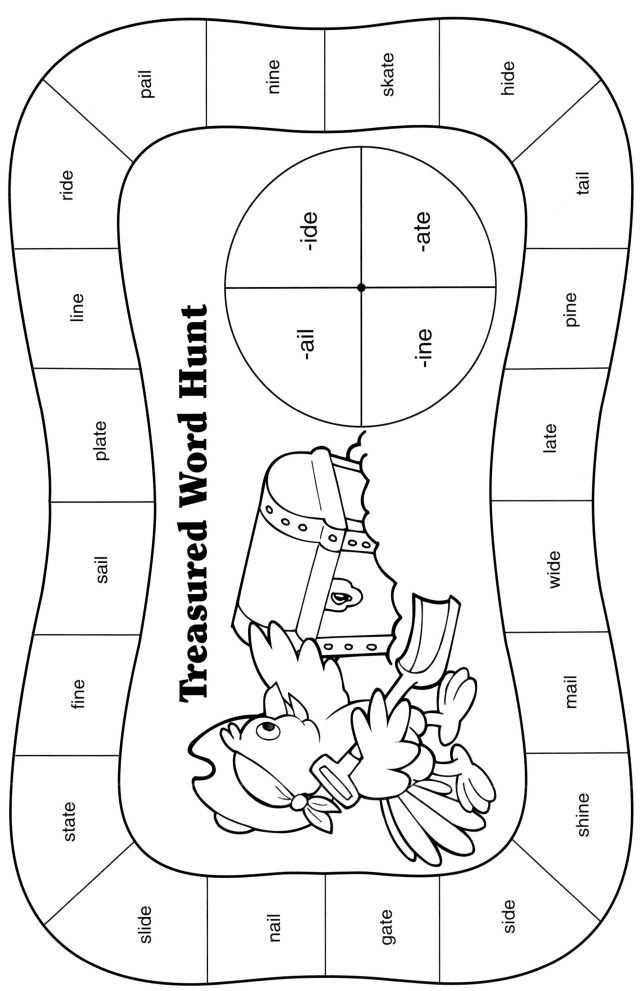

Spinner:
- -ide
- -ate
- -ine
- -ail

Board spaces:
pail · nine · skate · hide · tail · pine · late · wide · mail · shine · side · gate · nail · slide · state · fine · sail · plate · line · ride

**Note to the teacher:** Use with "Treasured Word Hunt" on page 89.

# Game Cards

Use with "Digraph Lineup" on page 90.

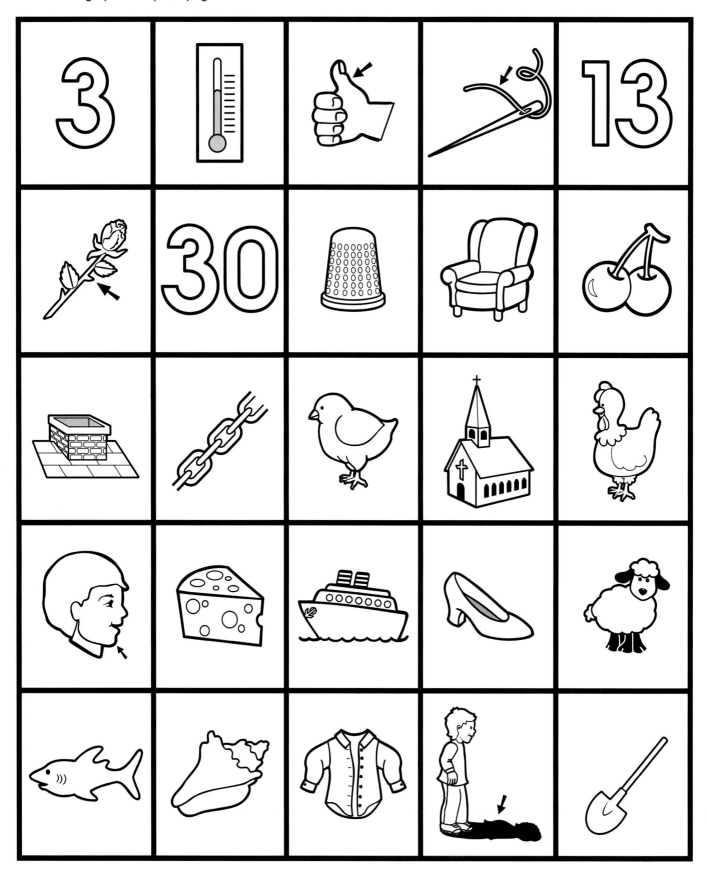

# SKILLS FOR THE SEASON

# Skills for the Season

## Language Arts and Math Ideas

### Melon Math

Here's **addition** practice fresh off the vine! Have each student trim a half sheet of paper to resemble a slice of watermelon. Instruct him to label it with an assigned number. Then ask him to color his watermelon, incorporating illustrations of the appropriate number of seeds.

Next, pair students and give each youngster a blank sheet of paper. Each student displays his number to his partner. He uses this number and his partner's number to write one or, if possible, two different addition sentences on his paper. He refers to the illustrations to check his work. At your signal, each student finds a different partner and repeats the process. The activity continues as time allows. For later reinforcement, tack the watermelon slices to a prepared bulletin board in groups of two or three. Then have students use the groups of numbers to write addition sentences. Cool!

$$5 + 7 = 12$$
$$7 + 5 = 12$$

### Compound-Word Giants

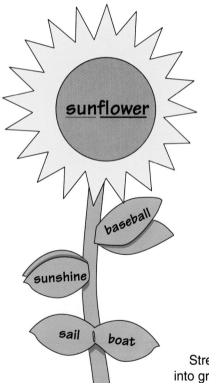

These giant sunflowers provide bright examples of **compound words!** Each student writes "sunflower" on a five-inch brown construction paper circle. He draws a different-colored line under each smaller word in the compound word. Next, he folds a 9" x 12" sheet of green construction paper in half lengthwise. He cuts out three leaf shapes along the fold. He writes a compound word on each folded leaf, then writes the two smaller words inside as shown.

To complete his project, the youngster glues his circle onto a ten-inch yellow construction paper circle. He makes cuts in the larger circle to resemble sunflower petals. He glues the resulting blossom onto a 1" x 12" construction paper stem, then staples his leaves to the stem so that they can open. What a nifty reminder of compound words!

### Vocabulary Work

Stretch **vocabularies** from *A* to *Z* with this Labor Day activity! Divide students into groups of three or four and give each group one sheet of paper. Have each group list the letters of the alphabet vertically. Then challenge the students to write an occupation for each letter. Explain that each correctly identified word earns one point. If only one group writes the word, it earns two points.

At the end of the allotted work time, ask each group to announce its word for the letter *a*. Award the appropriate points. If no group has a response for the letter, help students identify a job-related word for it. Continue the scoring process with the remaining letters. Then lead students in a round of applause for the top-scoring group. Now that's putting students' vocabularies to work!

# Skills for the Season

## Language Arts and Math Ideas

### I-Spy Pumpkin

This idea is just "ripe" for reinforcing seasonal **vocabulary!** In advance, make a pointer by taping a pumpkin cutout to one end of a ruler. Draw the outline of a pumpkin on a large sheet of unlined paper. Write several grade-appropriate seasonal words on the pumpkin and display it within student reach.

To begin, read the words with students. Then secretly choose one word and announce a skill-related clue for it, such as "I spy a word that ends with *-ake*" or "I spy a compound word." Invite a student to name the word and use the pumpkin pointer to indicate it on the poster. Challenge students to identify the remaining words in a similar manner. Repeat the activity on each of several days to harvest increased reading and writing vocabularies!

pumpkin
candy          treat
spooky
rake
leaf       fall
football
costume

### Scarecrow Stories

Put an entertaining spin on **writing** with mix-and-match story elements. Prompt a class discussion to explore what students know about scarecrows, providing additional background information as needed. Then announce that each student will write a creative story about a scarecrow. To identify a main character for his tale, a student uses a pencil and small paper clip to spin the pumpkin-shaped spinner on a copy of page 105; he draws an X in the indicated section. Next, he marks his choices for a story setting and problem. He incorporates the chosen details into a story that he pens on writing paper. Then he staples his completed work inside a construction paper folder and adds a title and illustrations. Now that's something to crow about!

### "Sum" Turkeys!

Student-made turkeys give **addition with three addends** a fine-feathered twist! To make a turkey, each student traces on white construction paper one hand with fingers outstretched. She draws an eye on her thumb tracing and labels each of three finger tracings (feathers) with a digit from 0 to 9. She colors the turkey, cuts it out, and then signs the back of it. She uses construction paper scraps to add a wattle, a beak, and two legs.

Next, have each student write on provided paper an addition problem with her three digits. After she solves the problem, ask her to trade turkeys with a nearby classmate. Instruct her to write an addition problem with her classmate's digits and then write the sum. Have students continue the trading and math process for a desired number of problems. Then display the "handsome" gobblers for more addition practice. Gobble! Gobble!

Laura Bianchi—Gr. 2
Ridgebury School
Lyndhurst, OH

Grace

$3 + 5 + 2 = 10$

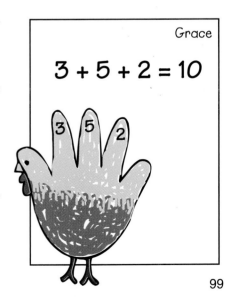

# Skills for the Season

## Language Arts and Math Ideas

### Mouthwatering Spelling

This versatile **spelling** idea prompts visions of sugarplums and sweet success. Each student labels the cards on a copy of page 106 with his spelling words (provide additional cards if necessary). After he checks his work, he signs the jar and adds crayon details. He then cuts out the jar and cards.

Next, the youngster folds a 4½" x 12" piece of paper in half to 4½" x 6". With the fold at the bottom, he glues his jar onto the paper so that the bottom edge aligns with the fold. He trims the paper to the shape of the jar. Then he staples the sides and stores his cards inside. He uses his words to complete assigned spelling activities, such as sorting by letter patterns or listing the words in ABC order. Spelling practice has never been so tempting!

**Kwanzaa Principles**
1. Unity
2. Self-determination
3. Working together
4. Sharing
5. Purpose
6. Creativity
7. Faith

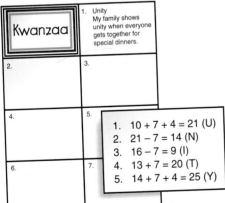

### Ways With Seven

The number seven is featured in this mathematical introduction to Kwanzaa! In advance, display an alphabet code in which A = 1, B = 2, and so on. Use the code to prepare grade-appropriate **math problems with the number seven** so that the answers spell the first principle of Kwanzaa (unity).

To begin, explain that Kwanzaa is a seven-day holiday with seven principles. Have each student divide a sheet of paper into eight sections as shown. Ask him to title the first section "Kwanzaa," decorate it as desired, and then number the remaining sections. Next, instruct each student to solve the prepared problems and use the code to identify the first principle. Discuss the principle's meaning as a class. Then have each youngster label his first numbered section with the principle and write one way in which it may be demonstrated. Plan to use different problems to continue the activity on later days and familiarize youngsters with the remaining principles.

1. 10 + 7 + 4 = 21 (U)
2. 21 − 7 = 14 (N)
3. 16 − 7 = 9 (I)
4. 13 + 7 = 20 (T)
5. 14 + 7 + 4 = 25 (Y)

### New Year Notes

Welcome the New Year the **"write"** way! To prepare a two-sided booklet, each youngster folds a 9" x 12" sheet of construction paper and an 8½" x 11" sheet of white paper in half lengthwise. He staples the white paper inside the folded construction paper. He titles the resulting covers as shown. To reflect on the past year, he lifts the appropriate cover and writes about a memorable occasion on the front of each booklet page. To look ahead to the coming year, he flips his booklet and writes about his hopes on the remaining pages. He completes his booklet with cover illustrations. Happy New Year!

Goodbye, 2003!

Hello, 2004!

# Skills for the Season

## Language Arts and Math Ideas

### "Heart-y" Work

With this Valentine's Day activity, it's a treat to work with **words and letters.** Give each youngster a copy of page 108 and a plastic snack bag that contains four conversation heart candies with different messages. Have each youngster follow the activity directions to complete his paper; then invite him to enjoy his candy snack. How sweet!

Sherry Olfert—Grs. K–7
School District 34
Abbotsford, British Columbia, Canada

### March Math

**Number sentences** sprout from these shamrocks! For each student, label each leaf of a shamrock cutout with a different number. Divide students into small groups and provide each group with two dice. Give each youngster a prepared shamrock and a sheet of paper.

To begin, one student in each group rolls the dice. He announces the total and a desired operation. Each group member uses this number and operation along with a chosen number on his shamrock to write an equation. The activity continues in this manner, with the group members taking turns rolling the dice and announcing the task, until each student has written a designated number of different equations. After each group completes its work, display students' shamrocks and papers with the title "March Math."

adapted from an idea by Amy Emmons—Gr. 2
Enon Elementary
Franklinton, LA

$$9 + 6 = 15$$
$$12 - 9 = 3$$
$$10 + 10 = 20$$
$$9 - 4 = 5$$
$$9 + 8 = 17$$
$$12 + 7 = 19$$

Winter
When I walk on the snow, it crunches like potato chips.

Spring
The buds on the trees are as tiny as bugs.

### Seasonal Similes

Usher in spring with this wild and woolly **simile** idea! Prompt a class discussion to ensure students' understanding of the expression "March comes in like a lion and goes out like a lamb." Point out that a comparison of two unlike things that uses *like* or *as* is a simile. Then invite students to suggest words to use in the expression in place of *lion* and *lamb*.

To follow up, each youngster writes "Winter" at the top of a half sheet of writing paper and writes a winter-themed simile below it. She leaves space below this simile, then titles and writes a springtime simile. She staples her completed writing in the center of a vertically positioned 9" x 12" sheet of paper. She adds wintry illustrations above her writing and springtime illustrations below it. Bind students' completed work into a class book titled "Seasonal Similes" and add it to your classroom library.

Linda Butler—K–6 Special Needs
Community Therapeutic Day School
Lexington, MA

# Skills for the Season

## Language Arts and Math Ideas

### Word Hunt

This egg hunt leads straight to **word-building** practice! In advance, obtain a class supply of plastic eggs. Inside each egg, place a slip of paper programmed with a chosen onset. Hide the eggs in various classroom locations.

To begin, divide students into groups and have each group find one egg for each of its members. Then, in each group, one student draws a large egg on a sheet of paper and titles it with an assigned rime. Each student opens his egg and announces his onset. Below the rime, the students list any words that they can form with the rime and their onsets. Then they return the onsets to their eggs, trade them with another group, and list any additional words they can form. They repeat the trading and listing process a designated number of times to complete their "egg-cellent" word reference.

adapted from an idea by Mandy Jones
Oldtown, MD

### Sweet Data

Here's a sweet approach to **collecting data.** Draw a large jar on a sheet of duplicating paper and give each student a copy. Have her draw ten jelly beans in her jar. Then list four colors on the board and ask each student to use a desired combination of them to color her jelly beans. For example, she may color five blue, one green, one orange, two yellow, and one red. After each student completes her coloring, pair students. Instruct the partners to complete a tally chart similar to the one shown and then write three sentences analyzing their data.

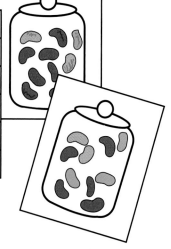

| Jelly Bean Colors | | |
|---|---|---|
| Color | Tally | Number |
| red | ⧻⧻ \|\| | 7 |
| green | \|\|\|\| | 4 |
| purple | ⧻⧻ | 5 |
| orange | \|\|\|\| | 4 |

### Colorful Creations

Brighten a rainy day with **poetry writing.** List these colors on the board: red, orange, yellow, green, blue, purple. On a half sheet of writing paper, each student uses the format shown to incorporate the colors into an original poem titled "Rainbow." Next, he uses a red crayon to trace the arc of an eight-inch half circle on a piece of drawing paper. He draws a rainbow, using the red line as the outer edge. Then he cuts out the rainbow, mounts it along with his poem on a 9" x 12" sheet of paper, and glues on cotton clouds. Beautiful!

Pam Susman—Gr. 1
The Shlenker School
Houston, TX

| Rainbow |
|---|
| Red as a sunset. |
| Orange as juice. |
| Yellow as a baby chick. |
| Green as a bunch of grapes. |
| Blue as the ocean. |
| Purple as a juicy plum. |

# Skills for the Season

## Language Arts and Math Ideas

### Cool Shopping

This refreshing approach to **adding money amounts** is sure to please! Display a poster that lists several frozen treats with grade-appropriate prices. Then designate one student as Cool Shopper. Invite her to announce two or three listed items that she would like to purchase and ask her to write them on the board. Have each student use scrap paper and, if desired, imitation coins to determine the total cost. Next, invite students to help you add the money amounts on the board or use overhead manipulatives to identify the correct answer. Repeat the activity with different shoppers for more tempting math fun.

adapted from an idea by Michelle Bassham
Houma, LA

**Treats**

| | |
|---|---|
| ice-cream cone | $.75 |
| milk shake | $1.25 |
| ice-cream sandwich | $.98 |
| sundae | $1.75 |
| nuts | $.20 |
| sprinkles | $.15 |

### Fishy Prompts

Reel in **writing** practice with this ongoing activity. Program several fish cutouts with writing prompts. Place the cutouts in an unbreakable fishbowl in a prominent classroom location. Each day, invite a student to remove one or two fish, read aloud each prompt, and then tape the fish to the board below the heading "Catch of the Day." Have each student write a response on provided paper; remove the displayed fish at the day's end. Every few days, serve fish-shaped crackers for students to enjoy as volunteers read aloud their favorite responses.

Elizabeth Searls Almy
Greensboro, NC

### Patriotic Picnics

With the Fourth of July right around the corner, a picnic is in order—**ABC order,** that is! Remind students that picnics have been a part of Fourth of July celebrations for many years. After students brainstorm a list of picnic-related words, have each youngster use a template to make two red, two white, and two blue construction paper stars from 5½-inch squares. Ask him to write a different listed word or phrase on each star.

Next, each student chooses one star of each color and vertically positions a 1½" x 18" strip of paper. He glues on the three stars in ABC order, leaving space at the top of the strip. He turns the strip over and glues his remaining stars in ABC order. Then he folds over the top portion of the strip, staples it in place, and threads a length of string through the resulting loop to make a hanger. After suspending students' completed projects from the ceiling, have each youngster complete a copy of page 110 for additional reinforcement.

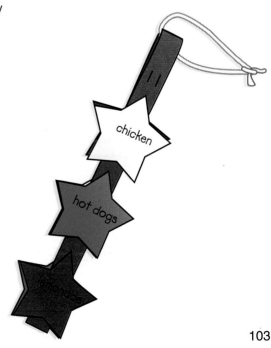

chicken

hot dogs

lemonade

# A Slice of Math

Solve the problems.
Outline the watermelon slices by the code.

**Color Code**
= red
= yellow
= orange

**Note to the teacher:** Make one copy of this page. Program it with chosen computation problems and fill in the code. Give each student a
104  copy of the sheet to complete.

Name _____

# Scarecrow Story Planner

Follow your teacher's directions to plan a story.

**Settings**

☐ a rainy day on a farm
☐ the school playground
☐ a huge store
☐ the town park

**Problems**

☐ wants a different job
☐ gets lost
☐ needs new clothes
☐ wants a friend

**Characters**

| smart scarecrow | lazy scarecrow |
| mixed-up scarecrow | funny scarecrow |

©The Education Center, Inc. • *THE MAILBOX*® • *Primary* • Oct/Nov 2003

**Note to the teacher:** Use with "Scarecrow Stories" on page 99.

# Jar Pattern and Cards

Use with "Mouthwatering Spelling" on page 100.

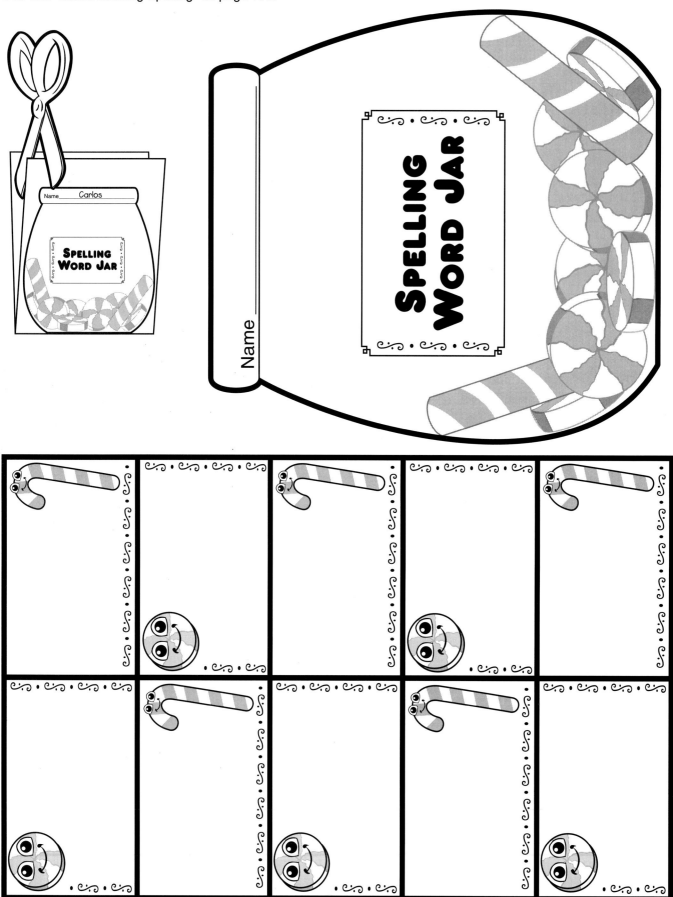

Name _____

# Time for Spring?

Read each sentence. Write the time.
Then number the clocks to show the correct order.

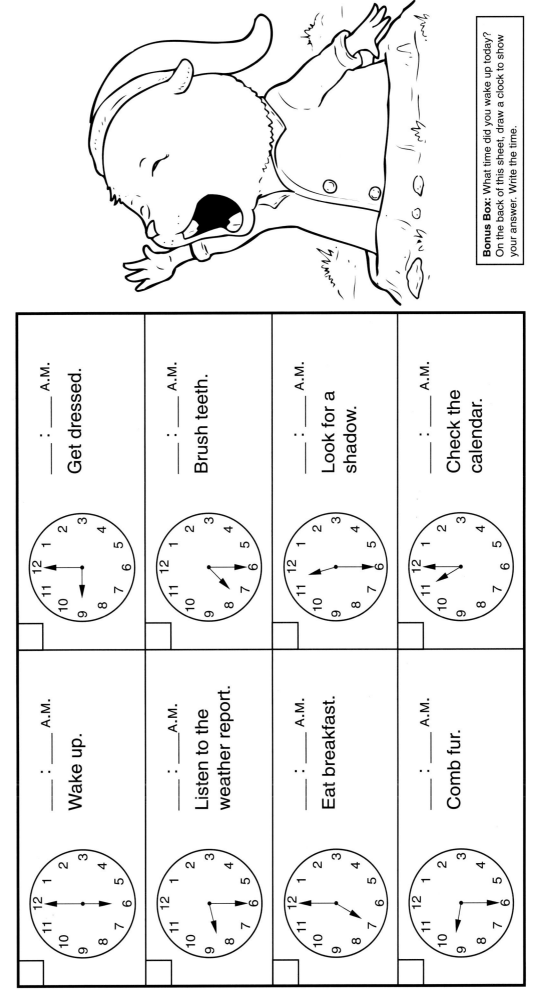

___ : ___ A.M.
Wake up.

___ : ___ A.M.
Get dressed.

___ : ___ A.M.
Listen to the
weather report.

___ : ___ A.M.
Brush teeth.

___ : ___ A.M.
Eat breakfast.

___ : ___ A.M.
Look for a
shadow.

___ : ___ A.M.
Comb fur.

___ : ___ A.M.
Check the
calendar.

**Bonus Box:** What time did you wake up today?
On the back of this sheet, draw a clock to show
your answer. Write the time.

©The Education Center, Inc. • THE MAILBOX® • Primary • Feb/Mar 2004 • Key p. 311

Name _____

108

# How Sweet!

Read your candies.
Write each message on the Valentine.
Follow the directions in each box.

**Messages**

1. _____
2. _____
3. _____
4. _____

♥ Count the words in the messages. Write the total. ☐

♥ List the words in ABC order.

♥ Use the letters in the messages to form at least five new words. List the words.

♥ Choose three of the messages. Use each one in a different sentence.

a. _____

b. _____

c. _____

©The Education Center, Inc. • THE MAILBOX® • Primary • Feb/Mar 2004

**Note to the teacher:** Use with "Heart-y' Work" on page 101.

Name _____

# Spring Cleaning

Solve the problems.
Look at the answers.
Color the eggs by the code.

**Color Code**

even = blue

odd = green

| | | |
|---|---|---|
| ① | ④ | ⑥ |
| | ② | ⑦ |
| | ⑤ | |
| ⑫ | ⑧ | ⑩ |
| ⑬ | ⑨ | ⑪ |
| ⑭ | ③ | |

**Note to the teacher:** Make one copy of this page. Program it with chosen computation problems. Have each student complete a copy of the sheet.

109

Name _____

# Ant Antics

Read each set of words.
Circle the word that comes first in the dictionary.

1. pickles
   plates
   pie

2. crowd
   crackers
   cups

3. salad
   soda
   sandwich

4. bugs
   brownie
   bread

5. grill
   grapes
   ground

6. banana
   berries
   basket

7. hot dog
   happy
   hamburger

8. trees
   talk
   table

9. potato
   play
   plums

10. forks
    friends
    food

11. cups
    cherries
    chicken

12. chips
    cheese
    cookies

©The Education Center, Inc. • *The Mailbox*® • Primary • TEC43013 • June/July 2004 • Key p. 311

**Note to the teacher:** Use with "Patriotic Picnics" on page 103.

110

WRITE ON!

# Write On!

## Ideas and Tips for Teaching Students to Write!

### Timely Prompts

Tempt your young writers with cool **prompts!** Tell students that the ice-cream cone was invented about 100 years ago and its anniversary is in September. Then invite students to share their thoughts about the tasty invention. Next, each youngster uses a scoop-shaped template to make two booklet covers from construction paper and two pages from writing paper. He staples the scoops together, as shown, and responds to a provided prompt inside. He lifts the pages and glues a cone cutout to the back cover. Then he adds a title and desired crayon details.

- Explain how to fix and eat an ice-cream cone. Tell what to do if the ice cream begins melting!
- The ice-cream cone is a handy invention. What other ice-cream inventions might be popular? Write your ideas.
- Imagine that you invented the ice-cream cone. How would you convince people that it was an important invention?

### Writers' Station

Here's a simple strategy for increasing **writing motivation!** Place one or more chairs at a designated table. To the back of each chair, attach a sign labeled "Author at Work." To complete the station, display colorful posters with writing and proofreading tips. Set out various publishing supplies, such as blank booklets, pens, novelty pencils, and crayons. Add several laminated magazine images for writing inspiration and a file box that contains story starters or writing prompts. Secure a supply of paper in a three-ring binder that you have titled "Class Diary." Encourage each student who visits the station to add an entry. As students' interest in writing grows, their skills are bound to increase too!

*Brandy Fessler—Gr. 2, Sandymount Elementary, Finskburg, MD*

### Descriptions With Character

Add character to **descriptive writing!** Draw a circle on the board and label it with the name of a familiar book character. Ask students to imagine that they will describe the character to someone who has never heard of him or her. On the board, make a web of student-generated details. Model how to use the web to write an image-evoking paragraph.

To follow up, each youngster makes a web for a favorite book or TV character on a blank sheet of paper. Then she titles a sheet of story paper with the character's name and incorporates the details into a paragraph. After each youngster illustrates her work, bind students' papers into a class book titled "Meet Our Favorite Characters!"

*Patricia Rigueira—Gr. 3, Southern Cross School, Buenos Aires, Argentina*

Ramona

Ramona is nine years old, but she wishes she were older. She is in fourth grade this year. She has brown hair, brown eyes, and no cavities. She has calluses on her hands from the rings at the park. Ramona never likes to miss anything. She doesn't like spelling and isn't very good at it

If all the kids were in the same room, I think it would be fun. It would be neat to see what the older kids do. The big kids could help the little kids with their work. Sometimes it would be hard, though. With just one teacher, kids would have to wait awhile for their turns. It would be hard for the teacher to help everyone.

Emily

Things I Like

Soccer
Comic books
Walking my dog, Lucky
Baseball
Pizza
Riding my bike down the hill
Root beer floats

Luis

# Write On!

## Ideas and Tips for Teaching Students to Write!

### Timely Prompts

These **prompts** about the past are a perfect addition to a study of colonial times. To familiarize students with childhood during this time period, share a book such as *...If You Lived in Colonial Times* by Ann McGovern. Next, each student responds to a provided prompt on a piece of writing paper that is approximately 6" x 7". She staples her writing to a 9" x 12" sheet of brown construction paper, about one inch from the top. Then she trims the construction paper to resemble a hornbook. What an interesting look at the past!

- Colonial children had many chores. Which would you have liked better: outdoor or indoor chores? Explain.

- What would you have liked the most about living during colonial times? The least?

- A colonial school had only one teacher and one room for children of all ages. What do you think that would be like? Write your ideas.

### Likable Poetry

Every student can be a poet with these festive **list poems!** To begin, a student brainstorms a list of things he enjoys. Then he titles a half sheet of writing paper "Things I Like." He refers to his list as he organizes his thoughts in a list poem; then he signs his name. To showcase his work, he cuts a piece of gift wrap that is slightly larger than a 9" x 12" sheet of tagboard. He staples the gift wrap to the tagboard and then trims the excess gift wrap. Finally, he staples his writing in the center of the prepared tagboard. Post students' work on a board titled "Poetry That Pleases." Use the eye-catching display to prompt discussion about students' unique and shared interests.

*Dawn Maucieri—Gr. 3, Signal Hill Elementary School, Dix Hills, NY*

### At the Top

Fee-fi-fo-fum! Here's an imaginative way to help **descriptive-writing skills** grow! Read aloud your favorite version of *Jack and the Beanstalk*, stopping just before Jack reaches the top of the beanstalk. Then have each youngster describe on a half sheet of writing paper what she imagines Jack will see at the top. After volunteers read their writing to the class, share the rest of the book. At the book's conclusion, each youngster tapes two sheets of paper, end to end, to the bottom of her paper. She illustrates the extraordinary beanstalk and Jack's house on the resulting blank strip. She staples the top of her writing paper in a 6" x 9" construction paper folder as shown. She accordion-folds the entire length of paper, tucks it inside the folder, and then titles her project. Impressive!

*Nicole Miner—Grs. 1–2, Painted Sky Elementary, Albuquerque, NM*

# Write On!

## Ideas and Tips for Teaching Students to Write!

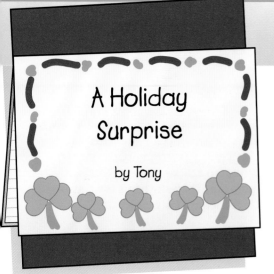

### Timely Prompts

Sprightly leprechauns are the focus of these St. Patrick's Day **prompts.** Tell students that according to legend, a person who catches a leprechaun can ask the wee creature to reveal where he hid his pot of gold. Invite students to share their thoughts about this leprechaun lore. Then have each youngster write a response to a chosen prompt. To showcase his work, the student staples his writing inside a construction paper folder and writes a title on the front. For decoration, he glues construction paper hearts on his folder to resemble shamrocks and adds desired crayon details.

- What would you do if you discovered a leprechaun's pot of gold? Explain.
- Some people believe that a leprechaun is the size of a person's thumb. What would a day at school be like if you were this size?
- Imagine that you saw a leprechaun on your way to school. Write a letter to a friend about what happened.

### Poetic Tributes

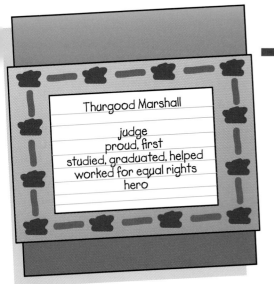

During Black History Month (February), honor famous Americans with this **poetry-writing** activity. Use selected picture book biographies by David A. Adler or other grade-appropriate resources to familiarize students with the achievements of chosen Black Americans. To pay tribute to the featured people, give each youngster a copy of page 118. The student identifies a chosen Black American as his poetry topic. Then he follows the activity directions to draft a poem about the person. After he edits his poem, he writes a final draft on a half sheet of writing paper, mounts it onto a sheet of construction paper, and then decorates his work as desired.

*Traci A. Guth—Gr. 2, McPherson Elementary School, Chicago, IL*

### From Picture to Paragraph

**Writing paragraphs** is sure to be a snap for students when they start with pictures. Display a picture from a magazine or another chosen resource that shows an activity. As a class, form one sentence that tells what the picture is mostly about; write the sentence on the board. Explain that this will be the topic sentence for a paragraph. To identify supporting details, invite youngsters to name pictured or inferred details; list them on the board. Then, with students' help, use chosen details to write a paragraph on a sheet of chart paper. To follow up, give each youngster a different picture to study and have him use it to develop his own picture-perfect paragraph.

*Susan DeRiso, Barrington, RI*

# Write On!

## Ideas and Tips for Teaching Students to Write!

A Perfect Home

If I were a robin, I would build my nest in a tree that's beside a house. I would try to find a branch that is near a window. I could watch the kids play outside. I could look in the windows too. I could see what the people are doing. Maybe I could peek in and watch TV!

Diego

### Timely Prompts

These **prompts** are sure to inspire fine-feathered writing. Invite students to tell about any birds that they have seen recently. Point out that robins are a sign that winter is ending. Then distribute half sheets of writing paper and have each youngster write a response to a provided prompt. After the student edits his work, he fashions a bird's nest from a 6" x 9" piece of construction paper and prepares a few construction paper eggs. Then he staples his writing near the top of a vertically positioned 9" x 12" sheet of paper and glues his nest and eggs below it.

- Robins are one sign of spring. Write about three other signs.
- Imagine that you are a robin. Write about what you see as you fly from place to place.
- A robin often builds its nest in the same spot, year after year. If you were a robin, where would you build your nest? Why?

### Rainy-Day Writing

Splish, splash! Pitter, patter! It's a shower of **writing motivation!** Label both sides of several construction paper raindrops with rain-related words. Embellish the raindrops with silver glitter. Then suspend a large, open umbrella above a table and hang the raindrops from it. Complete the writing area with desired supplies. Invite a few students at a time to gather under the umbrella and write rainy-day poems or stories!

*Sherry Olfert—Grs. K–7, School District 34, Abbotsford, British Columbia, Canada*

downpour     puddles

### Chatter Bugs

What's all the chatter about? **Writing dialogue!** Pair students. Have each youngster illustrate a chosen insect and then cut it out. Instruct the partners to glue their insects onto one large piece of paper. Next, the partners imagine that the insects are having a conversation. They use two speech bubbles to show a question-and-answer exchange. The partners glue the speech bubbles in place. Then they write the dialogue on provided paper, expanding the sentences as appropriate and using the correct punctuation. Finally, they mount their writing on the illustrated paper. Now that's an idea guaranteed to be the talk of the class!

*Jodi Smigelsky—Gr. 2, Schirra Elementary School, Old Bridge, NJ*

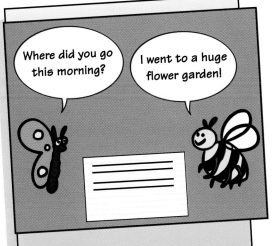

Where did you go this morning?

I went to a huge flower garden!

# Write On!

## Ideas and Tips for Teaching Students to Write!

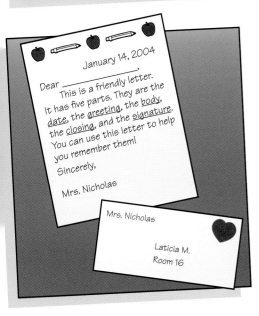

Tony

Respect is when you treat people nicely. It's treating people the way you want them to treat you. Dr. King said that we should respect people even if they are different from us. It would make the world a happier place!

January 14, 2004

Dear _____,
This is a friendly letter. It has five parts. They are the date, the greeting, the body, the closing, and the signature. You can use this letter to help you remember them!
Sincerely,
Mrs. Nicholas

Mrs. Nicholas

Laticia M.
Room 16

Look Inside for Bright Ideas!

### Timely Prompts

These **prompts** for Martin Luther King Jr. Day are sure to lead to thoughtful discussion and writing! Remind students of Dr. King's dream for peace and justice. Explain that the anniversary of this leader's birthday is a time to honor him and his achievements. Use the questions below to guide a class discussion; then ask each student to write a response to a chosen prompt. Invite him to mount his writing on a sheet of construction paper along with an illustration. Happy birthday, Dr. King!

- If you could make a dream come true for your country, what would it be? Why?

- What do you think are the two most important things to remember about Dr. King and his work? Tell why they are important.

- Dr. King believed that people should be treated with respect. What does respect mean to you? Explain.

### "Send-sational" Introduction

Begin a **letter-writing** unit with a special delivery! Prepare a letter similar to the one shown and copy it to make a class supply. For each student, personalize a letter; then fold it in thirds and seal it with a decorative sticker. Address the outside of the letter; add your name in the upper left-hand corner and a sticker in the upper right-hand corner. To begin, announce that you have a special delivery and give each youngster her letter. After students open and read their mail, direct each youngster to mark the parts of her letter in a chosen manner. For example, you might have her circle the date with a red crayon and underline the greeting with blue. In the end, she'll have a first-class letter-writing reference!

*Linnae Nicholas, Cuba, NY*

### Bright Ideas

Make writer's block a thing of the past with this suggestion for sparking **ideas!** Cut out a supply of pictures from discarded greeting cards, calendars, or magazines. Place the pictures in a decorated box that you have labeled as shown. When a student has difficulty thinking of a writing topic, encourage him to select a picture from the box. After the youngster studies the picture, he jots down questions he has about it or thoughts that come to mind. Then he uses his notes to guide his writing. The youngster keeps the picture with his edited writing. Or, if desired, he returns it to the box for another student to use. To keep the box freshly stocked, invite parents or classroom volunteers to make contributions. What a bright idea!

*Christine Vaughn—Gr. 2, Cedar Hill Elementary School, Lawrenceville, GA*

# Write On!

**The Day I'll Never Forget**

One day it was so hot that the water in Parker Pond started boiling! I was in a boat with my friend. We took the boat to shore to be safe. We were really hot, so we went to get some ice cream. The bottoms of our sneakers melted when they touched the ground. Ouch! The ice cream melted as soon as we took it out of the freezer. We had to drink it with straws!

Kiera

It is as bright as the sun.
It is as smooth as a tabletop.
It is as yellow as a dandelion.

MARKER

It is a yellow marker.
Michael

Introducing _____ (character's name)

Birthdate: _____
Place of Birth: _____
Proud Parents: _____
Other Family Members: _____

_____

Looks: _____

Describing Words

_____

_____

A Future Life Event: _____
A Future Problem: _____

## Timely Prompts

Heat up writing practice with summertime **prompts**. Lead students in a class discussion about favorite activities for this time of year. Then have each youngster write a response to a prompt listed below. After the student edits her work, she staples it to a sheet of construction paper. For decoration, she illustrates a head-and-shoulders cutout to resemble herself wearing a pair of sunglasses; then she glues her self-likeness and two hand cutouts to her paper as shown. Cool!

- What three things would you most like to do on a hot summer day?
- A lot happens during the summer! Use describing words to write about what you might see outside.
- Write a paragraph about the hottest day ever. Include unbelievable details and begin with "One day it was so hot that…"

## Mysterious Similes

**Similes** can make writing vivid descriptions as easy as pie! In advance, have each student bring in a small item from home, such as a school tool, souvenir, or toy. To begin, ask each youngster to write on a folded piece of paper three similes that tell about his item without revealing its identity. Encourage him to describe with the similes details such as the item's size, color, or texture. After he completes his writing, have him unfold his paper, write what the item is, and sign his name. Display students' items and collect their papers. Next, read aloud a chosen set of similes. Ask each of several volunteers (excluding the author) to guess which item the similes describe. Then reveal the answer. Investigate the identity of each remaining item in a similar manner.

*Liz Harrell, Cornwall on Hudson, NY*

## A Special Announcement

When it comes to creating story characters, this **prewriting** idea delivers! Prepare a birth announcement form similar to the one shown. Each youngster completes the form with details about an original character that she would like to include in a story. Then she folds the paper in half so that her writing is inside and positions her paper so that the fold is at the top. On the front of the resulting card, she writes "Look Who's Here!" and adds an illustration. When the student is ready to write her story, she'll have lots of details at her fingertips!

*Vicki Dabrowka, Palm Harbor, FL*

# Poetry Planner

Write your topic on the line below.
List words that tell about your topic in the correct columns.

| Topic: _____ | | |
|---|---|---|
| **Nouns** | **Adjectives** | **Verbs** |
| | | |

Now use words from the chart to write a poem below.

_____
(noun)

_____ , _____
(adjective)                              (adjective)

_____ , _____ , _____
(verb)                        (verb)                          (verb)

_____
(four-word phrase)

_____
(noun)

**Note to the teacher:** Use with "Poetic Tributes" on page 114.

# LANGUAGE ARTS UNITS

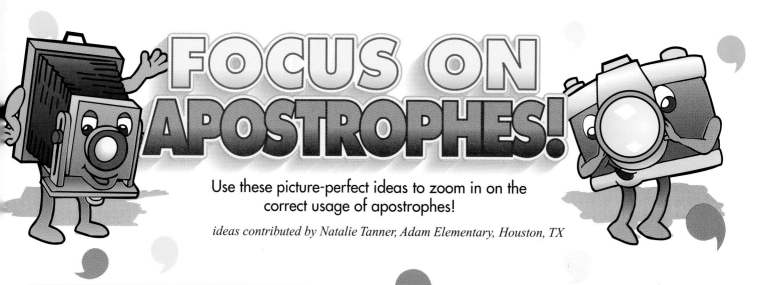

# FOCUS ON APOSTROPHES!

Use these picture-perfect ideas to zoom in on the correct usage of apostrophes!

*ideas contributed by Natalie Tanner, Adam Elementary, Houston, TX*

## Places, Everyone!
*Forming contractions*

This dramatic approach to forming contractions gives apostrophes a starring role! Prepare a set of large letter cards and an apostrophe card. To begin, suggest that an apostrophe has an important role in a contraction because it holds a place for one or more letters. Next, give volunteer student actors the appropriate letter cards to spell "is not." Have these students hold the cards at the front of the classroom to form the words. Ask a seated student to use the apostrophe card to help change the words to a contraction. To do this, she dramatically remarks to the student who is holding the letter that needs to be omitted, "I'm sorry, [letter name], but I can make this shorter." The letter holder returns to his seat and the apostrophe holder takes his place.

Invite a seated student to say an original sentence that uses the resulting contraction, pausing for the card holders to say the featured word in unison. Then ask the card holders to return to their seats. Instruct each student to write the two words and contraction on provided paper. Use the list shown and a similar process to explore different contractions. No doubt every youngster will want a role!

## Possessives on the Go
*Forming singular possessives*

What do you pack for a trip? Possessions! Make this point to help students remember that apostrophes are needed to form possessives. Encourage students to imagine that they are helping a group of animals pack for a vacation. On the board, use the format shown to write a sentence with a singular possessive. Confirm that students understand the placement of the apostrophe. Next, each youngster draws a line a few inches from the bottom of a provided sheet of paper. Below the line, he uses the displayed format to write an original sentence about a chosen animal. Then he adds an illustration above the sentence. Display students' work and a jumbo suitcase cut-out on a bulletin board titled "Packing Up With Apostrophes!"

**Sentence Format**

I packed the [singular possessive] [item] [reason].

### Sample Contractions

| are | is | not | will |
|-----|-----|-----|------|
| they're | here's | can't | I'll |
| we're | he's | couldn't | she'll |
| you're | where's | doesn't | we'll |
| | who's | haven't | you'll |

I packed the giraffe's sunscreen so he does not get sunburned.

**Barry Slate**

## The Bee's Knees
*Forming and using possessives*

Is forming possessives a laughing matter? Sure it is—when you make this humorous booklet project! Guide students to brainstorm a list of animal-related noun phrases that rhyme. (See the examples.) Use a selected phrase to review how to form singular and plural possessives.

To make a booklet, each youngster staples three half sheets of white paper together. She opens the booklet and uses a ruler to mark four equal horizontal sections on the right-hand page. She carefully cuts along each section just to the stapled side and labels each resulting flap with two listed rhyming words. On the back of each flap, she uses the corresponding words in a sentence that includes a singular or plural possessive. In the space opposite each sentence, she adds an illustration. She completes her booklet with a title and cover illustration. Who knew apostrophes could be such fun?

## Apostrophes at Work
*Identifying uses of apostrophes*

For such tiny punctuation marks, apostrophes do big jobs! Remind students that apostrophes have jobs in two types of words: contractions and possessives. Write student-generated examples of these types of words on the board. Then, as a class, write a brief explanation of the apostrophe's job in each one. Use a word-processing program to type the explanations and then give each student a copy. After he adds examples, have him keep the reminder in his writing folder for later reference.

**Apostrophes**

Contraction
    An apostrophe shows where one or more letters are left out. Example: can't (can not)
Possessive
    An apostrophe helps show ownership.
**Examples: one dog's toy, two dogs' toys**

The pigs' wigs are curly.

goat, coat

bear, hair

bee, knee

Don't forget to say cheese!

Possessive

Contraction

## The "Write" Form
*Forming and using possessives*

Put apostrophe skills to the test with sentence-writing practice! Give every group of two or three students an individual whiteboard or chalkboard and appropriate writing supplies. Draw a three-column chart on the board. Title the first column "Noun," the second column "Belongs to One," and the third column "Belongs to More Than One."

To begin, write a noun in the first column. Then have each group write an original sentence on its board that includes either the singular or plural possessive form of the word. In turn, ask each group to hold up its board and read its sentence aloud. Challenge the other groups to tell whether the possessive is singular or plural, providing assistance as needed. After each group shares, write the appropriate possessive form in each column. Then ask each group to erase its board. Repeat the process with different nouns.

The camera's flash is ready.

121

# It's Picture Day!

Use the words to make contractions.
Write the contractions on the lines.

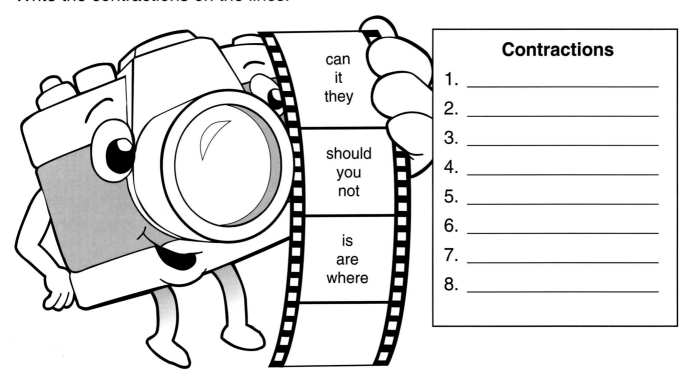

| can it they |
| should you not |
| is are where |

**Contractions**

1. _____
2. _____
3. _____
4. _____
5. _____
6. _____
7. _____
8. _____

---

Complete each sentence with the correct contraction.

a. Tom and Tina are glad _____ Picture Day. (it is)

b. Tina _____ wait to get her pictures. (can not)

c. _____ be presents for her family. (They will)

d. Ms. Snap said, "_____ forget to say 'Cheese!' " (Do not)

e. "We _____," answered Tom and Tina. (will not)

f. Then the teacher announced, "_____ go." (Let us)

g. "_____ line up by the library," she explained. (You will)

h. "_____ going to be first in line," said Tina. (We are)

i. "It _____ take long," said Ms. Snap. (should not)

j. "I bet _____ be back in a flash!" joked Tom. (we will)

---

**Bonus Box:** Choose three contractions from above. On the back of this sheet, use the contractions in different sentences.

# Spelling Practice That Sticks!

If your students tend to forget spelling words after tests, this unit is for you! The following ideas present skill-boosting practice with letter patterns and high-frequency words—just what students need to make spelling skills stick!

*ideas contributed by Starin Lewis, Phoenix, AZ*

## Letter-Perfect Changes
*Short-vowel patterns*

Letter patterns can make forming words a snap! Place a blank transparency on an overhead projector and set a supply of magnetic letters nearby. Draw three lines on the transparency for letter spaces, and have each youngster do the same on a sheet of paper. Announce a consonant-vowel-consonant word. As you guide students to identify the letter that goes in each blank, set the corresponding magnetic letter in place on the transparency. Direct each youngster to write the word.

Next, announce a different three-letter word that has the same rime and have each student draw three more letter blanks. Lead students in the provided chant to review the previously spelled word and prepare to spell the new word. Ask a volunteer to remove and add the appropriate magnetic letters to spell the new word, and instruct each youngster to write it. Repeat the process with several more words; then have students identify the letter pattern.

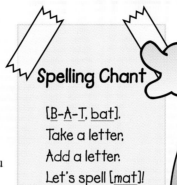

### Spelling Chant

[B-A-T, bat].
Take a letter,
Add a letter.
Let's spell [mat]!

## Sunny Spelling
*Short-vowel patterns*

Brighten spelling practice by helping students recognize the word-making possibilities of rimes! With students' input, list on the board several three-letter words that have a familiar short-vowel rime. Point out that knowing how to spell one word with the rime can help students spell other words with the same letter pattern. Erase the board. Then list three rimes and five onsets for each one (see the suggestions).

To practice using the rimes, each student glues five ¾" x 4" yellow strips onto a five-inch yellow semicircle to resemble a sun. She labels the semicircle with a rime and each strip with a different onset. Next, she cuts a cloud from a 6" x 9" piece of white paper. She glues it onto the lower part of the sun. Then she uses the onsets and rime to write five words on the cloud. Display students' completed work on a blue-backed bulletin board to create a sunny reminder of letter patterns!

-an

can ran fan
man pan

| Rimes | Onsets |
|-------|--------|
| *-an* | c, f, m, p, r |
| *-ot* | c, d, h, n, p |
| *-ug* | b, h, m, r, t |

## Blend Friends
### Blend patterns

Have students join together to spell with blends! Draw a two-column chart on the board. List the words *lay, lip, pan* in the first column and *clay, flip, plan* in the second column. Ask students to identify the spelling pattern. Lead them to conclude that each word in the first column begins with one consonant, and each word in the second column begins with two consonants—a blend.

Next, give each youngster a sheet of paper and set out letter cards. Announce a chosen *l*-blend word. Ask volunteer cardholders to spell the word for their classmates. Signal the blend by having the corresponding cardholders link arms or stand together in a similar way. Have the seated students help the cardholders make any needed spelling corrections; then lead them in a round of applause for the volunteers. After the volunteers are seated, have each youngster write the word. Continue with different volunteers and a desired number of words. To line up more spelling fun, plan to repeat the activity with other groups of blend words.

pam crane

## Boning Up on Silent *E*!
### Long-vowel patterns

This silent-*e* activity develops top-dog spellers! Pair students and then have each twosome cut out a copy of the cards and doghouse on page 126. Instruct the partners to divide the cards between them. Name each picture, in turn, and write the word on the board. If a student has this card, he writes the word on the back for later reference.

To begin, the partners set the doghouse between them. They scramble their cards and stack them on the doghouse, picture side up. Partner 1 takes a card and names the picture. Partner 2 spells the word aloud. If he is correct, Partner 1 sets the card beside the doghouse. If he is not correct, Partner 1 reveals the correct spelling and places the card at the bottom of the stack. The partners alternate turns until they spell all of the words correctly.

ai
rain
pail
snail
chain

## Pattern Search
### Long-a patterns

Long-*a* patterns are the topic of this ongoing investigation. Post a three-column chart. Label a column for each of the following: *ai, ay, a-consonant-e*. Remind students that words with these letter patterns have the long-*a* sound; then list student-generated examples. Next, have each student staple three quarter sheets of white paper between two 4½" x 6" pieces of construction paper to make a booklet as shown. Instruct her to title it "Long-*a* Patterns" and label a page for each pattern. Encourage students to be on the lookout for words with these patterns. When a student sees one, she writes it on the corresponding page in her booklet. Periodically add newly found words to the chart. The result will be grade A spelling references!

| Double-Consonant Patterns | Single-Consonant Patterns |
|---|---|
| digging | eating |
| hopping | looking |
| running | raining |
| sitting | reading |

running

## It Takes Two!
*Double-consonant patterns*

With this sorting activity, students see double—double consonants, that is! Prepare a card for each listed word; then scramble the cards and stack them facedown. Draw a two-column chart on the board. Label one column "1" and the other column "2."

Show students a pair of novelty eyeglasses and suggest that they help the wearer see the double-consonant pattern. Invite a volunteer to don the eyeglasses and take a card. Have the youngster read the word aloud, announce whether it has single or double consonants, and then tape it in the correct column. Continue with different volunteers until all of the cards are displayed. Then help students identify the pattern: if a word ends with a single vowel and consonant, the consonant is doubled before adding *-ing*. To check understanding, place verb cards (without *-ing*), the eyeglasses, and paper at a center. Have students sort the cards and then write the corresponding *-ing* words. They're sure to see the pattern clearly!

## Guess and Check
*High-frequency irregular words*

Here's an approach to spelling irregular words that's perfect for small groups! For each student, cut the top layer of a manila folder into three equal-size columns and label them as shown. Have each student slide a sheet of paper into her folder. Instruct her to lift the second flap, trace the sides of the section revealed, and then close the flap. Explain that some words are "sticky" because they don't follow letter patterns. Provide examples such as *been* and *friend*.

To practice spelling irregular words, each youngster writes a dictated word under her first flap. Under the second flap, she writes the word as you spell it aloud. She rewrites the word under the third flap, then lifts the second flap to check her spelling. After writing a desired number of words, each youngster removes her paper and presents it for teacher approval.

Tara Smith—Gr. 1, Orange Beach Elementary, Orange Beach, AL

| High-Frequency Irregular Words | |
|---|---|
| again | are |
| been | come |
| friend | does |
| know | said |
| very | they |
| was | were |

## Partner Practice
*High-frequency irregular words*

When it comes to spelling irregular words, practice makes perfect! Pair students. Give each student in a twosome a sheet of paper and a different list of irregular words (see the suggestions). Partner 1 announces a word and Partner 2 writes it on his paper. If the spelling is correct, Partner 1 draws a smiley face beside the word on his list. If it is not, he spells the word aloud and Partner 2 writes it on his paper. Next, the partners switch roles. They continue as time allows and then trade the lists to use for take-home spelling practice.

125

# Cards and Doghouse

Use with "Boning Up on Silent *E*!" on page 124.

Long-Vowel Words

# Wild About R-Controlled Vowels

Unlock students' awareness of vowel patterns with these "zoo-rific" ideas!

*ideas contributed by Starin Lewis, Phoenix, AZ*

## "Grrreat" Word Sort
### Skill: sorting

Investigate *r*-controlled vowel patterns with a little help from the animal kingdom! For every two students, label a blank card with a different word from the chart shown (not including the headings) so that there is at least one card for each vowel pattern. To begin, write the word *tiger* on the board. Read it aloud, emphasizing the *r*-controlled vowel sound. Point out that the letter *r* changes the sound of the *e*. Next, suggest that other animal words can help students remember different vowel patterns. Draw a five-column chart on the board and label the columns as shown. Then pair students and distribute the cards. Ask each pair, in turn, to use its word in a sentence and then tape it below the correct heading.

| ti**ger** | sh**ark** | b**ir**d | st**or**k | t**ur**tle |
|-----------|-----------|----------|-----------|------------|
| after | art | dirt | corn | curl |
| her | far | first | short | hurt |
| herd | star | girl | torn | turn |

## Word Hunt
### Skills: identifying and categorizing

Students track down vowel patterns with this booklet project. Give each student a booklet that has construction paper covers and five white pages stapled inside. Ask her to label one page for each of the following: *ar, er, ir, or, ur.* On the front cover, have her illustrate a type of animal whose name includes a featured vowel pattern. Invite her to add desired details, such as a zoo sign or narrow strips of paper that resemble cage bars. Next, set out several animal-related books. Over a few days, allow time for each student to look in the books for words with the featured vowel patterns. When she finds one, she writes it in her booklet. The result will be a "paws-itively" handy word reference!

## Missing Letters
### Skill: spelling

This missing-letter activity leads to improved spelling. Give each student a sheet of paper and a blank card labeled with one of the following vowel patterns: *ar, er, ir, or,* or *ur.* (Be sure that there is at least one card for each vowel pattern.) Have each youngster divide his paper into five sections, labeling each section with a different vowel pattern. On the board, write a word that has an *r*-controlled vowel, substituting a blank for the vowel and *r.* At your signal, each student who has letters that will correctly complete the word holds up his card. Scan the cards and then confirm the correct answer(s). Ask each student to write the word(s) in the correct section on his paper. Continue the activity with a desired number of additional words.

128 Name _____

# At the Zoo

Cut. Read.
Glue each word onto the correct house.

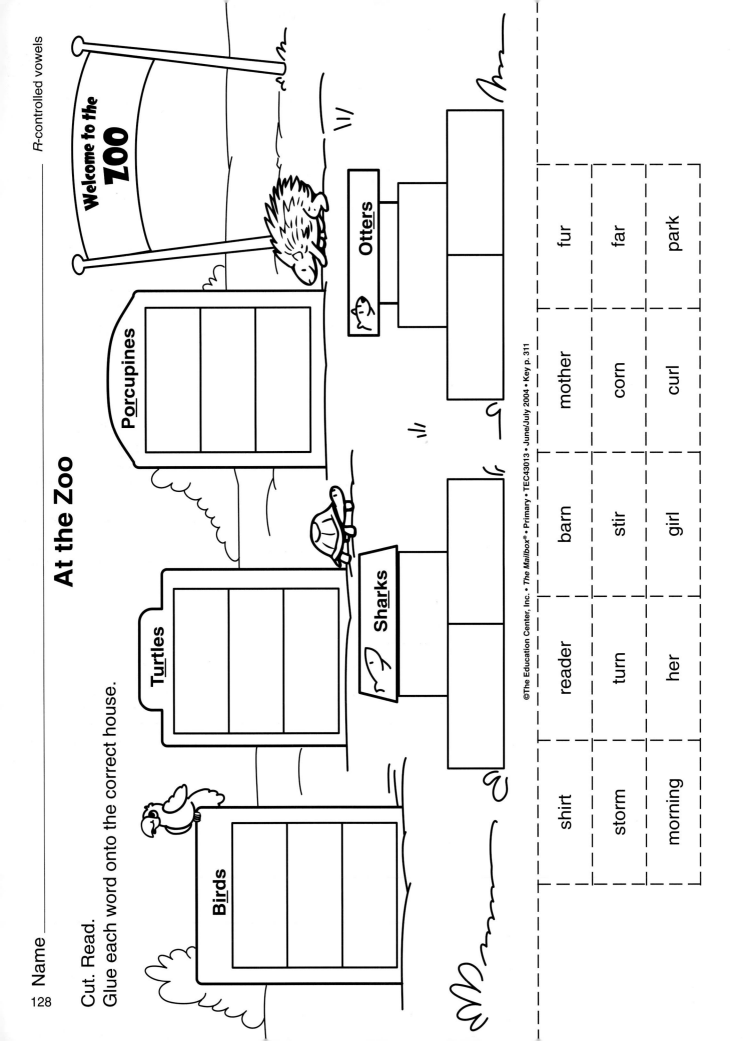

Welcome to the ZOO

Porcupines

Turtles

Birds

Sharks

Otters

| fur | mother | barn | reader | shirt |
| far | corn | stir | turn | storm |
| park | curl | girl | her | morning |

# Follow the Signs

Write **ar**, **ir**, or **or** to complete each zoo sign.

1. No P___king

2. B___dhouses

3. See the newb___n bear cubs!

4. Trail st___ts here.

5. M___e Animals

6. Postc___ds sold here.

7. T-sh___ts for sale!

8. Zoo St___e

9. Do not touch the b___s of the cage.

10. Rain F___est

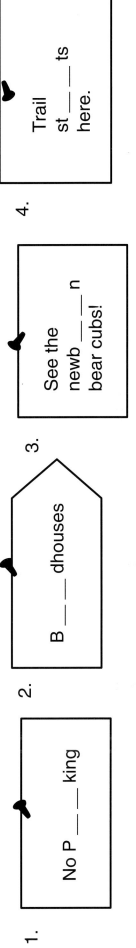
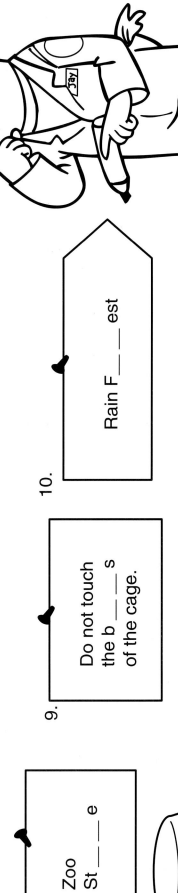
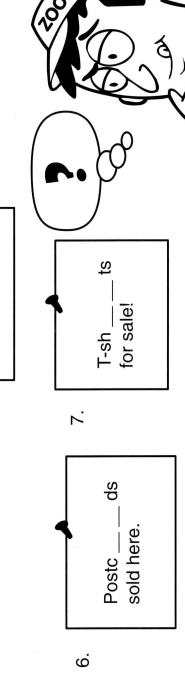

**Bonus Box:** Look at these words: *cord, dart, shirt.* Change the vowel in each word to make a new word. Write the new words on the back of this sheet.

# It's a Word Workout!

Encourage students to flex their word-building
muscles with these kid-pleasing activities!

*ideas contributed by Starin Lewis, Phoenix, AZ*

## Ready Letters

Before launching into the word-building exercises
on this page, use this idea to outfit your students with
individual sets of letters. Give each youngster a copy of
page 132, a 6" x 9" piece of construction paper, scissors,
crayons, glue, and access to a stapler. The student
vertically positions the construction paper and folds up
the bottom approximately four inches. He staples the
sides and folds down the top to make a pocket for letter
storage. He signs and colors the label; then he cuts out
the label and letters. He glues his label onto his pocket
and places his letters inside.

Tanner's
Word Workout
Letters

## Nouns

| | |
|---|---|
| ant | nest |
| drop | plan |
| flag | plant |
| frog | trap |

WORD
POWER

## Word Warm-Up
### Reviewing letter-sound correspondence

Use this plural-forming activity to warm up students'
letter-sound skills. Have each student spread out her letters
from "Ready Letters" on this page. Announce a noun from the
provided list and the corresponding number of letters. After
each student forms the word, ask a volunteer to announce
the correct spelling. Write the word on the board. Encourage
students to check their work and make any needed corrections.
Then announce each sound in the word, in turn, pausing to
have each youngster slide her corresponding letter forward.
Next, instruct each youngster to add a letter to change her
word to its plural form. Confirm the correct spelling; then
continue in the same manner with several other listed nouns.

## Word Stretchers
### Reviewing letter-sound correspondence

Stretch students' word-building skills, letter by letter! Have each youngster spread out
his letters on a work surface (see "Ready Letters" on this page). Announce the first word
in a listed word group and ask students to form the word. Write it on the board; have each
student check his work. Then announce the next word in the group. After each student adds
a letter to form the word, write it on the board below the first word. Explore the third word
in the same manner. Congratulate students on forming increasingly longer words and then
present additional word-stretching challenges as time allows.

## Word Groups

all, wall, walls
an, tan, stand
at, fat, flat
in, pin, spin
it, bit, bite

-ake

cake
bake
take
shake
lake
make

## Rime Stations
### Using rimes to form words

Students will be on the move with this word-family activity! In each of four classroom areas, post a different rime. Divide students into four groups and give each group a sheet of paper. Have each group stand by a different rime. Then ask the students to brainstorm a list of words with their rime. At the end of the allotted time, direct each group to another rime and have the youngsters brainstorm a corresponding list. Continue in this manner until each group has written four lists. Then, with students' help, compile their words into one list for each rime, omitting any duplicate words. To keep students' vocabularies in tip-top shape, display the lists for ongoing reference.

## Flip a Letter!
### Forming short *a* words

This simple project has lots of word-forming possibilities! Give each student six two-inch construction paper squares, a 2" x 6" construction paper strip in a different color, a marker, and access to a stapler. Use the directions shown to help her make a minibooklet. Demonstrate how the pages can be flipped up, pointing out that some of the letter combinations form words. Then challenge her to see how many different words she can form.

### Directions for one minibooklet:
1. Label a square for each of the following: *fl, r, tr.*
2. Position the strip horizontally. Stack the squares on the left end and staple them at the top to make pages.
3. Label a square for each of the following: *n, p, sh.*
4. Stack the squares on the right end of the strip and staple them at the top.
5. Write *th* under the left-hand pages. Write *t* under the right-hand pages.
6. Write *a* in the center of the strip.

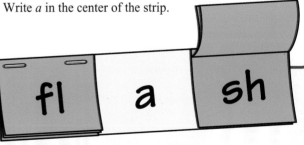

fl   a   sh

| | |
|---|---|
| rip | trip |
| pin | pan |
| top | stop |
| tall | ball |
| pin | spin |

WORD POWER

## Word Transformations
### Adding or changing letters to form new words

What a difference one letter makes! Pair students. Give each twosome two sheets of paper and a supply of letter manipulatives. Post a desired list of consonant-vowel-consonant words. To begin, each partner divides his paper into two columns. Partner 1 uses the letters to form a chosen listed word. Each partner writes the word in his first column. Then Partner 2 adds or changes one letter to make a new word. He reads it aloud and each partner writes it in his second column. The activity continues as time allows, with the partners taking turns forming the words for the first column and being careful not to repeat words in the second column. Now that's a letter-perfect approach to exploring words!

Kelly Rienks—Grs. 2–3 Looping
De Beque Elementary School, De Beque, CO

## Letters and Label
Use with "Ready Letters" on page 130.

| | | | | |
|---|---|---|---|---|
| a | e | i | o | u |
| b | c | d | f | g |
| l | l | n | p | p |
| r | s | s | t | w |

_____'s

**Word Workout
Letters**

# Building Word Family Skills

Set a solid foundation for reading and writing with these easy-to-adapt word family ideas. For added fun, begin by reading aloud your favorite version of *The Three Little Pigs*!

## Words With Character

*Forming words with onsets and rimes*

A twist on familiar storybook lines makes forming words a class act! Label a blank card "Wolf" and each of three blank cards "Little Pig." Use a hole puncher and a length of string to make each card into a necklace. Program a large blank card with a chosen rime and set out several letter cards to be used as onsets. Give each youngster a sheet of paper. To assign roles, have each of four volunteers wear a necklace and stand at the front of the room. Ask two pig actors to hold the rime card in clear view. Give the third pig actor a letter card that can be used to form a word with the rime. Have her stand apart from the other actors.

Next, the actors say the provided lines. As the wolf dramatically blows air toward the cards, the pigs move together so that the cards form a word. Lead the remaining students in reading and spelling the word aloud. After each seated youngster jots it down, repeat the process with different onsets and student actors.

**Characters' Lines**
**Wolf:** Little pigs, little pigs, make a word.
**Pigs:** Not by the hairs on our chinny chin chins.
**Wolf:** Then I'll huff and puff and blow the letters together!

## Speaking of Word Families

*Sorting by word families*

These three little pigs don't have houses made with different supplies. Instead, they have words made with different rimes! To prepare this small-group activity, make a set of word cards for three chosen word families. Shuffle the cards and stack them facedown near the board. Embellish three construction paper circles to make simple pig faces similar to the ones shown. Tape the pigs to the board to establish column headers.

To begin, tell students that the pigs like different word families. Draw a speech bubble for each pig and write a different rime in each one. Invite each youngster, in turn, to take a card, read it aloud, and use a loop of tape to display it below the appropriate pig. Continue until all of the cards are sorted in this manner; then lead students in reading each group of words. Now that's a "swine" plan for increasing reading vocabularies!

133

## Recipe for Words
*Identifying real and nonsense words*

Students cook up a happily-ever-after ending at this partner center when they identify real and nonsense words. Place in a large cooking pot a wooden spoon, a set of consonant cards, and one card that you have labeled "Wolf!" Program each of several sentence strip lengths with a different rime. On the back of each one, write the real words that may be formed with the consonants and rime. Set the prepared pot and rimes at a center stocked with paper and pencils.

Each student takes a rime. To take a turn, he stirs the cards and then removes one of them. If he removes a consonant card, he uses the letter and his rime to write a word on his paper. He reads the word and announces whether it is a real or nonsense word. If it is a real word, he draws a pig face beside it before returning the card. If a student removes the "Wolf!" card, he takes an extra turn. The activity continues until one student has three pig faces. After each student reads his real words to his partner, he flips his rime to check them.

**Step 1**

## "Write" at Home
*Writing consonant-vowel-consonant words*

This homemade booklet idea gives students practice writing short-vowel words! Use the provided directions to help each youngster make a booklet. Then have her write an assigned rime at the top of her first booklet section. Announce a word that has this rime and have her write it. Confirm the correct spelling; then explain that students can use this word to help them write other words in the same word family. Dictate additional words for students to write in the first section of their booklets. After checking students' work, invite each youngster to move her pig beside each word as she reads her list to herself. To store her booklet, direct her to refold it with the pig tucked inside. Plan to use a similar process with different word families to complete the remaining sections.

---

**Booklet directions:**
1. Accordion-fold a 6" x 18" strip of white construction paper into four sections as shown.
2. Cut away the top corners of the folded strip to make a roof.
3. Keeping the strip folded, illustrate the cover to resemble a favorite little pig's house.
4. Decorate a two-inch pink construction paper circle to resemble a pig.
5. Tape an 18-inch length of yarn to the back of the pig. Unfold the strip. Tape the free yarn end to the last section.

Name _____

# Three Little Houses

Cut. Read.
Glue each word on the correct house.

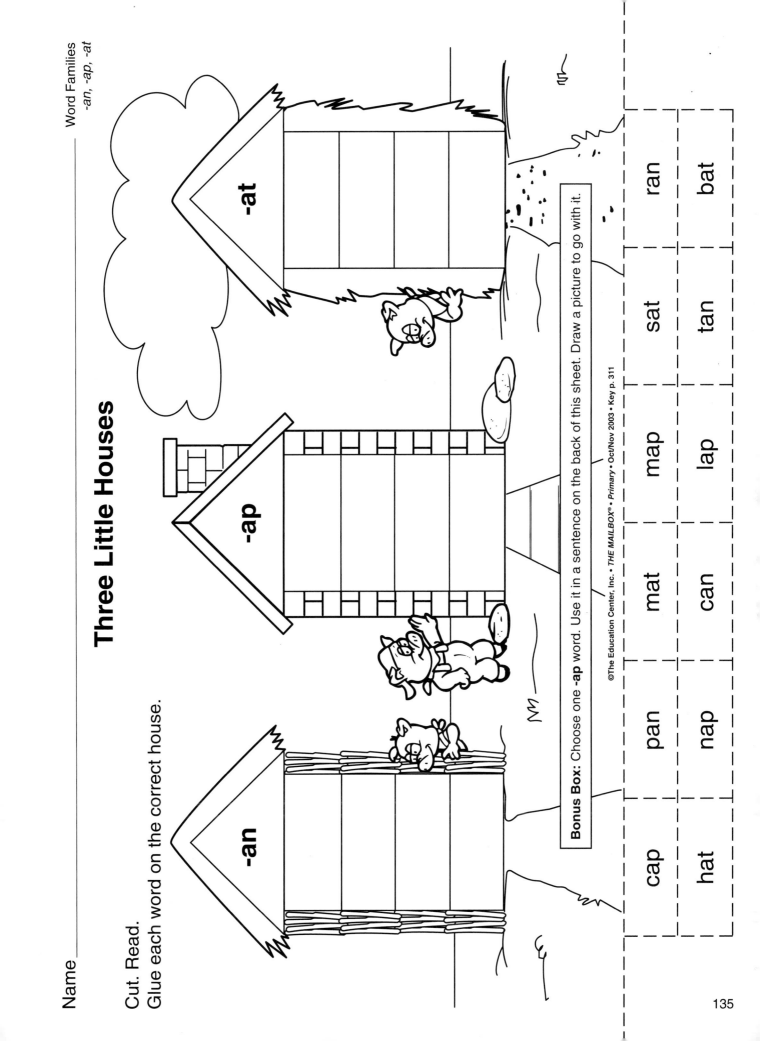

**-at**

**-ap**

**-an**

**Bonus Box:** Choose one **-ap** word. Use it in a sentence on the back of this sheet. Draw a picture to go with it.

©The Education Center, Inc. • THE MAILBOX® • Primary • Oct/Nov 2003 • Key p. 311

| ran | sat | map | mat | pan | cap |
|-----|-----|-----|-----|-----|-----|
| bat | tan | lap | can | nap | hat |

135

# All Aboard for Story Writing!

Use these specially engineered ideas to help students move ahead with story writing!

*ideas contributed by Peggy Morin Bruno—Language Arts Consultant*
*Squadron Line School, Simsbury, CT*

### Begin With Books
*Identifying story elements*

Favorite storybooks are just the ticket to prepare students to write stories! Set out several familiar picture books that have plots with clearly established problems and solutions. Good choices include *Strega Nona* by Tomie de Paola and *Swimmy* by Leo Lionni. On the board, draw and label a story-element web similar to the one shown. Write the title of a chosen book in the blank circle. Encourage students to listen for the story elements as you read the book aloud. At the book's conclusion, have them identify each element and relevant details; incorporate the information into the web.

For additional reinforcement, set aside time for each youngster to study a displayed book and use an individual version of the web to identify the story elements. When students write their own stories, they'll have plenty of great models!

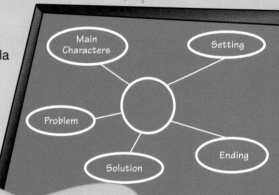

### Stories With a Twist
*Collaborating on a story innovation*

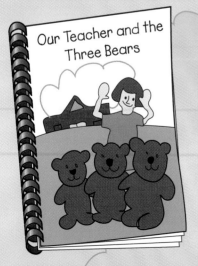

If your budding authors aren't quite ready to write stories on their own, why not help them make an old story new again? Share a familiar folktale such as *Goldilocks and the Three Bears* or *Jack and the Beanstalk*. Then wonder aloud what the story would be like if it had a different character or setting, or if there were a different turn of events. Ask students to brainstorm ideas for creating a new version of the tale; select one idea by student vote. Then, with students' help, write and illustrate the story on large sheets of paper and bind it into a class book. Or write the story on an overhead transparency, use a word-processing program to type it, and then make student copies. Now that's a surefire strategy for story-writing success!

## Tell About It!
*Developing a plot*

Warm up students' plot-development skills with picture-perfect storytelling. Pair students and give each twosome four sheets of drawing paper. To plan their story, the partners label a sheet of paper for each of the following: beginning, middle, and end. Then they determine a story idea and discuss possible events for each part of the story. On each labeled sheet, they illustrate their ideas and add a caption. Finally, they write a title on the remaining sheet of paper and sign their names.

After each twosome completes its work, invite the partners to tell their story to the class, using their posters as props. Then collect their posters and clip them together. On a classroom wall, periodically showcase a different set of sequenced posters below the title "The Story Station."

A Trip to the Castle

by Dajuan & Alicia

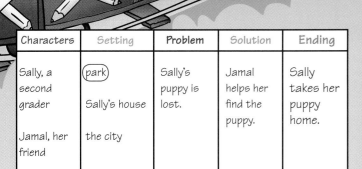

| Characters | Setting | Problem | Solution | Ending |
|---|---|---|---|---|
| Sally, a second grader<br><br>Jamal, her friend | (park)<br><br>Sally's house<br><br>the city | Sally's puppy is lost. | Jamal helps her find the puppy. | Sally takes her puppy home. |

## Time to Plan!
*Using a graphic organizer*

Help students get their writing on track with first-class story plans! Post a five-column chart that you have labeled with the headings shown. To plan a class story, list two or three characters in the first column. Then complete the chart with student-generated details. Narrow down the suggestions in chosen columns, as needed, by circling students' top choices. With students' help, use the identified elements to write a brief story on an overhead transparency. Later, read the story aloud and remind students that the plan provided the framework. Then have each youngster plan an original story on a copy of the graphic organizer on page 140 and refer to it as she writes and illustrates her tale.

## Three-Part Story
*Writing a well-organized story*

With this booklet project, each student develops a plot from the beginning to the end. First, each youngster uses a desired prewriting strategy to identify a story idea. Next, he cuts a 9" x 12" sheet of paper in half to 4½" x 12". He folds each resulting strip in half and then unfolds it. He places the two strips end to end and tapes them together. He writes a title in the first section and illustrates it as desired. He writes "Beginning," "Middle," and "End" to label the next three sections in order. He writes each part of his story in the corresponding section. Then he accordion-folds his strip (see the illustration).

To decorate his booklet covers, he signs a copy of the engine pattern on page 139 and illustrates himself as the conductor. He colors the engine and caboose patterns and cuts them out. Then he glues his engine to the front of his booklet and his caboose to the back of it.

# Route to Success

*Using the writing process*

These suggestions are perfect for getting students on board with the writing process!

- To familiarize students with the writing process, post a list of the various stages. Periodically ask youngsters who are at different parts in the process to tell the class about their progress.

- Make revisions inviting for students by having them use sticky notes to add details to their work instead of writing another draft.

- Have students edit for only a few details at first. As students sharpen their skills, increase their editing responsibilities.

- After a student puts the finishing touches on his writing, ask him to tell the class how he got the idea for his story; then encourage him to read his story aloud.

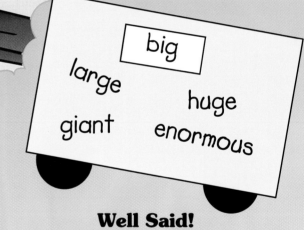

# It's in the Details!

*Revising for details*

Students bring characters to life with this revision strategy. After a student drafts a story, she folds a blank sheet of paper in half and then unfolds it. She lists each story detail about a chosen character on one half of the paper and illustrates the character on the other half. Next, she studies the illustration and adds to her list any new details that come to mind. Then she reads her story to a classmate and invites her to ask questions about the character. She jots down any new details prompted by the questions. She circles the details she'd like to add to her story and uses carets to insert them in her writing. A more interesting story will be the result!

# Well Said!

*Revising for word choice*

With well-chosen words, it's full speed ahead to vivid stories! Explain to students that one way to improve a story is to use a variety of specific words. To promote use of this strategy, divide students into small groups. Give each group a 9" x 12" sheet of light-colored paper and a paper strip bearing a commonly overused word such as *big, pretty, said,* or *walk.* Have the youngsters glue their word near the top of their horizontally positioned paper and brainstorm a list of more specific alternatives. Then ask them to glue on construction paper wheels to make a boxcar.

Next, have each group read its words aloud. Guide students to name any other suitable words and have the team members add them to their boxcar. Arrange an engine cutout and students' boxcars on a classroom wall to resemble a train. Encourage students to check out the resulting word reference whenever it's time to polish their writing.

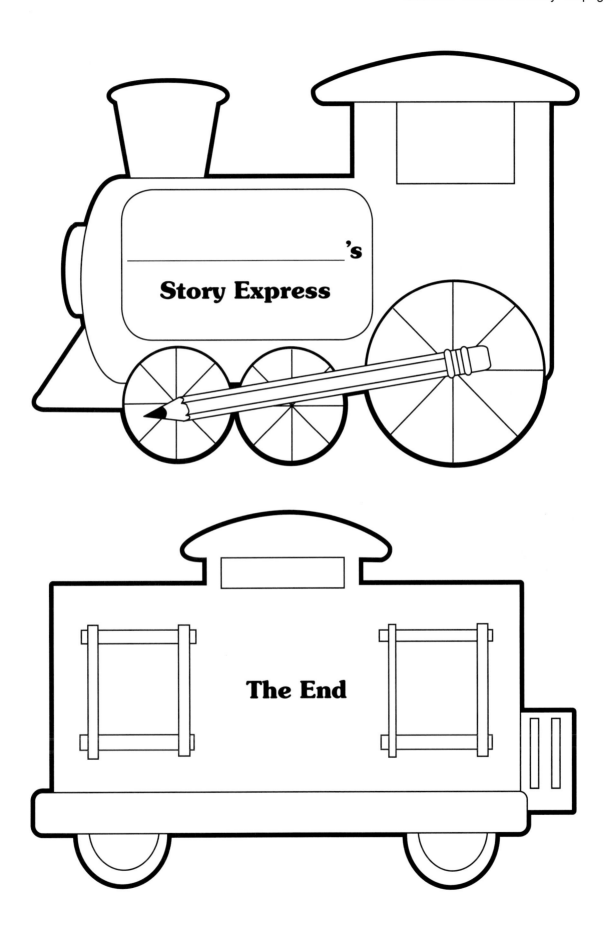

_____'s

**Story Express**

**The End**

Name _____

# First-Class Story Plan

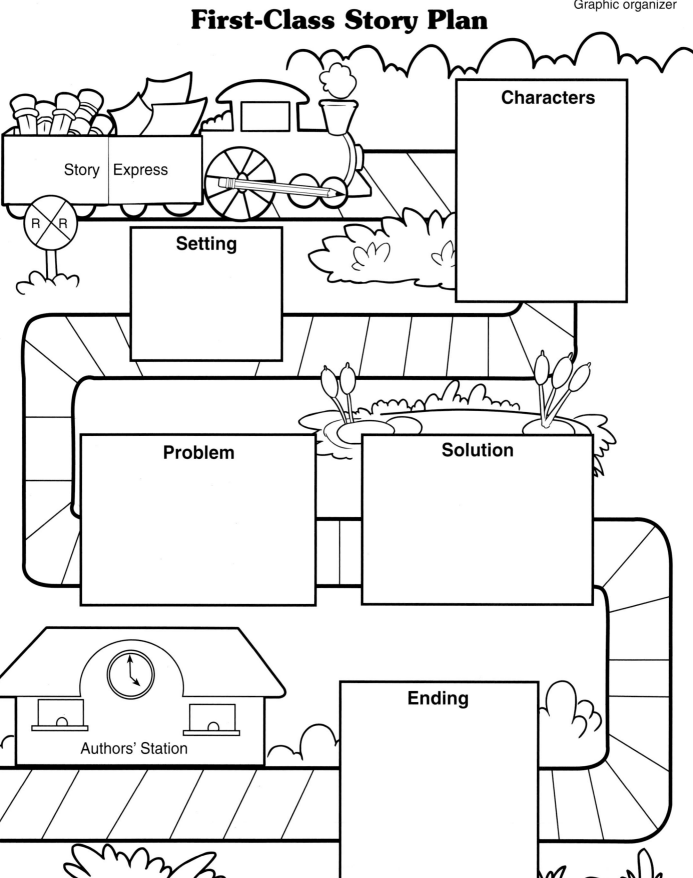

Story Express

Characters

Setting

Problem

Solution

Authors' Station

Ending

**Note to the teacher:** Use with "Time to Plan!" on page 137.

# Blueprint for Editing Success

This handy unit is just the "write" tool to build editing skills! Use the activities below to provide capitalization and punctuation practice. Then choose from the remaining ideas to guide your students' editing efforts!

## Sentence Repairs

**Punctuation** know-how helps youngsters repair these sentences. For half of your students, write a variety of telling, asking, and exclamatory sentences on sentence strips. Cut off the ending punctuation. Then randomly distribute the sentences and punctuation. (Plan to participate if you have an odd number of students.)

Next, challenge each student to find a classmate who has a sentence strip piece that can be used with his piece. When he finds one, the two youngsters tape their assembled sentence to the board and write their initials by it. After each sentence has been repaired in this way, invite each pair to read its sentence aloud and explain how the partners determined the correct punctuation.

Cindy Kovach—Gr. 1, St. Marys Elementary, St. Marys, GA

## Punctuation Warm-Up

Put **punctuation** practice in motion! Establish a signal for each ending punctuation mark. For example, represent a period with clasped hands, an exclamation mark with raised arms, and a question mark with one hand curved over your head. To begin, have each student stand. Display a sentence without ending punctuation and read it aloud. On your count, ask each youngster to signal the appropriate punctuation. Confirm the correct response. Then continue with additional sentences for a fast-paced skills check.

Lauren Fiamingo—Gr. 3, St. Angela School, Mattapan, MA

## Capital Clues

This idea helps students develop an eye for correct **capitalization!** Display on an overhead transparency a passage that reflects various uses of capitalization and give each student a copy of it. Announce, "I spy with my editor's eye a capital [letter] for [chosen word]." Have a volunteer find the word on the transparency and use a wipe-off marker to circle it. (She circles only one instance of the word.) Ask each student to circle the word on her paper; then invite one youngster to tell why it is capitalized. Explore a desired number of other capital letters in a similar manner.

# Sentences Under Construction

Self-editing can be challenging for youngsters new to the task. So why not have your students start out editing work that's not their own? Use the **practice sheet** on page 143 to help them feel right at home with editing.

## The Sentence Train

With this cargo of **editing reminders,** it's full speed ahead to good work! Post on a classroom wall a train similar to the one shown. Suggest to students that it can help them check their writing. Then present this analogy:

- The train starts with an engine. A sentence starts with a capital letter.
- The train cars need space between them. Words need spaces between them.
- The caboose signals the end of the train. Ending punctuation signals the end of the sentence.

If your students are ready for other editing responsibilities, label the boxcars with additional details. All aboard!

Sara Kvern—Gr. 1, Hilltop Elementary, Inver Grove Heights, MN

## Clever Reminder

This simple **checklist** prompts young authors to give their work a careful second look. To introduce the checklist, familiarize students with the acronym CUPS (complete sentences, uppercase letters, punctuation, spelling). Display a poster similar to the one shown and place a supply of CUPS checklists in your writing area. When a student finishes a writing assignment, she completes a checklist and staples it to her paper. You'll know at a glance whether she edited her work!

Erin Reppert—Gr. 3, Brecknock Elementary School, Shillington, PA

Name _____
Date _____
I checked my work for
☐ **c**omplete sentences
☐ **u**ppercase letters
☐ **p**unctuation
☐ **s**pelling

C U P S

## Writer's Toolbox

Set the foundation for first-rate editing with these easy-to-adapt **writing folders.** To prepare one, a youngster colors the labels on a copy of page 144 and then cuts them out. He signs the folder label and glues it to the front of a manila file folder. He glues each page label onto a separate sheet of writing paper. He stacks the papers atop any other desired references, such as a high-frequency word list. Then he staples the stack at the top to secure it in his folder.

On the appropriate pages, he begins ongoing lists of words that he often misspells, capitalization reminders, and punctuation rules. When it's time to write, he'll have plenty of editing help!

Michele Fernandez, Cahoon Elementary School, Tampa, FL

# Under Construction

Read the sentences.
Mark each letter that should be capitalized.
Add the missing punctuation.
Use the checklist to help you.

1. where does Mr. Beaver live

2. Mr. Beaver and his wife, Betty, live in lakeville

3. they live with their kids, Ben and bob.

4. Mr Beaver is building a new house on river Road.

5. Are Ben and bob happy about moving

6. ben helps Mr. Beaver every saturday.

7. He bought the wood from Mrs. forest in april.

8. Mr. Beaver wants to move in july

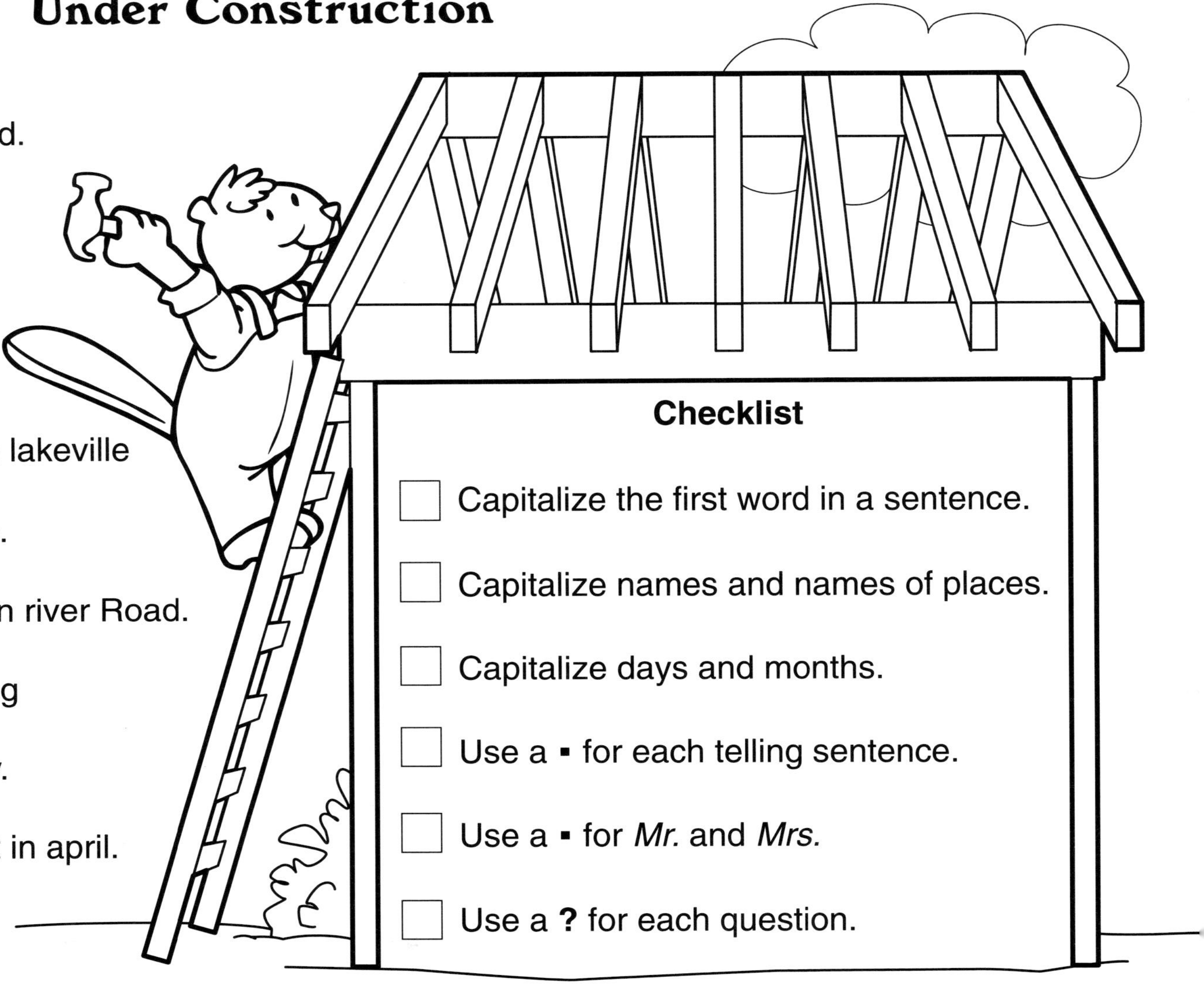

## Checklist

☐ Capitalize the first word in a sentence.

☐ Capitalize names and names of places.

☐ Capitalize days and months.

☐ Use a ▪ for each telling sentence.

☐ Use a ▪ for *Mr.* and *Mrs.*

☐ Use a ? for each question.

©The Education Center, Inc. • *The Mailbox*® • Primary • TEC43012 • April/May 2004 • Key p. 311

**Note to the teacher:** Use with "Sentences Under Construction" on page 142. If students are familiar with standard editing symbols, have them use the symbols to indicate the needed corrections. If they are not, ask them to write each needed punctuation mark as they normally would and circle each letter that needs to be capitalized.

# Folder and Page Labels

Use with "Writer's Toolbox" on page 142.

## Writer's Toolbox

Name _____

Spelling Helper    s a i d

Using Capital Letters    A M L T

Using Punctuation    . ? ! ,

# HOMOPHONES BY THE PAIR

Take a bite out of these "a-peel-ing" homophone ideas!

*ideas contributed by Starin Lewis, Phoenix, AZ*

## Hear, Here!
### Skills: recognizing and using homophones

When it comes to identifying pairs of homophones, this activity is sure to help students make clear connections! For each child, program a paper strip with a word that is a homophone for one other student's word. (If you have an odd number of students, prepare a strip for yourself and plan to participate.) Give each youngster a small foam cup. Have him turn the cup upside down and use a pencil to poke a hole in the part that is now the top. Instruct him to label the upside-down cup with his assigned word. Then ask him to find the classmate who has the corresponding homophone and sit with him.

Next, give each twosome a three-foot length of yarn and access to tape. Each partner threads one end of the yarn length through the hole in his cup and then tapes it in place to make a play phone. Each partner, in turn, speaks to his partner through his cup, using his homophone in a sentence. Allow time for each twosome to have several homophone-related exchanges; then tack the student-made phones onto a bulletin board titled "Calling All Homophones!"

### Homophones

| | |
|---|---|
| blew—blue | meat—meet |
| brake—break | one—won |
| cent—scent | right—write |
| close—clothes | sail—sale |
| fir—fur | sea—see |
| flour—flower | some—sum |
| for—four | son—sun |
| grate—great | stair—stare |
| heard—herd | tail—tale |
| knight—night | threw—through |
| made—maid | wait—weight |
| mail—male | wear—where |

I blew out the candles.

Use these word pairs throughout this unit!

## Pairs of Pears
### Skill: defining homophones

Homophone definitions take root with this idea! Give each student a large sheet of drawing paper and a yellow construction paper copy of page 147. The youngster chooses a word from the word bank and writes it in the box on one pear. She labels another pear with the corresponding homophone. Then, referring to a grade-appropriate dictionary as needed, she writes a definition of each homophone in her own words. She uses another set of homophones to prepare the two remaining pears in a similar manner. To display her work, the student cuts out the pears and illustrates a large, leafy tree. She glues the cutouts onto the tree in pairs. What a "tree-mendous" way to cultivate students' vocabularies!

# Undercover Sentences
### Skill: using homophones

Take the "write" approach to homophones! Assign each student a pair of homophones. To feature the word pair in a minibooklet, the youngster cuts a sheet of paper in half (to 5½" x 8½"). He staples the two halves to another sheet of paper as shown. He labels each resulting flap with a different homophone and uses crayons to add decorative borders. Under each flap, he uses the corresponding homophone in a sentence and then underlines it. He illustrates his work and signs his booklet.

After helping students edit their work, set the booklets in a designated location for interested students to enjoy. When a student reads a booklet, encourage him to silently recall the meaning of each featured homophone before lifting the flaps to read the sentences.

# Memorable Spelling Strategies
### Skill: developing spelling strategies

If your students need help remembering which homophone is which, why not leave them to their own mnemonic devices? Pair students and assign each twosome a different pair of homophones. Challenge the youngsters to determine a way to help them distinguish the spelling of the two words, sharing examples, such as the ones shown, for inspiration. Have each twosome use provided arts-and-crafts materials to make a poster that conveys its strategy. Invite partners to share their posters with the class; then display the eye-catching reminders for student reference.

# To Be or Not to Bee?
### Skill: spelling homophones

This creative twist on spelling bees will have students abuzz with enthusiasm for homophones! Divide students into small groups and confirm that each group has markers and paper. For scorekeeping purposes, assign each group a number. On the board, draw one bee without stripes per group and label it with the appropriate number.

To play one round, announce a selected homophone. Use the word in a sentence that conveys its meaning. Invite the students in each group to quietly confer with each other about the word's spelling. Ask them to keep their paper from view as they write the word in large letters. At your signal, have each group display its word. If a group spelled the word correctly, draw a stripe on its bee. Continue play for a desired number of rounds. The group that earns the most stripes wins.

146

# Word Bank

| sea | eight | sale | hear | hour |
|-----|-------|------|------|------|
| meet | right | son | whole | won |

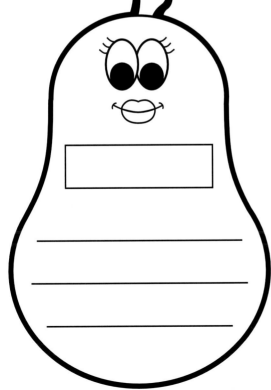

**Note to the teacher:** Use with "Pairs of Pears" on page 145.

# Spice It Up With Adjectives!

Help students add flavor to their writing with these enticing adjective ideas!

## What a Sight!
### *Identifying and using adjectives*

This introductory activity brings adjectives onto the scene! In the center of a large sheet of paper, mount a colorful image of a scene from a discarded calendar or magazine. Display the poster and ask students to tell what they see. Around the image, use a black marker to write the nouns that students name. Next, suggest that additional details would be helpful in describing the scene. Read aloud each noun, in turn, and have students name words that describe it. Use a colored marker to list each word near its corresponding noun. Point out that the words written in color are adjectives. Then, with students' input, incorporate the adjectives into a description of the scene. It's true—a picture is worth a thousand words!

Naomi Pridemore—Gr. 1
L. B. Johnson School, El Paso, TX

## Writing Resource
### *Identifying adjectives*

A few well-chosen adjectives can add just the right touch to writing. And these student-made booklets provide plenty of choices! To make a booklet, each student places three half sheets of paper between two 6" x 9" pieces of construction paper and staples the stack along a short side. She titles one page for each of the following: people, places, things. She writes "Awesome Adjectives" on the front cover and signs her name.

After each youngster assembles her booklet, remind students that adjectives describe nouns. If desired, read aloud *Hairy, Scary, Ordinary: What Is an Adjective?* by Brian P. Cleary for additional reinforcement. Encourage students to be on the lookout for adjectives whenever they read. When a student finds one she may want to use later, she writes it on an appropriate page in her booklet. How handy!

## What's in a Word?
### *Exploring word choice*

Here's a poetic strategy to help students realize how adjectives influence meaning! Choose a favorite poem that has several adjectives (or ask your school's media specialist for a grade-appropriate selection). Write the poem on a sheet of chart paper and then read it with students. Next, have students use sticky notes to cover the adjectives. Ask them to brainstorm adjectives to replace the covered words and write their suggestions on the sticky notes. Then lead students in reading the revised poem. Wow! Adjectives really do make a difference!

Sandy Scarborough—Gr. 2, Brennen Elementary School, Columbia, SC

## Letter-Perfect Challenge
*Brainstorming adjectives*

With this adjective game, expanding students' vocabularies is as easy as A, B, C! On each of several blank cards, write a different frequently used consonant. Divide students into equal-size teams, and provide each team with a marker and sheet of chart paper. Explain that the object of the game is to list the greatest number of adjectives that begin with a designated letter.

To begin a round, write a chosen noun on the board. Select a card at random and announce the letter. At this signal, each team begins listing adjectives for the noun. After a predetermined amount of time, ask each team to read its list aloud. Award one point for each appropriate adjective and a bonus point if no other team wrote it. Invite the highest-scoring team to name a noun for the next round and select another letter card. Continue play as time allows.

## Special Ingredients
*Revising to provide more descriptive detail*

If your students' writing is missing vivid details, have them shake it up! Label a large, unbreakable lidded jar as shown. Inside the jar, place strips that you have programmed with adjectives. Set the jar at a writing center. When it's time for a student to revise her writing, she shakes the jar and then removes several strips. She uses the words to prompt her thinking as she fine-tunes her writing. Then she returns the strips to the jar. Invite youngsters to add their favorite adjectives to the jar to keep the supply freshly stocked!

Kelly Chapman—Gr. 1
Concord Elementary School
Anderson, SC

## Clothes-R-Us
*Writing a brief description*

Dress up students' descriptive-writing skills! Display two or three articles of clothing. Ask students to imagine that they write clothing descriptions for a catalog company. Then guide students to brainstorm a list of adjectives for a selected article of clothing. Model how to use the adjectives to write a brief description. Next, give each youngster a sheet of story paper. The youngster illustrates either a displayed article of clothing or one that he is wearing. Then he writes a brief description of it. Bind students' completed work into a class catalog to "sell-ebrate" their use of adjectives!

adapted from an idea by Karoleigh K. Allison
Remedial Reading
Russell Elementary, Hurtsboro, AL

149

# Camp Capers
## Reading and Writing Fun

Your students are sure to be happy campers when you gear up for summer with these literacy ideas!

ideas contributed by Stacie Stone Davis
Lima, NY

Laws' Lodge

### Setting Up Camp

Set the stage for learning fun by establishing a mock campsite in your classroom. Pitch a small tent or drape a blanket over a table. Nearby set out a few flashlights and a backpack or carryall that you have stocked with summer-related books. Plan for students to use the tent for independent reading. In an open area of the classroom, arrange stones, cardboard tubes, and construction paper flames to resemble a campfire. Invite students to bring in sleeping bags, and encourage them to wear camping attire such as visors, sunglasses, and bandannas.

After setting up camp, sit with students around the campfire. As a group, decide on a camp-themed name for your classroom, such as [teacher's name]'s Lodge. Plan for one or more volunteers to make a pennant to display the name. Then guide students to write a camp song or chant. Or dim the lights and lead students in retelling favorite stories that they read earlier in the year, asking each youngster to hold a flashlight when it's his turn to speak.

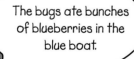

The bugs ate bunches of blueberries in the blue boat.

A ants
animals
art

B boats
blueberries
bugs
backpack
bunk bed

C compass
cabin
campfire

### A Is for Ants, Art, and Animals!
#### Writing a list

This list-making idea results in a pack of kid-pleasing word activities. To begin, invite students to tell about any camping experiences they have had. Guide the discussion to build on students' background knowledge. Then assign each student a letter of the alphabet, omitting less frequently used letters and repeating letters as appropriate. Challenge him to list things that he might see or do while camping, explaining that the words need to begin with his assigned letter. Allow time for each student to list several words.

Next, compile students' words by letter on a length of bulletin board paper. Frame the completed list with construction paper logs to give it a rustic look. During the next few days, use the words for activities such as a phonics version of the I-Spy game, syllabication practice, or writing silly alliterative sentences. What letter-perfect possibilities!

150

## Brochure Questions

1. How many cabins does Camp Learn-a-Lot have?
2. Does the camp have tennis lessons?
3. Can a five-year-old stay at the camp?
4. What should each camper bring for her cabin?

# Read All About It!
### Reading for information

A reproducible brochure is just the ticket for informing would-be campers! Have each student sign a copy of page 152. Ask her to cut out the brochure on the bold lines and then fold it on the thin lines as shown. Next, display several relevant numbered questions (see the examples). Each student looks for the answers in her brochure. When she finds one, she labels the information with the corresponding question number. After each student completes her work, ask volunteers to announce the answers and where they found them. Then have each youngster color her brochure and write on the back of it what she likes most about the camp.

# Some More S'mores, Please!
### Following written directions

A camp experience doesn't seem complete without making s'mores, so why not pair the tempting tradition with skill reinforcement? To prepare, hide the needed ingredients and supplies in various school locations, with the help of other staff members as needed. (See the recipe on this page.) Write multistep directions to each hiding place on a separate blank card. Divide students into groups so that there is one group for each card. Instruct the group members to read the directions and follow them step-by-step. After each group returns with its find, display the recipe and arrange for each youngster to prepare his snack. For practice with sequencing directions, have each student complete a copy of page 153.

### Simple S'Mores
**Materials for one snack:** whole graham cracker, spoonful of marshmallow creme, miniature chocolate bar, plastic knife, small paper plate

**Directions:**
1. Break the graham cracker in half. Spread the marshmallow creme on one half.
2. Set the candy bar on the creme.
3. Place the second graham cracker half on top.

# Camp Correspondence
### Writing a friendly letter

Letter-writing know-how can come in handy for young campers! Read aloud *Arthur Goes to Camp* by Marc Brown to share how Arthur puts his letter-writing skills to use. Then review the format of a friendly letter. Next, have each student write a letter from Arthur's perspective to his parents. Instruct her to fold her completed letter into thirds and then initial it. Collect students' letters in a paper sack labeled "Special Delivery." Redistribute the letters so that no student receives her own. After a youngster reads the letter she receives, she assumes the role of one of Arthur's parents and writes a response. She delivers her completed correspondence to the appropriate classmate. Mail call!

151

# Camp Brochure
Use with "Read All About It!" on page 151.

## Lots to Do!
The camp has lessons for
- swimming
- hiking
- horseback riding
- sailing
- craft projects
- cooking on a campfire

## Mark Your Calendar!
The camp starts in the second week of July. It ends on August 30.

## Directions
Camp Learn-a-Lot is ten miles east of Sunny Town. From Snowville, drive south.

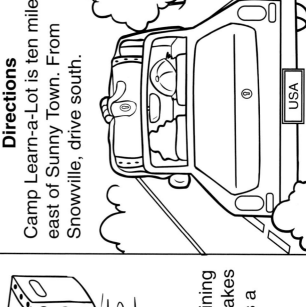

## Where, Oh Where?
Camp Learn-a-Lot is on Loon Lake. It is just minutes from Mile-High Mountain.

## Campers' Cabins
The camp has six log cabins with bunk beds. Twelve campers can sleep in each cabin. Each camper should bring a pillow and sheets.

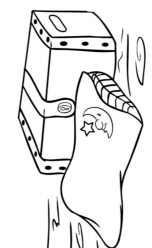

## Chow Time!
All meals are served in the dining hall. Our peanut butter pancakes are the best! Fish surprise is a favorite any time of day.

## Come to Camp Learn-a-Lot!

At Camp Learn-a-Lot, the learning is fun and the fun never ends. It's the best summer camp for children ages 6–10!

Name _____

©The Education Center, Inc. • *The Mailbox®* • Primary • TEC43013 • June/July 2004

# Lead the Way!

Help the campers find their way!
Study the map. Read.
Number each set of directions in the correct order.

A.  Roxie is in the cabin. She wants to go swimming.

_____ Next, turn onto Lake Lane.

_____ First, leave Hilltop Cabin.

_____ Finally, walk up the lane to the lake.

_____ Then walk on Raccoon Road to Lake Lane.

B.  After Roxie swims, she wants to eat lunch in the dining hall.

_____ Walk past Tiny Trail.

_____ Walk on Pines Way to the dining hall.

_____ Turn onto Pines Way.

_____ Walk from the lake to Raccoon Road.

C.  Rita is in the dining hall. She wants to tie-dye a shirt at the craft center.

_____ Walk on Pines Way to Raccoon Road.

_____ Walk down Tiny Trail to the craft center.

_____ Turn onto Tiny Trail.

_____ Walk on Raccoon Road to Tiny Trail.

D.  When Rita is done at the craft center, it is time for bed.

_____ Stop at the end of Raccoon Road.

_____ Turn left onto Raccoon Road.

_____ Walk from the craft center on Tiny Trail.

_____ Walk past Pines Way.

**Bonus Box:** Rita is in the cabin. She wants a sandwich. On another sheet of paper, write directions from the cabin to the dining hall.

# Pondering Reports

With this creative collection of ideas, students will be eager to leap into report writing. Whether youngsters research pond life or you modify the activities for a different topic, strong report-writing skills are sure to surface!

*ideas contributed by Laura Wagner, Raleigh, NC*

**Pond Words**
frogs
cattails
pollution
turtles
dragonflies
ducks
fish
lily pad

## Words to Ponder
*Generating appropriate report topics*
What's one strategy for writing "toad-ally" terrific reports? Narrowing down a topic! This brainstorming activity helps students do just that. Have students generate a list of pond-related words. Supplement students' suggestions as needed. Next, give each student a copy of page 156. Using the list for inspiration, the youngster writes a different pond-related topic on the first line of each lily pad. Below each topic he writes one or more relevant questions. Then he considers all of his questions and chooses the topic that he would most like to research. He writes his topic on the log and presents his paper for teacher approval. Now that's getting a report off to a great start!

## Look for the Signals!
*Using features of nonfiction text*
Invite students to leap into research with this "ribbiting" look at nonfiction text. In advance, gather nonfiction materials about pond life or another desired topic. Instruct each student to cut a lily pad shape from each of four two-inch construction paper squares. Have her glue each lily pad onto one end of a narrow construction paper strip. Ask her to initial the resulting bookmark. After each student prepares her bookmarks, explain that a lily pad resting on a pond's surface signals where the rest of the plant is underwater. Suggest that in a similar way, features of nonfiction text point out where certain information is. Provide examples such as a table of contents, an index, and boldfaced words.

Next, divide students into small groups and distribute the previously collected resources. Have the students look through the materials for features that are helpful in finding information. When a student finds one, she marks the page with a bookmark. After each group marks several pages, invite the group members to report their findings to the class. Then encourage students to use a similar strategy to uncover information about their research topics.

# Sticking to the Topic
*Organizing relevant information*

Here's a kid-pleasing strategy for organizing notes. Each student folds a 9" x 12" sheet of white paper in half (to 6" x 9") and then in half again (to 4½" x 6"). After he unfolds it, he draws a lily pad in the center of his paper and labels it with his topic. He lightly colors the lily pad and uses a blue crayon to trace the fold lines as shown. He titles each section with a question that will guide his research about the topic. As he researches his topic, he writes relevant facts in each section. If he finds useful information that relates to his topic but not to his questions, he writes it on the back of his paper. With this approach to note-taking, it will be snap to develop a multiparagraph report!

Where do frogs live?

How do frogs grow?

Frogs

What do frogs eat?

What kinds of frogs are there?

# Pooling Facts
*Planning a report*

Help students get their facts in order with this simple suggestion. As students find information about their topics, instruct them to take notes on writing paper, skipping lines between facts. When a student's research is complete, she cuts her facts apart and groups related facts on provided paper. Then she arranges the facts in each group in a logical order. After she is satisfied with the groupings and each sequence, she tapes the facts in place. If desired, help her label each group of facts and suggest that she use the labels as report headings. What a nifty way to piece together a writing plan!

# Pond Presentations
*Reporting on a topic*

Culminate students' research efforts with presentations that are sure to make a splash! To prepare, each student staples half sheets of writing paper (one for each of his report's subtopics) inside a 6" x 9" blue construction paper folder. With the fold at the top, he draws a large pond shape on the front cover, being careful to enclose the staples. He cuts along the tracing through all the thicknesses. He writes information about a different subtopic on each page in his resulting booklet. He titles and signs the cover; then he uses provided arts-and-crafts materials to embellish it as desired. When it's time to present his report to the class, he'll have his information at his fingertips.

My Pond Report

Freddy

# Pondering Report Topics

My topic: _____

**Note to the teacher:** Use with "Words to Ponder" on page 154.

# LITERATURE UNITS

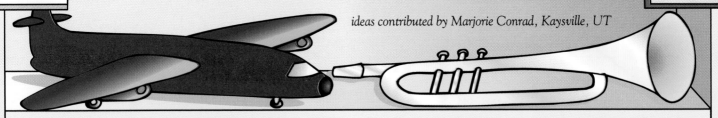

# Corduroy

### Written and illustrated by Don Freeman

*Day after day, Corduroy waits with the other department-store toys, eager for someone to take him home. When the overalls-clad teddy bear realizes that a missing button might jeopardize his chances of being purchased, he sets off in search of it. Happily, he discovers that a new friend likes him just the way he is—missing button and all!*

*ideas contributed by Marjorie Conrad, Kaysville, UT*

## At the Store
### Skill: building on background knowledge

Poor Corduroy! Will a shopper ever choose him? Prompt students to think about a similar shopping situation with this story introduction. Designate a classroom area as a toy department. Arrange in a row several stuffed animals, including one that is worn or has a missing part. Set a small container in front of each toy and place a class supply of pennies nearby.

To begin, direct students' attention to the display. Ask them to imagine that they are shoppers in a toy department. Give each student a penny to "spend," pointing out that stuffed animals actually cost more. Have each youngster indicate which toy he would buy by dropping his penny into the corresponding container. Count the pennies, and then lead a class discussion about your youngsters' choices. Next, explain that you will read a story that takes place in a department store. Display the first page that shows Corduroy. Invite students to tell what they notice about the bear and predict what will happen. Then read the story to check the predictions. Students are sure to develop a new perspective on shopping!

## "Beary" Important Feelings
### Skill: inferring a character's feelings

From waiting at the store to happily gaining a friend, Corduroy has many different experiences. At the book's conclusion, use this inference activity to explore Corduroy's reactions to various events. Give each student a large button and a copy of the feelings strip (page 160). Confirm that students are familiar with the words on the strip. Then retell the story, stopping at key points to have each youngster conclude how Corduroy feels. Ask her to place her button in the corresponding box on her strip, explaining that there may be more than one correct answer. Invite students to share their responses and explain their reasoning. Now that's a "pawsitively" simple way to enhance understanding!

happy    sad    scared    surprised

# The Bear Facts
### Skill: identifying the beginning, middle, and end
Students review the plot from cover to cover with these minibooklets! Each student uses a five-inch circle template to prepare three white and two brown paper circles. He sandwiches the white circles between the brown circles, staples the stack at the top, and then numbers the pages. He illustrates and labels the first page with the beginning of the story, the second page with the middle, and the third page with the end. He illustrates a bear face on the front cover and glues two construction paper ears in place. He uses his resulting bear friend to tell his family about *Corduroy!*

# Watching for Friends
### Skill: exploring a story theme
Shed light on the story's theme of friendship! Sit with students in a circle on the floor. Show them a flashlight and explain that it reminds you of the night watchman in *Corduroy.* Prompt students to recall how the watchman and Lisa befriend Corduroy. Next, dim the lights and turn on the flashlight. Summarize a real-life or hypothetical example of friendship; then pass the flashlight to the student seated next to you. Ask this youngster to identify a different example of friendship. Continue around the circle until every student has taken a turn. Encourage students to "stay on duty" and watch for friendly behavior throughout the year!

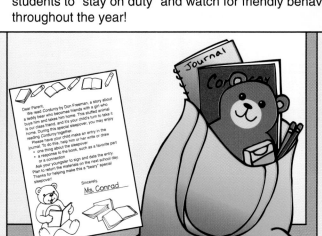

# Overnight Journal
### Skill: making a journal entry
A stuffed animal is a perfect prop for helping students relate to the story. Obtain a small stuffed animal and have students name it. Establish a rotating schedule for students to take the toy home overnight. To prepare the toy for transport, place it in a carryall along with a parent note (page 160), a copy of *Corduroy,* a journal, and a supply of pencils and crayons. A student makes a journal entry as described in the note. After she returns the toy, she shares her entry with the class. No doubt students will be as eager as Lisa to spend time with a furry friend!

# Connecting With *Corduroy*
### Skill: making text-to-text connections
Once students are familiar with *Corduroy,* it's a sure bet they'll notice similarities with other stories. Display a sheet of chart paper titled "Reminders of *Corduroy.*" As you share additional books with students, keep a running list of the connections they make. For example, when the bear in *Somebody and the Three Blairs* by Marilyn Tolhurst mistakes a faucet for a stream, it may remind students of when Corduroy mistakes an escalator for a mountain. Or students may recognize similarities between the plots in *A Pocket for Corduroy* and *Corduroy.* With each connection, students will become more thoughtful readers!

# Parent Note and Feelings Strip

Use the note with "Overnight Journal" on page 159.

Use the feelings strip with "'Beary' Important Feelings" on page 158.

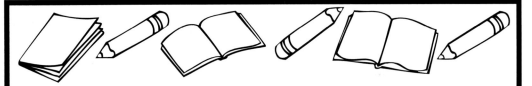

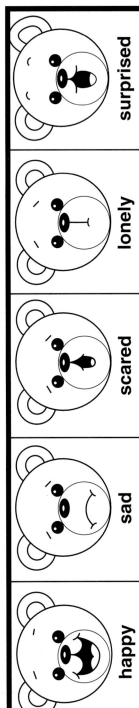

Dear Parent,

We read *Corduroy* by Don Freeman, a story about a teddy bear who becomes friends with a girl who buys him and takes him home. This stuffed animal is our class friend, and it's your child's turn to take it home. During this special sleepover, you may enjoy reading *Corduroy* together.

Please have your child make an entry in the journal. To do this, help him or her write or draw
- one thing about the sleepover
- a response to the book, such as a favorite part or a connection

Ask your youngster to sign and date the entry. Plan to return the materials on the next school day. Thanks for helping make this a "beary" special sleepover!

Sincerely,

_____

©2003 The Education Center, Inc.

# My Name Is María Isabel

Written by Alma Flor Ada
Illustrated by K. Dyble Thompson

*María Isabel Salazar López is proud of her name! Her new teacher decides to call her Mary Lopez, though, since there are already two Marías in the class. María Isabel gradually adjusts to her new school, but not to the unfamiliar name. In the end, a writing assignment presents a perfect opportunity for the youngster to reclaim her name and cultural heritage.*

*ideas contributed by Tara Kenyon—Reading, MA*

**Read Aloud**

## Cultural Ties

**Skill: building on background knowledge**

Puerto Rico is special to María Isabel. Now she lives on the mainland, but she began school in Puerto Rico and enjoys visiting her relatives who live there. Enhance students' understanding of María Isabel's heritage with this prereading activity. Point out Puerto Rico on a globe or world map. Explain that the main character lived there before moving to the United States. Then write on the board the first word listed on the chart shown. Ask students to speculate how it relates to Puerto Rico. Use the provided information to confirm their ideas or clarify any misconceptions. Repeat the process with the remaining words.

Throughout the book, encourage students to consider the influence of María Isabel's heritage. Periodically invite youngsters to share their observations. Increased comprehension will be the result!

| Word | How It Relates to Puerto Rico |
|---|---|
| island | Puerto Rico is an island about 1,000 miles from Florida. |
| Spanish | Spanish is usually spoken in Puerto Rican schools, but English is also taught. |
| citizens | Puerto Ricans are U.S. citizens. |
| tourists | Many tourists visit Puerto Rico for its pleasant climate and beaches. |

## Journal Connections

**Skill: making connections**

From adjusting to a new school to proudly taking part in a school event, students are sure to relate to many of María Isabel's experiences. Use this ongoing journal idea to explore the connections they make. Post the provided code and confirm that students are familiar with the three types of connections. Next, have each youngster fold three sheets of white paper in half and then staple them inside a 6" x 9" construction paper folder. Ask her to personalize the front cover of the resulting journal as desired.

At the conclusion of each reading session, invite each student to write in her journal about any connections she made. Have her label each connection with the appropriate symbol. Then ask volunteers to explain how their connections helped them understand the story.

**Connection Code**

= text-to-self

= text-to-text

= text-to-world

## Between Friends
**Skill: analyzing a character**

Despite blossoming new friendships, María Isabel still misses her old friends. If she decides to keep in touch by sending letters, what could she write? Pose this question to students after reading chapter 5. To identify what María Isabel might share with her friends, ask students to brainstorm a list of story events and discuss the character's corresponding reactions. Have each youngster refer to the list as he writes a letter to either Virginia or Clara from María's perspective. Invite students to share their completed letters in small groups. What a "send-sational" approach to character analysis!

## Sticky Situations
**Skill: discussing a story's themes**

Reading *Charlotte's Web* prompts María Isabel to relate her problems to a sticky spiderweb. After reading chapter 8, have students create a web of their own with this discussion activity. Obtain a ball of yarn and sit with students in a circle. Announce one of the prompts shown; then give the yarn to a student who wants to respond. When she finishes speaking, instruct her to hold the end of the yarn and gently toss the ball to another student. When that student finishes speaking, he will hold the yarn and toss the ball to a third student, and so on. Continue forming the web until every student has had an opportunity to talk, using additional prompts as needed to keep the discussion going.

Next, suggest that the resulting yarn web represents María Isabel's web of problems. To untangle it, invite each yarn holder to toss the ball of yarn to the previous youngster as students share possible solutions to María Isabel's problems.

### Prompts
- María Isabel faces several problems. Which one do you think is the most important? Why?

- How does María Isabel feel about being called Mary Lopez? Explain how you would feel if someone called you by a different name.

- Chapter 8 is titled "Trapped in a Spider's Web." Do you think this is a good title? Explain.

## Wish Upon a Star
**Skill: responding to literature**

No doubt María Isabel's careful reflection on her wishes will lead students to think about their greatest wishes. At the conclusion of chapter 9, remind youngsters that María Isabel's first two wishes—to make a snowman and to participate in the pageant—are not as meaningful to her as her wish to be called by her real name. Next, have each student list several of his wishes on provided paper. Ask him to mark the most significant wish. Then instruct him to write the wish on one side of a provided star cutout and sign his name. Ask him to illustrate the other side of the star as desired, hole-punch the top of it, and then add a length of string for a hanger. Suspend students' stellar work from the ceiling to create an inspiring display!

My greatest wish is to become an astronaut.

Aaron

# What's in a Name?

María Isabel's full name is important to her.
For each part of her name, write one reason why it is special.
You may use the book to help you.

| María | _____ |
| Isabel | _____ |
| Salazar | _____ |
| López | _____ |

Now think about your full name.
Write it in the box.

Write to complete at least three boxes below.

| How many syllables are in your full name? _____ | How many vowels are in your full name? _____ Consonants? _____ |
|---|---|
| What do you like most about your name? Explain. _____ _____ _____ _____ _____ | Write about a nickname that you have or would like to have. _____ _____ _____ _____ _____ |

## Staging Events

Read the story events. Number them to show the correct order.
For each event, choose the word from the code that best tells how María Isabel feels.
Use the code to color the musical note.

**Color Code**
happy = red
unhappy = blue

_____ A new friend takes María Isabel to the school library.

_____ On her first day of school, María Isabel trips and falls.

_____ Mrs. Salazar gives María Isabel a key to the apartment.

_____ María Isabel's teacher calls her Mary Lopez.

_____ María Isabel sings in the pageant.

_____ The teacher does not give María Isabel a part in the pageant.

_____ The Salazars visit the old neighborhood.

_____ The librarian tells María Isabel to take a book.

**Note to the teacher:** Use at the completion of the book.

# Stories for the Season

**Rake in heaps of learning fun with these picture books and related activities!**

## The Hallo-Wiener
Written and illustrated by Dav Pilkey

*Oscar doesn't look like most dogs. He's half-a-dog tall and one-and-a-half dogs long! The other pooches tease him about his appearance, and they tease him even more when they see his embarrassing Halloween costume. But Oscar rises above it all to become the hero of this hilarious tale.*

### "Bone-a Fide" Comprehension

*Identifying the beginning, middle, and end of a story*

At first the neighborhood dogs tease Oscar, but later they declare him a hero. What prompts them to change Oscar's nickname from Wiener Dog to Hero Sandwich? Students sum up the events with this comprehension-boosting idea! To begin, read the book aloud for students' enjoyment. Invite them to comment on the story; then revisit the book to explore the humor conveyed in the illustrations and text.

To check understanding, guide students to tell what happens at the beginning, in the middle, and at the end of the story. Have each youngster summarize this information with a pooch-themed trick-or-treat bag. To do this, he writes his name and the book title on a brown paper lunch bag. After he adds desired illustrations, he uses a dog bone template (approximately 3" x 8") to make three white construction paper bones. He illustrates a scene from the beginning of the book on one side of a bone and summarizes the corresponding part of the story on the other side. On the two remaining bones, he recaps the middle and end of the story in a similar manner. He numbers the illustrated side of each bone to show the sequence and then places the bones in his bag. He takes his unique doggie bag home and uses it to share the story with his family.

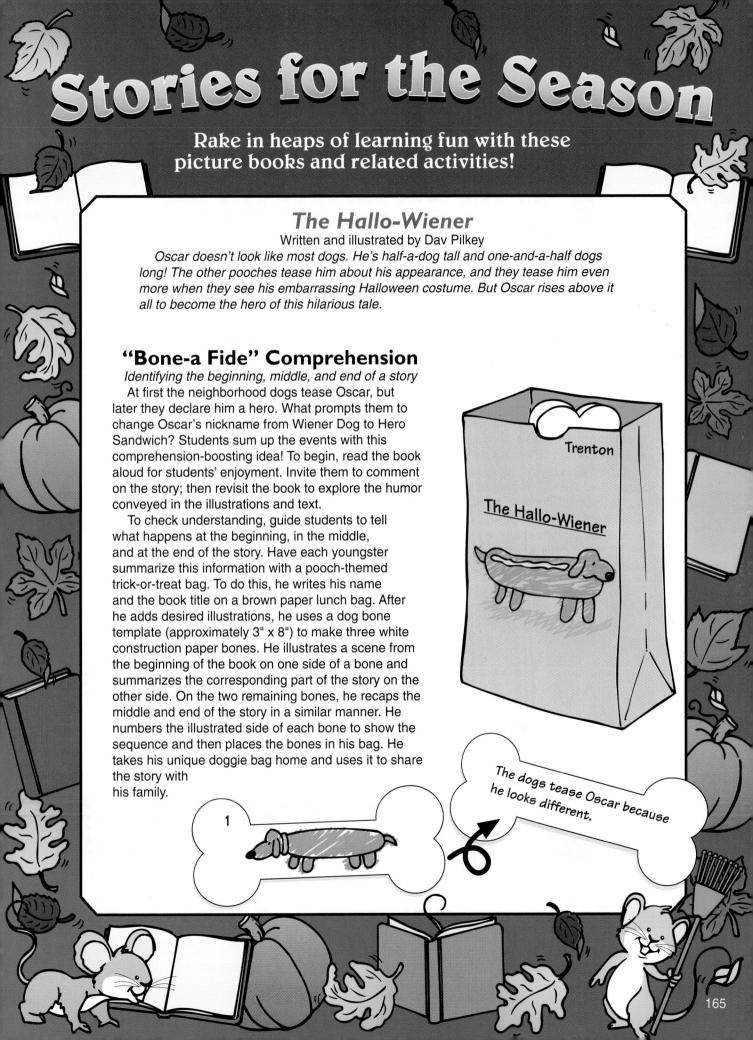

Trenton

The Hallo-Wiener

1

The dogs tease Oscar because he looks different.

165

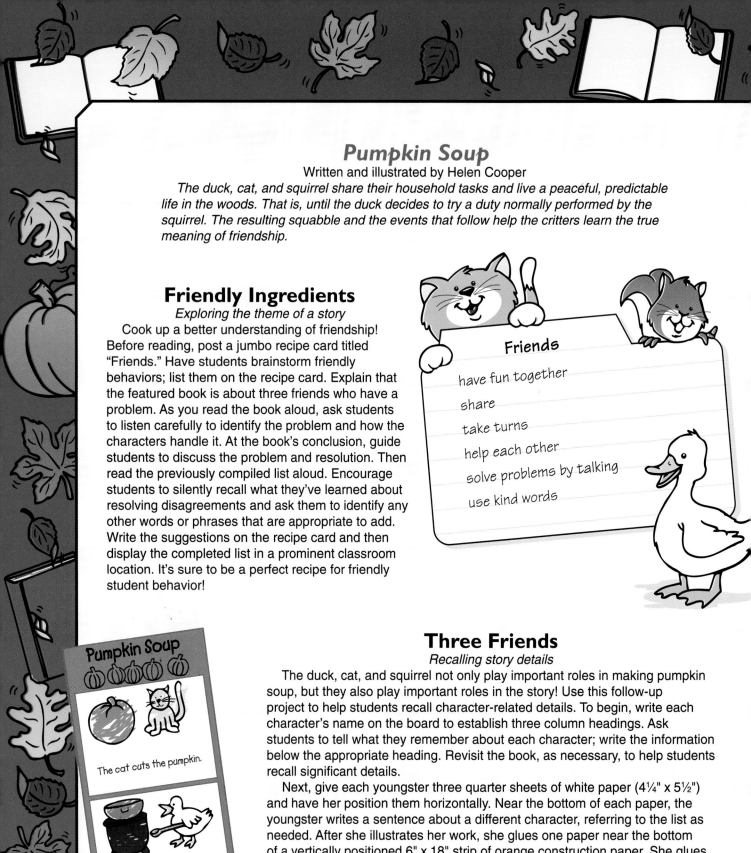

## Pumpkin Soup

Written and illustrated by Helen Cooper

*The duck, cat, and squirrel share their household tasks and live a peaceful, predictable life in the woods. That is, until the duck decides to try a duty normally performed by the squirrel. The resulting squabble and the events that follow help the critters learn the true meaning of friendship.*

### Friendly Ingredients

*Exploring the theme of a story*

Cook up a better understanding of friendship! Before reading, post a jumbo recipe card titled "Friends." Have students brainstorm friendly behaviors; list them on the recipe card. Explain that the featured book is about three friends who have a problem. As you read the book aloud, ask students to listen carefully to identify the problem and how the characters handle it. At the book's conclusion, guide students to discuss the problem and resolution. Then read the previously compiled list aloud. Encourage students to silently recall what they've learned about resolving disagreements and ask them to identify any other words or phrases that are appropriate to add. Write the suggestions on the recipe card and then display the completed list in a prominent classroom location. It's sure to be a perfect recipe for friendly student behavior!

**Friends**

have fun together

share

take turns

help each other

solve problems by talking

use kind words

**Pumpkin Soup**

The cat cuts the pumpkin.

The duck wants to stir the soup.

The squirrel is sorry that they didn't give the duck a turn.

### Three Friends

*Recalling story details*

The duck, cat, and squirrel not only play important roles in making pumpkin soup, but they also play important roles in the story! Use this follow-up project to help students recall character-related details. To begin, write each character's name on the board to establish three column headings. Ask students to tell what they remember about each character; write the information below the appropriate heading. Revisit the book, as necessary, to help students recall significant details.

Next, give each youngster three quarter sheets of white paper (4¼" x 5½") and have her position them horizontally. Near the bottom of each paper, the youngster writes a sentence about a different character, referring to the list as needed. After she illustrates her work, she glues one paper near the bottom of a vertically positioned 6" x 18" strip of orange construction paper. She glues the other two papers above the first one, leaving space between them. In the remaining space at the top of the strip, she writes the book title and adds any desired decorations. Now that's a story reminder with character!

# I Know an Old Lady Who Swallowed a Pie

Written by Alison Jackson
Illustrated by Judith Byron Schachner

*A Thanksgiving dinner guest has a surprisingly voracious appetite in this silly cumulative story! Rollicking rhyming text coupled with whimsical illustrations make this read-aloud a favorite.*

## Line by Line

*Participating in a read-aloud, exploring rhythm and rhyme*

The lines of this incredible tale beg to be read aloud. And no doubt your students will be eager to chime right in! Invite them to participate with this speaking activity. To prepare, find in the book each sentence that has this pattern: "I know an old lady who swallowed [noun phrase]." For each identified sentence, write the next sentence in the book on a sentence strip. After reading the book aloud, divide students into nine groups (one group per sentence strip). Give each group a prepared sentence strip and a sheet of drawing paper. Confirm that the students in each group can read their strip. Ask them to illustrate their sentence and then practice reading it with rhythm and expression.

To prepare for a second reading, have members from each group hold their sentence and poster as students sit with you in a circle by group. Begin rereading the book, pausing for each group to stand, show its poster, and say its line at the appropriate time. When a group's item is mentioned in the book again, have the poster holder display the illustration. What fun!

"For goodness sake, a ten-layer cake!"

"I kid you not—she swallowed a pot!"

## More Rhymes, Please!

*Identifying rhyming words*

It's a Thanksgiving Day feast—a feast of rhymes, that is! To follow up the featured read-aloud, prepare one pie cutout for every two students. Program each pie with a rhyming word pair as shown so that each word rhymes with exactly one other word. Then cut each pie in half. Scramble the pie halves and then distribute them. Encourage students to listen carefully as you invite a volunteer to read his word aloud. The youngster who has the corresponding rhyme says his word in response. Then the two youngsters sit together and assemble their pie. Continue with additional volunteers until all of the pies are assembled. If appropriate, direct students' attention to chosen pairs of words and point out that rhyming words may have endings with different spellings.

For additional reinforcement, have the students in each twosome write on provided paper one sentence with both of their words. Instruct them to underline the rhymes. Then ask volunteers to read their sentences aloud. Display each twosome's pie and sentence on a bulletin board titled "Oh, My! It's Rhyme Pie!"

pot | not

The old lady should <u>not</u> eat a <u>pot</u>!

# Flat Stanley

Written by Jeff Brown
Illustrated by Steve Björkman

*Life changes dramatically for Stanley Lambchop after a bulletin board falls on him. Suddenly only half an inch thick, he can slide under doors, fit inside an envelope, and even fly like a kite! The Lambchops' matter-of-fact approach to Stanley's extraordinary condition makes this time-honored story a rib-tickling favorite.*

## Unusual Size

**Skills: exploring story details, making predictions**

Flat "as a pancake"! That's how Mr. Lambchop describes Stanley. In chapter 1, Mrs. Lambchop realizes that her son is so flat his clothes need to be altered. To help students size up Stanley's predicament at the end of the chapter, post his measurements: four feet tall, one foot wide, and one-half inch thick. Tack a four-foot length of adding machine tape to a wall to illustrate Stanley's height.

Next, pair students and give each twosome a ruler and a recording sheet similar to the one shown. Challenge the youngsters to find classroom items with dimensions of about one-half inch. Have each twosome measure chosen classroom items, record the measurements, and compare them to Stanley's thickness. As the students work, encourage them to use the posted reference to compare their heights with Stanley's. After every twosome completes its work, invite predictions about the problems that Stanley will now face. Then have students continue reading to check their ideas.

| Item | Measurement | Comparison |
|------|-------------|------------|
| crayon | 3" long | Stanley is thinner. |
| math workbook | ½" thick | This is the same as Stanley! |

| Adjective | Story Detail |
|-----------|-------------|
| helpful | helps his mother get her ring |
| smart | is third from the top in his class |
| polite | asks, "How do you do?" |
| brave | helps catch the sneak thieves |

## Super Skinny!

**Skills: understanding a book's theme, analyzing a character**

In chapter 5, Stanley goes from being a local celebrity to becoming a subject of ridicule. At the book's conclusion, ask students to silently recall any experiences they've had with teasing. Then prompt a class discussion about Stanley's reaction to being called names. Suggest that even though Stanley's appearance becomes unique after the bulletin board incident, his personality remains the same. On a two-column chart similar to the one shown, record student-generated adjectives that describe Stanley's nonphysical characteristics and the supporting story details. Students are sure to agree that whether a person is flat or round, it's what's on the inside that counts!

# Invisible Stanley

### Written by Jeff Brown
### Illustrated by Steve Björkman

*Stanley feels out of sorts one night, but he doesn't realize why until the next morning. That's when his family points out that he's invisible! In this hilarious installment of Jeff Brown's popular series, Stanley faces new opportunities and challenges as a result of his amazing transformation.*

## A Peculiar Case
### Skill: exploring the story's problem

Dr. Dan doesn't know what to make of Stanley's predicament. After all, the boy is his first invisible patient! But the puzzled physician encourages the Lambchops to look on the bright side. Have your students consider both sides of the unusual case with this follow-up to chapter 2. To begin, ask students to brainstorm advantages and disadvantages of Stanley's unusual situation.

Next, each youngster imagines that she is invisible. She illustrates a face on one side of a 9" x 12" construction paper balloon cutout to imitate the Lambchops' strategy for keeping track of Stanley. On a 3" x 5" card, she starts a paragraph by writing "If I were invisible." She continues by explaining at least one potential benefit and one challenge of being invisible, and then she glues the card onto the back of the balloon. Next, she tapes a length of curling ribbon to the bottom of the balloon and uses a hole puncher and length of string to make a hanger at the top. Suspend students' balloons from the ceiling to create a colorful reminder that there's more than one way to view a situation!

> If I were invisible, people might step on me. I could get squished! A good thing about being invisible is that I could spy on my sister. That would be cool!

## Thanks, Stanley!
### Skill: writing a thank-you letter

Invisibility has benefits—not just for Stanley, but also for some of the people he meets. At the conclusion of chapter 6, point out that over the course of the book Stanley helps several characters. Have students identify them *(Billy, the young couple, Arthur, the police).* Suggest that if all of the characters knew about Stanley's role in their successes, they'd undoubtedly agree that he deserves thanks.

After reviewing the parts of a friendly letter, ask each youngster to write a thank-you letter to Stanley from a chosen character's point of view. Instruct him to use provided arts-and-crafts materials to make a keepsake of the corresponding event for Stanley. For example, if Billy wrote a letter, he might enclose a picture of himself riding his bike. Or a police officer might enclose an honorary badge for Stanley. Display each student's letter with his memento on a bulletin board titled "Thanks, Stanley!"

From Billy

# More Fun With Stanley!

After your students read one or more books about Stanley Lambchop, follow up with the activities below. Learning fun is guaranteed!

## A Usual Family?
### Skill: comparing and contrasting

Mr. Lambchop considers his family to be usual—mostly, that is! Use this thought-provoking idea to compare the storybook family to other households. To begin, each student draws a Venn diagram. She labels one circle "The Lambchops" and one circle "My Family." She writes details about the families in the appropriate sections.

Next, she folds two sheets of white paper in half and staples them inside a 6" x 9" construction paper folder. With the fold at the top, she titles the resulting booklet "Family Album." She adds the names of the two families and desired illustrations. She lists all of the members of each family on the first page. Then, for each family, she illustrates a snapshot and summarizes the appropriate Venn diagram information on two facing pages as shown. She compares and contrasts the two families on a remaining page. While each family is unique, the households are bound to have a lot in common!

Stanley at the park with Arthur

There are two boys in the Lambchop family, Arthur and Stanley. Stanley is only one-half inch thick. Sometimes Arthur is jealous of Stanley. The mom and dad are very polite.

Giant Stanley

by Emily B.

New

Amazing!
Stanley is like most kids. But one strange day he grows and grows. He becomes a giant! Read this book to find out what happens.

Check out all of the books in this funny series!

Bartlett Book Company          $4.95

## Another Adventure
### Skill: generating ideas for sequels

Now that your youngsters are familiar with Stanley and his tendency to get into unusual situations, invite them to imagine that they're in the author's shoes. What adventures might lie ahead for Stanley? Explain that students will share story ideas by designing book covers.

To prepare, post a two-column chart. Label one column "Front" and one column "Back." Have students study the covers of several books and identify important cover elements. Write the information on the chart. Next, instruct each student to use provided arts-and-crafts supplies to make a book cover that includes selected elements. After students share their projects with the class, display their work on a table. With all the great story ideas, don't be surprised if students are inspired to pen their own creative tales!

## In the News
### Skill: summarizing significant story events

Help students get the scoop on Stanley's extra-ordinary adventures! Display a student-generated list of significant story events. Choose one event and help students identify the key details: who, what, when, where, why, and how. Then ask each of your cub reporters to complete a copy of page 171. Now that's newsworthy summarizing practice!

*ideas for this unit contributed by Julie Douglas, St. Louis, MO*

*Flat Stanley* and *Invisible Stanley*
Summarizing important story events

# The Inside Scoop

Stanley's adventures are making headlines!
To prepare a newspaper article, choose a story event.
Write notes about it below.
Then write a headline and an article.

BOY IS INVISIBLE!

FLAT AS A PANCAKE!

_____
(headline)

## Notes

| Who? | Where? When? |
|---|---|
| **What Happened?** | |
| Why? | How? |

©The Education Center, Inc. • *THE MAILBOX*® • *Primary* • Aug/Sept 2003

**Note to the teacher:** Use with "In the News" on page 170.

# The Henry and Mudge Books

Written by Cynthia Rylant • Illustrated by Suçie Stevenson

What do you get when you pair a red-haired boy and a 180-pound dog? Lots of entertaining adventures! Invite students to enjoy the stories about the charming duo, Henry and Mudge, with this collection of ideas. Use the first two activities to complement the featured titles and the last two suggestions to follow up any books in the series.

*ideas contributed by Julie Hays—Gr. 1*
*Foothills Elementary, Maryville, TN*

## Henry and Mudge: The First Book

*An only child named Henry decides that Mudge, a short, floppy-eared puppy, is just the right pet for him. As the lovable pooch grows, his friendship with the young boy grows too!*

Help students bone up on their **summarizing** skills with this look at how Henry and Mudge become faithful friends. In advance, prepare seven dog bone cutouts. Cover a small bulletin board with light-colored paper and title it as shown. To begin, ask students whether they have heard the expression "A dog is man's best friend." Clarify its meaning and explain that the expression reminds you of the book. Read the story aloud. At the book's conclusion, ask students to identify story details that convey the characters' friendship.

Later, encourage students to listen carefully for the main events as you reread the book one chapter at a time. At the end of each chapter, label a dog bone with the appropriate chapter number. Guide students to summarize the story events with a sentence or two; write the summary on the bone. Post the sequenced bones on the board in a zigzag arrangement and draw arrows between them as shown. Complete the display with small student-made illustrations of favorite scenes.

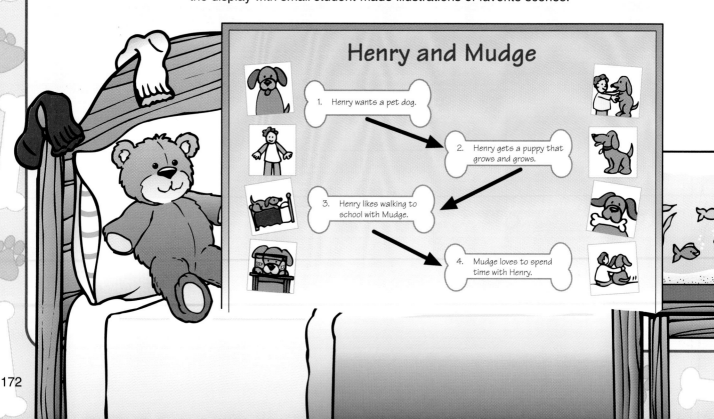

# Henry and Mudge
## and the Long Weekend

*One cold, wet day in February, Henry is bored until his mother suggests building a castle!*

Increase students' understanding of **story elements** with this royal project. After a discussion of the book's plot, help each youngster use the materials and directions shown to create a story-themed castle. Impressive!

**Materials for one castle:** copy of page 174, 6" x 12" construction paper rectangle (castle base), two 3" x 6" construction paper rectangles (towers), large sheet of drawing paper, crayons, scissors, glue

**Directions:**
1. Write the story elements on the patterns. Color the patterns as desired and then cut them out.
2. Make cuts along one long edge of the base and one short edge of each tower as illustrated to resemble castle walls.
3. Draw bricks on the base and towers; then glue the base and towers on the drawing paper (see the illustration).
4. Glue on the patterns as shown. Use crayons to complete the scene.

## "Paws" to Write

As students enjoy the various Henry and Mudge books, make **journal writing** a pet project! To make a journal, a student places a 4½" x 6" construction paper rectangle atop several quarter sheets of white paper (4¼" x 5½"). She staples the stack at the bottom of a 6" x 9" construction paper rectangle as shown. She signs the label (page 175), cuts it out, and then glues it onto the journal cover. To decorate her journal with a Mudge look-alike, she uses the patterns (page 175) to make a snout, two ears, two paws, and two eyes from construction paper. She glues the paws above the journal and then glues on a six-inch construction paper circle to make a head. After she glues the remaining cutouts in place, she adds crayon details to the eyes and snout. This adorable journal will be the perfect place to reflect on the stories!

## Story Celebration

Henry and Mudge love to snuggle up at night, so what better way to **culminate** a study of the series than with a bedtime-themed celebration? Suggest that each student wear slippers or a bathrobe and bring in a stuffed animal. (Arrange to have extra stuffed animals for students who do not bring any.) To begin, sit with students on the floor and invite them to recall favorite story events. Comment that Cynthia Rylant's son and dogs inspired her to write the books. Suggest that being familiar with a topic can help authors write engaging stories. Then have each youngster return to his chair and pen a story about a familiar topic. Serve crackers, one of Henry and Mudge's favorite snacks, as students work. To conclude the event, invite your young authors to share their story ideas.

# Castle Patterns

Use with *Henry and Mudge and the Long Weekend* on page 173.

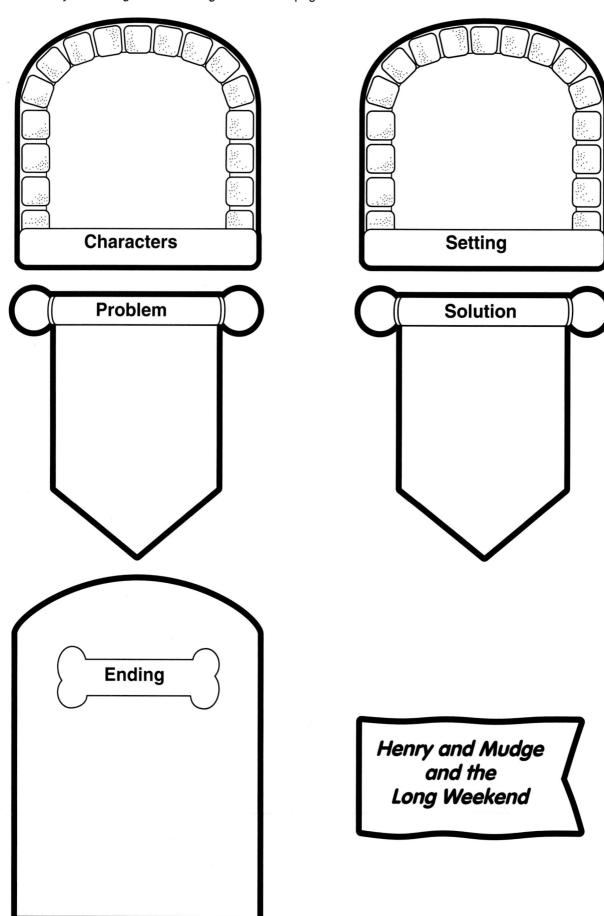

Characters

Setting

Problem

Solution

Ending

Henry and Mudge
and the
Long Weekend

snout

ear

paw

eye

label

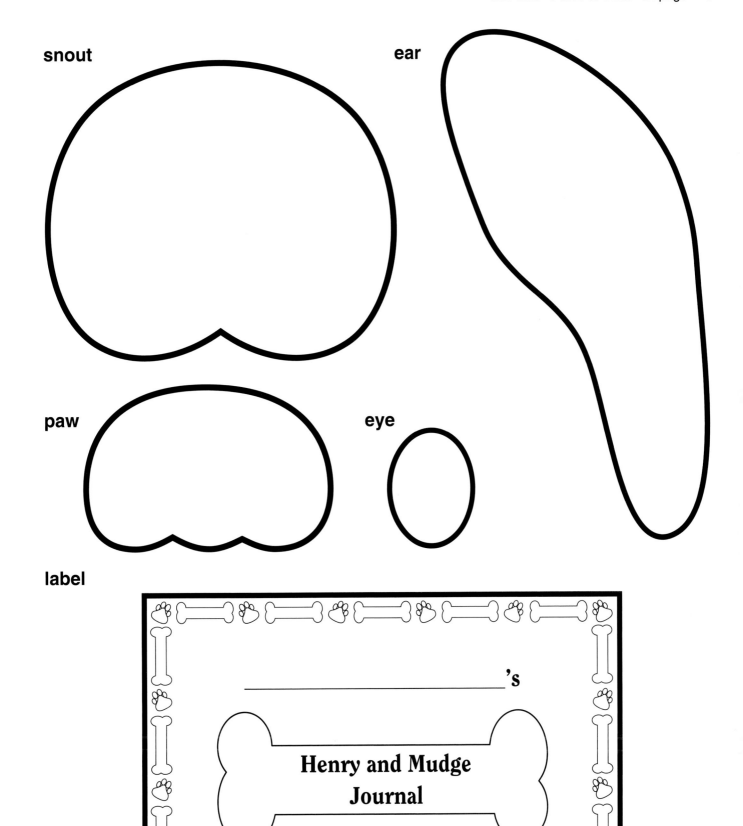

_____'s

**Henry and Mudge
Journal**

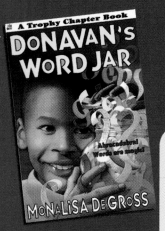

**A Trophy Chapter Book**

**DONAVAN'S WORD JAR**

Abracadabra! Words are magic!

MONALISA DEGROSS

# Donavan's Word Jar

**Written by Monalisa DeGross**
**Illustrated by Cheryl Hanna**

"Wordgatherer" Donavan Allen has a dilemma. He's been collecting words on strips of paper. Now his jar is overflowing and he doesn't know what to do. After a visit with his grandmother, he accidentally leaves behind his prized collection. When he goes to retrieve it, he not only discovers the power of his words, but he also finds a perfect solution to his problem!

*ideas contributed by Julie Douglas, St. Louis, MO*

## Cool Collections
### Skill: responding to literature

Donavan is so fascinated with words that he loves to collect them. His classmates also enjoy collecting things that intrigue them. After reading chapter 1, prompt students to recall these items. Then, to explore your students' interests, give each youngster a white jar cutout, a slightly larger piece of construction paper, scissors, crayons, and glue. At the top of her cutout, the youngster writes a few sentences about things she collects or would like to collect. She illustrates her collection below her writing. Then she glues her cutout onto the construction paper and trims the excess to make a narrow border. After each student completes her project, invite her to tell the class about her collection.

Julie

I collect rocks. I have rocks in all sorts of shapes and colors. I have over 20 rocks. Shiny rocks are the best!

## Picturing Words
### Skill: exploring word meanings

While looking in his father's tool chest in chapter 2, Donavan realizes that some things resemble their names. For example, the resemblance between a pair of pincers and a crab claw gives a hint about how pincers are used. Remind students of Donavan's realization; then write the word *fluffy* on the board with cloudlike letters. Comment that the shape of the letters helps convey the word's meaning. List the suggested words on the board and have students brainstorm how selected words might be written to reflect their meanings. Then add student-generated words to the list.

Next, give each student crayons and a sheet of drawing paper. Have him choose several words from the list and write them in a manner that suggests what they mean. Display students' resulting posters with the title "Picturing Words." What a creative way to increase interest in words!

shaky
timid
sparkle
skinny
tall
jump

### Suggested Words

| | |
|---|---|
| bloom | sparkle |
| lazy | tall |
| round | timid |
| shaky | wiggle |
| snuggle | windy |

marbles

tasty

shells

insects

nutrition

**Sam's Word Jar**

It looks cool when he <u>swirls</u> the paint.

I ate an <u>enormous</u> candy bar.

a trip

## Noteworthy Words
### Skill: developing vocabulary

Donavan won't be the only "wordgatherer" after this display idea! For each child, tack a personalized jar cutout to a bulletin board. After reading chapter 2, ask students to name ways that Donavan gathers words and recall places where he finds them. Then reveal that students will collect words for the displayed jars.

When a student comes across an interesting word, he folds a colorful index card in half lengthwise. With the fold at the top, he writes a sentence with the word, using a dictionary as needed. He underlines the word, unfolds the card, and then defines the word inside. After his work receives teacher approval, he attaches it to his jar with loops of tape. Encourage students to use the words in their conversations and writing. After each student collects several words, invite him to take his jar home. Or arrange for him to trade words with classmates for more vocabulary-boosting fun!

## What a Dilemma!
### Skills: problem solving, writing a letter

What should Donavan do with his growing collection of words? At the end of chapter 3, have students name the solutions that Donavan considers and why he feels they won't work. Then ask each student to write a letter to Donavan proposing a solution and explaining her reasoning. Collect students' completed letters for safekeeping. At the end of the book, have each youngster compare her suggestion with the actual solution.

## Word Power
### Skill: making connections

At the book's conclusion, Donavan excitedly discovers that his words are powerful. Not only do they help his grandmother's neighbors resolve their problems, but they also make people feel better. Discuss with students why Donavan's words are important to the neighbors. Then have each student think of two words that are especially meaningful to her, such as words that make her smile or remind her of a goal. Guide her to use the provided directions to showcase her words on a desktop reminder. How inspiring!

**Directions:**
1. Fold a 9" x 12" sheet of white paper in half and then unfold it. Fold in the ends to meet in the center. Refold the paper in half.
2. Position the paper with the opening at the bottom. Label it with a word and add desired illustrations. Turn the paper over. Then label and decorate the blank side in a similar manner.
3. To stand the project, unfold it slightly, overlap the blank flaps, and glue them together (see the illustration).

**Step 1**

practice

**Step 2**

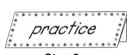

recital

**Step 3**

sneeze drizzle slumber cuddle treasure hush

Name _____

# Which Jar?

Read. Look at each underlined word.
Decide whether it is a noun, verb, or adjective.
Write the word on the correct jar.

1.  Donavan <u>collects</u> many words.
2.  His <u>jar</u> is full of words.
3.  Donavan's father uses <u>orange</u> paint.
4.  <u>Nikki</u> has a bad cold.
5.  Donavan <u>teaches</u> his sister new words.

6.  Grandma's <u>home</u> is cozy.
7.  Mr. Bill and Miz Marylou <u>shout</u>.
8.  Grandma <u>carries</u> a brown paper bag.
9.  The <u>happy</u> neighbors laugh.
10. Donavan is <u>proud</u> to use Grandpop's jar.

**Adjectives**

**Verbs**

**Nouns**

**Bonus Box:** Choose one word from two different jars. On the back of this sheet, use the words in a sentence.

©The Education Center, Inc. • *The Mailbox®* • Primary • TEC43012 • April/May 2004 • Key p. 311

**Note to the teacher:** Use at the conclusion of the book.

# A Way With Words

Write the words in the correct order to make sentences.
Remember when to use capital letters and periods.
The first one has been done for you.

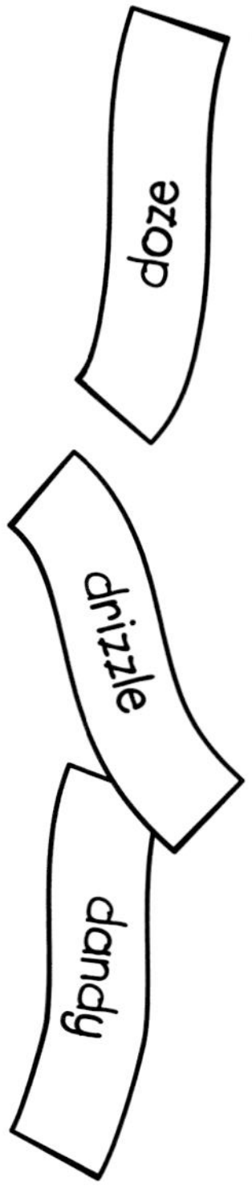

decide

delay

deep

delight

disappoint

Donavan

dines

discover

1. ate apes hungry apples
   *Hungry apes ate apples.*

2. boys bubbles both blew big

3. leap long lambs logs little over

4. travel on trains tracks tiny

5. sleep silly seven seals

6. flew from flies fields the five

7. dig dogs Don's in dirt the

8. on cats cute climb couch the

doze

drizzle

dandy

**Bonus Box:** On the back of this sheet, list seven words that begin with the same letter. Use some of the words to write and illustrate two sentences.

©The Education Center, Inc. • *The Mailbox*® • Primary • TEC43012 • April/May 2004 • Key p. 311

**Note to the teacher:** After sharing several chapters with students, point out that the author used alliteration for the chapter titles. Then have each student complete a copy of this page.

# "Purr-using" Mr. Putter and Tabby Books

Use these "pet-acular" ideas with Cynthia Rylant's beginning chapter books about Mr. Putter and his faithful feline, Tabby. Once your students are familiar with this endearing series, no doubt they'll put it at the top of their summer reading lists!

*ideas contributed by Marjorie Conrad*
*Kaysville, UT*

CYNTHIA RYLANT
Mr. Putter and Tabby
Pour the Tea

ILLUSTRATED BY
ARTHUR HOWARD

### Mr. Putter and Tabby Pour the Tea

*When lonely Mr. Putter hears about an old yellow cat, he's sure that the feline will be the perfect companion. After all, neither of them is peppy or cute, and they both have bones that creak!*

This first installment of the series not only introduces Mr. Putter to Tabby, but it also introduces readers to Mr. Putter! At the book's conclusion, invite students to tell what they learned about Mr. Putter from the story and illustrations. Revisit the book as needed to prompt youngsters.

Next, have each student prepare a story sack. To do this, he uses a four-inch circle (head), construction paper, crayons, scissors, and glue to create a likeness of Mr. Putter on the smooth side of a paper lunch bag. Then he writes on each of four blank cards a word or phrase that tells about the character. He illustrates two of Mr. Putter's favorite pastimes on two additional cards and then places all of his cards in his bag. Encourage each youngster to take his completed story sack home and use it to introduce his family to Mr. Putter.

**Exploring a main character**

tells good stories

loves opera music

My
Mr. Putter and Tabby
Scrapbook

shows *When Zeke*
*and tugged, Mr.*
*ad a hard time*
*him.*

*Juanita*

part of the story is
*Mr Putter had to*
*ke a nap in the*
*hammock. Zeke wore him*
*out!*

### Scrapbook of Stories

Mr. Putter has lots of wonderful stories to tell and a perfect place to capture mementos of them—a scrapbook. To keep her own mementos of Mr. Putter's stories, have each youngster fold a 5" x 16" construction paper strip in half and staple several copies of the scrapbook page (page 182) inside. Ask her to title and decorate the front cover as desired and then sign her name. After reading a book from the series, the youngster illustrates a chosen scene on a blank scrapbook page and then writes to complete the page. She takes her scrapbook home and plans to complete additional pages for any Mr. Putter and Tabby books that she reads during the summer.

**Writing and illustrating responses to literature**

## What's the Problem?

The simple story lines of the Mr. Putter and Tabby books are perfect for young readers to use in an investigation of plot. Divide a length of bulletin board paper into four columns. Label the first column "Title," the second column "Problem," the third column "Solution," and the fourth column "Ending." Post the resulting chart within student reach. For each of several chosen Mr. Putter and Tabby books, enlist youngsters' help to write the indicated information on the chart. With each addition to the chart, students will become more familiar with story structure! *Exploring plot*

## Story Events in Bloom

Help students' summarizing skills grow with this display idea! After reading a chosen book from the series, each student uses the tulip pattern (page 182) to make three blossoms from light-colored construction paper. Then she numbers them from 1 to 3. On the first tulip, she writes what happens at the beginning of the story. She summarizes the middle and ending of the story on the second and third tulips, respectively. Then she glues on construction paper stems.

Next, she folds up two inches of a horizontally positioned 6" x 12" strip of green construction paper. She places her paper so that the two-inch portion is facedown. Along the bottom edge of the strip she writes the book title. She slides her tulip stems between the two green layers and glues the tulips in order to the two-inch portion of the paper. She fringes the top layer to resemble grass and then glues the bottom part of the paper closed. Display students' work on a bulletin board titled "Mr. Putter's Garden of Stories." *Identifying the beginning, middle, and end*

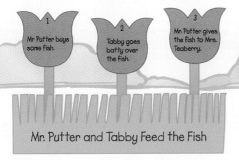

1. Mr. Putter buys some fish.
2. Tabby goes batty over the fish.
3. Mr. Putter gives the fish to Mrs. Teaberry.

Mr. Putter and Tabby Feed the Fish

## *Mr. Putter and Tabby Row the Boat*

*Mr. Putter and his neighbor, Mrs. Teaberry, find entertaining ways to cool off on an unbearably hot summer day.*

Mr. Putter and Mrs. Teaberry put a humorous spin on their tales by stretching the truth! To follow up this amusing book, point out that as the title of chapter 3 suggests, Mr. Putter's and Mrs. Teaberry's stories are greatly exaggerated. Then give each student a copy of page 183 and have him sign his name on the provided line. Instruct him to use the prompts to write his own outrageously exaggerated story. Next, sit with students in a circle and ask them to imagine that they're sitting by the edge of the big pond. Then invite youngsters to read aloud their tales for a sizzling storytime! *Writing to entertain*

CYNTHIA RYLANT

Mr. Putter and Tabby Row the Boat

ILLUSTRATED BY ARTHUR HOWARD

# Scrapbook Page and Tulip Pattern

Use the scrapbook page with "Scrapbook of Stories" on page 180.

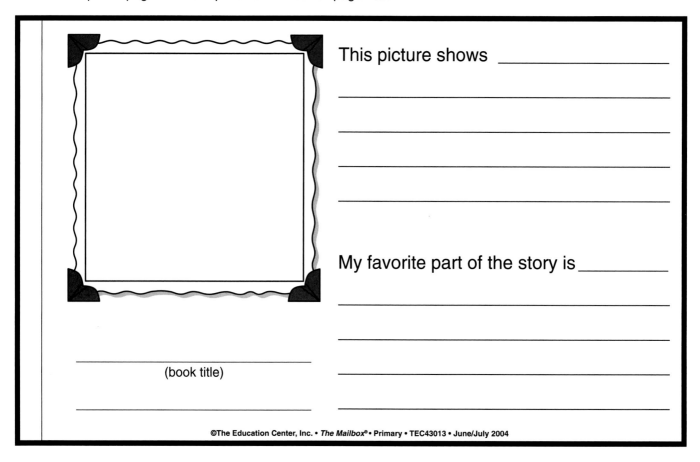

This picture shows _____

_____

_____

_____

_____

My favorite part of the story is _____

_____

_____

_____

_____

_____
(book title)

_____

Use the tulip with "Story Events in Bloom" on page 181.

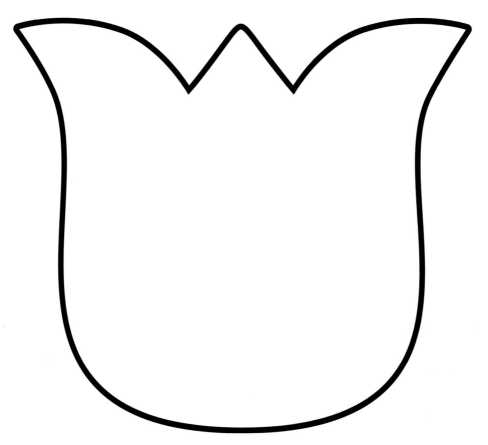

# Tall Tales

Told under the shady pines by _____

One summer day, it was so hot that _____

_____

_____

The pond was so _____

_____

The trees by the pond were very tall. In fact, _____

_____

_____

Tabby surprised Mr. Putter when _____

_____

_____

Then Zeke _____

_____

_____

What a fun day!

**Note to the teacher:** Use with *Mr. Putter and Tabby Row the Boat* on page 181.

# Sarah, Plain and Tall

by Patricia MacLachlan

*There hasn't been any singing in Anna and Caleb's prairie home since Mama passed away. That changes, though, when Sarah travels from Maine to answer Papa's advertisement for a wife. She brightens the home with songs and her spirited nature, quickly winning the family's love. But will she give up her life near the Maine coast to become part of the family? That's what Anna and Caleb anxiously wait to find out in this touching, award-winning book!*

*ideas contributed by Tara Kenyon, Reading, MA*

**Read Aloud**

## Rolling Land and Sea

*Exploring a story's setting*

The story takes Sarah from the rolling, open sea to the rolling, open prairie! Help students understand the importance of the story's setting with this ongoing project. Before reading the book, explain that Sarah lives near the sea but may move to the prairie. Invite students to tell what they know about the two geographical areas.

To explore related story details, each student folds a 9" x 12" sheet of white paper in half to 6" x 9". She unfolds it and traces the fold line. She folds the paper in half lengthwise and then trims the long side of the top layer with a wavy cut (see the illustration). She cuts the top layer to make two sections as shown. Then she positions the paper horizontally, adds the labels shown, and illustrates each flap to reflect the corresponding area. Periodically throughout the book, she writes relevant details under each flap. At the book's conclusion, she writes a paragraph on the back of her project to explain whether she would prefer to live by the sea or on the prairie. Students are sure to agree that Sarah has a lot to consider!

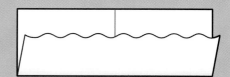

Prairie

Sea
Blue, gray and green are the colors

Chapter 2

News in the Mail

Special Letters

## Name That Chapter!

*Identifying appropriate chapter titles*

Encourage students to think like authors with this ongoing idea! Point out that the chapters of the book are numbered rather than titled. Guide students to identify characteristics of good chapter titles, such as interesting, brief, and related to the main idea. At the conclusion of each chapter, divide students into small groups and give each group a sentence strip. Have the students in each group consider the identified characteristics as they write an original title for the chapter. Then ask them to announce their title to the class and explain their reasoning. Arrange students' suggestions on a prepared bulletin board to create an overview of the story, chapter by chapter!

## It's in the Details!
### *Comparing and contrasting*

How does the story's setting compare with a contemporary town? Find out with this simple group activity! After reading chapter 6, post a large Venn diagram. Label one circle "Frontier," one circle "Our Town," and the center section "Both." Then divide students into small groups and give each group several sticky notes. Have each group program the sticky notes with details related to the frontier, the local community, or both settings. Then ask each group to read aloud its sticky notes and post them on the diagram, grouping any duplicate details. Invite students to analyze the displayed similarities and differences. Now that's a notable comparison of both time and place!

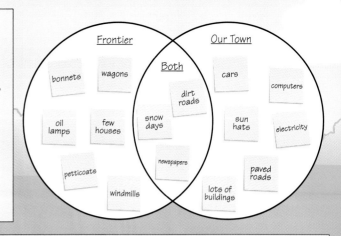

Frontier — Both — Our Town

bonnets · wagons · dirt roads · cars · computers · oil lamps · few houses · snow days · sun hats · electricity · petticoats · newspapers · paved roads · windmills · lots of buildings

## Things to Miss
### *Writing from a character's point of view*

In chapter 7, Maggie tells Sarah that there are things to miss wherever she is. If Sarah were to return to Maine, what would she miss most? Pose this question to students. Have each youngster respond by writing a paragraph from Sarah's point of view on a half sheet of writing paper. Instruct him to staple his writing in a 4½" x 6" construction paper folder and then decorate the front of the folder as desired. Arrange for students to share their work in small groups. Then poll the youngsters to find out whether they predict Sarah will stay with the family or return to Maine. After volunteers share their reasoning, read the rest of the book aloud to check students' ideas.

Swimming!

I would miss swimming in the cow pond. It's so much fun when it's hot! I like to show Caleb and Anna how to float. Caleb makes me laugh when he pretends he's a whale!

## Drawing on Imagery
### *Using imagery to increase comprehension*

With this picturesque approach to comprehension, students follow Sarah's example by illustrating memorable images. At the book's conclusion, ask each student to picture in her mind a favorite scene from the story. Have her make a pencil sketch of her image and then embellish it with blue, gray, and green crayons or colored pencils. Instruct her to write a description of her image on the back of her paper. Next, ask each of several students to show her classmates her artwork and tell about the corresponding story details. Suggest that imagery not only deepens understanding, but it also helps commit stories to memory. Then compile students' work into a class book to create a unique memento of the story. Sarah would be proud!

185

# Talk on the Prairie

Read the characters' statements.
Write the correct letter in each blank.

**A** = Anna

**P** = Papa

**S** = Sarah

**C** = Caleb

| | |
|---|---|
| _____ 1. "I've placed an advertisement in the newspapers." | _____ 6. "I want to learn how to ride a horse." |
| _____ 2. "What if she thinks we are loud and pesky?" | _____ 7. "Of course she's coming back." |
| _____ 3. "Tomorrow I want to see the sheep." | _____ 8. "Scared? Scared! You bet I'm not scared." |
| _____ 4. "*I* would have named you Troublesome." | _____ 9. "Women don't wear overalls." |
| _____ 5. "I've forgotten the old songs." | _____ 10. "I know about roofs. I am a good carpenter." |

**Bonus Box:** Look at the statements for numbers 8 and 10. What do they tell you about the character? Explain on the back of this sheet.

Name _____

# Picture This!

A **simile** uses *like* or *as* to compare two unlike things.
Each sentence in the box uses a simile to tell about a story detail.
Use the word bank to complete each sentence.

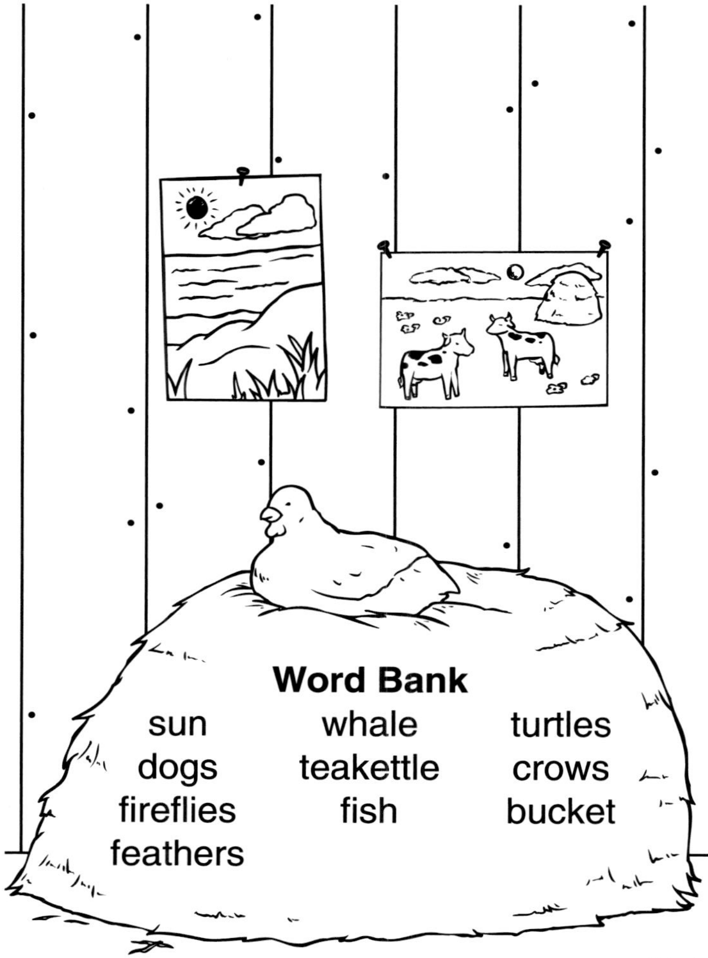

1. The cows walk as slowly as _____ .

2. The housekeeper snores with a whistle like a _____ on glass.

3. The sea shines like the _____ .

4. The seals slide through the sea like _____ of water.

5. Anna sinks in the pond like a _____ .

6. Caleb blows water like a _____ .

7. Sarah says that seals bark like _____ .

8. The dandelions are as soft as _____ .

9. The stars blink like _____ at night.

10. Sarah's three old aunts squawk like _____ .

**Word Bank**

| | |
|---|---|
| sun | turtles |
| dogs | whale |
| fireflies | teakettle |
| feathers | crows |
| | fish |
| | bucket |

©The Education Center, Inc. • *THE MAILBOX®* • *Primary* • Dec/Jan 2003–4 • Key p. 312

**Note to the teacher:** At the conclusion of the book, remind students that Patricia MacLachlan and other authors sometimes use similes to create vivid images. Then have each student complete a copy of this page.

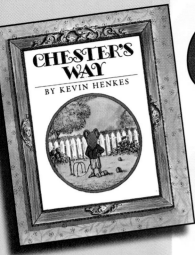

# Chester's Way

by Kevin Henkes

*Chester does things his way, and his best friend Wilson does things exactly the same way. The two pals happily share many routines and experiences. Then, one day, they meet Lilly. Lilly has a unique way of doing things that prompts the boys to avoid her. That changes, though, when she comes to their rescue and they learn a valuable lesson about friendship.*

*ideas contributed by Marjorie Conrad*
*Kaysville, UT*

## Delicious Differences
### Prompting prior knowledge

Serve up this prereading activity to help students understand that friends may have different likes and interests. To begin, ask students whether they prefer to have sandwiches cut into squares or triangles. Designate a classroom area for each choice and ask each youngster to respond by standing in the appropriate area. Allow time for the youngsters to notice who is in each group. Then, in a similar manner, announce two other sandwich-related categories and have each student indicate his preference. After students observe the new groupings, have them sit with you in your storytime area. Prompt discussion about the sandwich survey to help students realize that sometimes friends like different things.

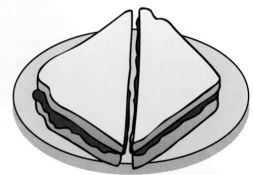

Next, reveal that the book is about two friends who do everything the same, including the way they cut their sandwiches. Explain that they meet someone who has a different way of doing things. Welcome students' predictions about what will happen; then read the story aloud.

## Friendship Journals
### Responding to writing prompts

There's no doubt about it—Chester and Wilson are the best of friends! After a first reading, revisit the illustrations to help students recall story details that reflect the characters' friendship. Then give each youngster a copy of page 190 and three additional copies of the journal page. To make a journal, the student cuts out the pages and stacks them inside a 6" x 9" construction paper folder on the right-hand side. She staples the stack at the top. She personalizes the cover label as desired, cuts it out, and glues it onto her folder's front cover. She cuts out each prompt and glues it onto the box on a journal page.

Date April 22

I was a good friend when...

I shared my jump rope with Meg at recess. We took turns counting for each other. It was really fun!

For student reference, place the book at a center. Periodically set aside time for each youngster to write and illustrate a response to a chosen prompt. Students are sure to strengthen their friendships along with their writing skills!

# Two Peas in a Pod
### Exploring a story theme

Chester's mother thinks that the phrase "two peas in a pod" is a fitting description of Chester and Wilson. After completing this display idea, your students will be sure to agree! Return to the page where the expression is mentioned and guide students to identify its meaning. Next, each youngster uses a template to make three five-inch white paper circles. He illustrates each circle to provide a story-related or real-life example that depicts the expression "two peas in a pod" and writes a caption. He uses a template to make a construction paper pea pod that is approximately 8" x 18". Then he glues his illustrations in place. Display students' work on a prepared board along with twisted paper vines and the title "Peas in Pods."

Chester and Wilson are always together.

They both like picnics.

They use the same umbrella.

# Chester's Way?
### Comparing and contrasting

At first, Chester and Lilly seem as different as night and day. But later it's clear that they have several things in common. To explore the similarities and differences, each student divides a horizontally positioned sheet of paper into three columns. She labels the first column "Chester," the second column "Lilly," and the third column "Both." Then she writes and illustrates two or more relevant details in each column. After each youngster completes her paper, encourage students to refer to their work as you lead a discussion comparing and contrasting the two characters. For added fun, invite students to compare themselves with either character.

| Chester | Lilly | Both |
|---------|-------|------|
| cuts his sandwich into triangles | uses cookie cutters to cut her sandwich | have night lights |
| eats toast with jam and peanut butter | wears funny disguises | have special mouse cups |

# Chester and Changes
### Evaluating a character's behavior

Does Chester always make the best choices? Find out what your students think with this discussion idea. First, have youngsters give thumbs-up or thumbs-down signs to indicate how they would rate Chester's behavior at the beginning of the story. After students respond, ask volunteers to share their reasoning. In a similar manner, invite students to share their thoughts about how Chester acts when he first meets Lilly and how he treats her later in the story. Guide students to identify why Chester's behavior changes. Then ask them to brainstorm advice for Chester that would help him get to know Victor, his newest neighbor.

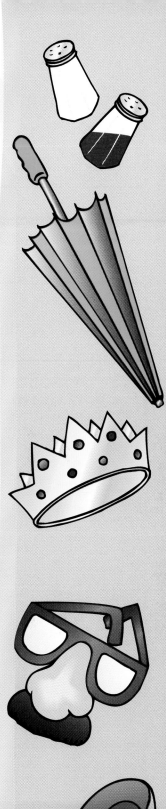

189

# Journal Prompts, Label, and Page

Use with "Friendship Journals" on page 188.

 I was a good friend when…

 *Chester's Way* makes me think of when…

 My friend and I like to…

 I have a lot of fun with my friends. We…

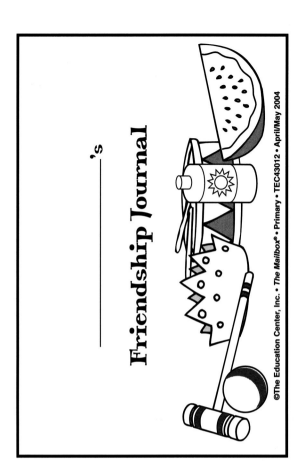

_____'s

**Friendship Journal**

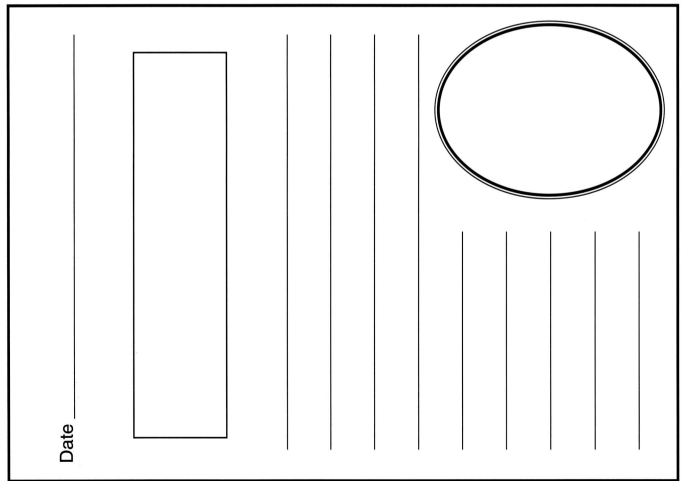

Date _____

# Ralph S. Mouse

Written by Beverly Cleary
Illustrated by Paul O. Zelinsky

Things aren't going well for Ralph S. Mouse at his home in the Mountain View Inn. He has trouble getting along with his relatives. Plus, he seems to be causing problems for the friendly handyman. The unusual rodent decides there's only one thing to do—move to his fifth-grade pal's classroom. Ralph soon discovers that he has a lot to learn!

**Read Aloud**

ideas contributed by Carol Stillings—Gr. 2
Bill Metz Elementary, Monte Vista, CO

## Nose for Fantasy
*Distinguishing between reality and fantasy*

This unbelievable tale about a motorcycle-riding rodent is perfect for an exploration of reality and fantasy! Before reading the book, post a two-column chart. Label one column "Reality" and one column "Fantasy." Have students brainstorm facts that they know about mice; then write the facts in the appropriate column. As you read aloud the first chapter, encourage youngsters to think about the distinction between fantasy and reality. Then list student-generated story details in each column of the chart.

Next, each student folds a 9" x 12" sheet of gray construction paper in half to 6" x 9". With the fold at the top, he draws a mouse head similar to the one shown and then cuts it out. He staples several half sheets of paper inside and then trims the excess. He uses provided arts-and-crafts materials to add two eyes, two ears, and a nose to the resulting booklet. After chosen reading sessions, he writes in the booklet at least one story detail that could be true and one that could not. He labels each detail with "R" for reality or "F" for fantasy. For additional reinforcement, he completes a copy of page 193. Fantastic!

How Ralph Feels at First
sad, brave, frightened, and nervous

How Ralph Feels Later
scared to be left alone
guilty for breaking his promise
angry about the maze

## Mixed Feelings
*Making text-to-self connections, analyzing a character*

Students are sure to relate to Ralph's tangled emotions at the end of chapter 2! Ask each student to think about times when, like Ralph, she had mixed emotions. Share a few of your experiences and invite volunteers to tell about times they recall. Then have students predict how Ralph's feelings will change. To track the character's feelings, have each youngster decorate a large white paper bookmark with a mouse cutout as shown. Then ask her to list Ralph's feelings when he first leaves the hotel. Throughout the rest of the story, have her jot down notes about Ralph's later feelings. Encourage her to check and revise her predictions as Ralph's school adventure unfolds.

## What Happened?
*Understanding cause and effect*

After Ryan's classmates learn about Ralph in chapter 3, one thing quickly leads to another. To identify the story's cause-and-effect relationships, each student writes the chapter number on a graphic organizer similar to the one shown. In the first box, he writes and illustrates a story event from the chapter. In the second box, he writes what happens as a result of the event.

After each student completes his paper, ask a volunteer to announce his event (cause) and the result (effect). Invite students to share any other cause-and-effect relationships. If desired, ask each youngster to store his paper in a personalized construction paper folder; have him complete a copy of the graphic organizer for each remaining chapter. Then instruct him to arrange the papers in order and staple them inside his folder. The sequence of events will be clear!

Chapter **3**          Colin

Cause
A student sees Ralph in Ryan's pocket.

Effect
Miss K plans a mouse exhibit.

## Through Ralph's Eyes
*Understanding a character's point of view*

With this imaginative follow-up to chapter 5, students consider things from Ralph's perspective! Have students recall how Ralph's small size and experiences influence his perceptions of many common items. For example, Ralph thinks that the inside of a mitten is a nice place to rest, and he compares a tape dispenser to a metal snail. Ask each youngster to illustrate a chosen classroom item and then write about it from Ralph's point of view. Showcase youngsters' completed work on a bulletin board titled "Mouse Sightings." Embellish the grin-inducing display with student-made illustrations of the tiny mouse.

Sometimes the art teacher puts out small bowls of water. I can take a bath in one of them. It's perfect! The water is not too hot or cold. Plus, it's not too deep. It's fun to splash in it.

## Surprising Friendships
*Exploring a story's theme*

New and renewed friendships give this mouse tale a happy ending! At the book's conclusion, have students recall the friendships among various characters. Point out that some friends, such as Ralph and Matt, may seem to be unlikely twosomes. To explore how friendships may develop, ask students to brainstorm characteristics of good friends. Then have each youngster answer the questions on a copy of page 194, pointing out that the responses may vary. After each student shares her ideas with a partner, talk about the questions as a class. No doubt Miss K would be pleased with students' thoughtful (and friendly!) discussions.

Name_____

# Amazing!

Show the mouse a path to the
motorcycle.
Read each sentence.
If it **could happen** in real life,
circle the number.
If it **could not happen** in real
life, color the box yellow.

| | | |
|---|---|---|
| 1. The mouse makes a soft nest. | 2. The mice scurry under the clock. | 3. A lonely boy hears the mouse talk. |
| 4. During the winter, the mouse lives indoors. | 5. The noise scares away the mouse. | 6. A mouse learns how to talk by watching TV. |
| 7. The mouse wears a crash helmet. | 8. All of the mice want to ride the motorcycle. | 9. The hungry mouse nibbles its food. |
| 10. The mouse fixes its motorcycle. | 11. Several mice live in the hotel. | 12. When it is warm, some mice go outside. |

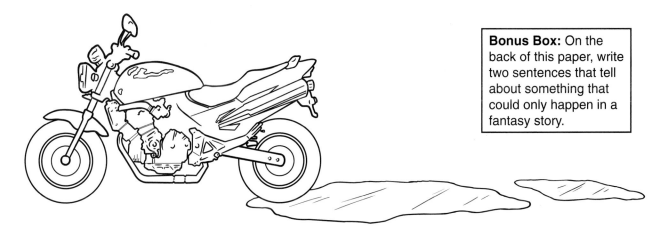

**Bonus Box:** On the
back of this paper, write
two sentences that tell
about something that
could only happen in a
fantasy story.

©The Education Center, Inc. • THE MAILBOX® • Primary • Feb/Mar 2004 • Key p. 312

**Note to the teacher:** Use with "Nose for Fantasy" on page 191.

# Time for Friendship!

Answer the questions.
Talk about your answers with a partner.

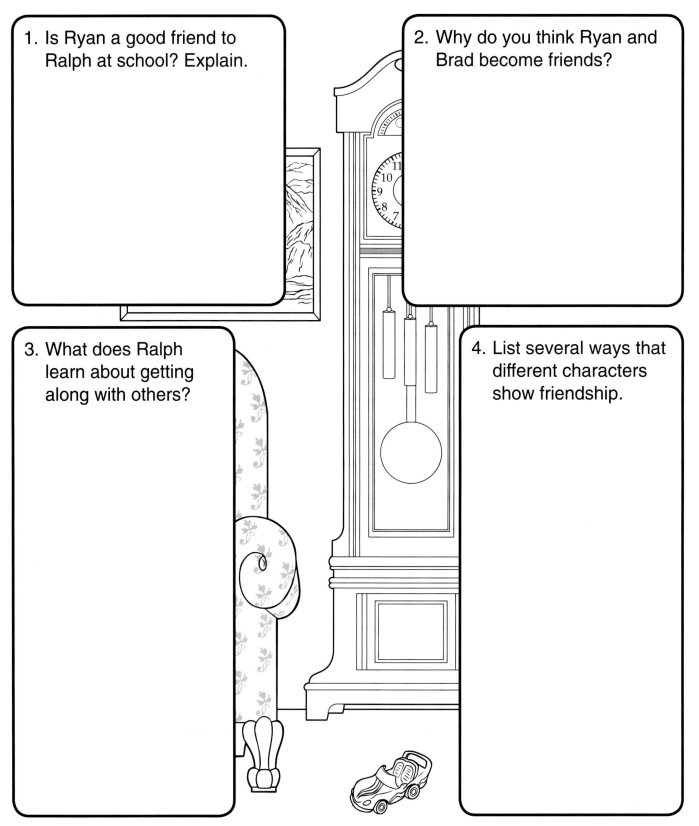

1. Is Ryan a good friend to Ralph at school? Explain.

2. Why do you think Ryan and Brad become friends?

3. What does Ralph learn about getting along with others?

4. List several ways that different characters show friendship.

# MATH UNITS

# Measurement at the Fairgrounds

What's the main attraction at this county fair?
An assortment of blue-ribbon measurement ideas!

*ideas contributed by Starin Lewis, Phoenix, AZ*

## Prized Comparisons

**Skill: comparing length**

Begin your measurement fair with this winning idea for comparing length! Give each student a recording sheet similar to the one shown, scissors, and a 6" x 9" piece of blue construction paper. Ask her to draw a blue ribbon and then have her cut it out. Next, challenge students to identify classroom items that are about the same length as their ribbons, longer than their ribbons, and shorter than their ribbons. To do this, each youngster holds her ribbon near a chosen classroom item and compares the lengths. She lists the item in the appropriate column on her recording sheet. She continues as time allows, trying to list three items per category.

At the end of the allotted time, prompt students to use measurement-related vocabulary as they tell the class about their findings. Guide any students who recorded the same items in different categories to realize that the discrepancies may be due to variations in the measurement tools (ribbons). Now that's a blue-ribbon strategy for making comparisons!

> The crayon box is shorter than my ribbon.

| Shorter Than My Ribbon | About the Same As My Ribbon | Longer Than My Ribbon |
|---|---|---|
| crayon box | pencil | ruler |
| eraser | block | desktop |
| paper clip | stapler | paper |

## Ticket Lengths, Please!

**Skill: using nonstandard units to measure length**

A length of tickets admits each student to this nonstandard-measurement event! In advance, purchase a roll of tickets (available at office supply stores). Give each student a strip of five tickets. To prepare a recording sheet, each youngster divides a sheet of drawing paper into two columns. He labels the first column "Item" and the second column "Length."

Next, each student measures to the nearest whole ticket several classroom objects of various lengths. He writes each item and length on his paper.

After he records several measurements, he identifies one item that is shorter than his strip of tickets and measures it to the nearest whole ticket. He tears off any extra tickets and discards them. He glues the strip of tickets in the middle of the blank side of his paper. Above the strip, he illustrates the item to show its actual length. Below the strip, he writes a sentence to tell the item's length in tickets. The result will be just the ticket to check students' use of nonstandard measurement!

This pencil is about 3 tickets long.

Kyle

## Sizable Snacks

**Skill: comparing customary and metric units of length**

Whet students' appetites for using customary and metric rulers. To begin, each student makes a construction paper cutout of a corn dog, a candied apple, or another county fair snack that is served on a stick. He glues a personalized craft stick to the back of it and labels a blank card with the type of snack. He measures his snack and stick to the nearest inch and then the nearest centimeter. He writes the measurements on the card and signs his name.

Next, have each student silently compare his two measurements and invite youngsters to speculate why they are different. Guide them to understand that it takes a greater number of smaller units than larger units to measure an item. For a mouthwatering follow-up, pair students. Have each youngster measure his partner's snack and use the prepared card to check his work.

corn dog
7 in.
18 cm
Robert

## Ounces or Pounds?

**Skill: determining the appropriate unit of measure**

Here's a fresh idea for introducing units of weight! Obtain two inexpensive produce items—one that weighs about an ounce (such as a cherry tomato) and one that weighs about a pound (such as a potato). Label a folded blank card for each unit of weight. Use the provided suggestions to program blank cards with several county fair sights that are appropriate to measure in ounces and several sights that are better measured in pounds. Code the back of the cards to make the activity self-checking. Set the produce and cards at a center.

A student briefly holds the two produce items to get a sense of their relative weights. She reads a card, decides whether the sight should be weighed in ounces or pounds, and then places the card near the appropriate produce item. She sorts the remaining cards in this manner. Then she flips the cards to check her work.

| County Fair Sights | |
|---|---|
| **Ounces** | **Pounds** |
| cotton candy | large pumpkin |
| box of popped corn | farmer |
| balloon | calf |
| cookie | whole watermelon |
| hot dog | pig |

## Weighing In With Estimates

**Skill: estimating weight**

Invite students to step right up and investigate weight! To prepare for this small-group activity, obtain an ounce scale, several objects to be weighed, and a one-ounce weight for students to use as a benchmark. Have each student prepare a three-column chart labeled as shown and ask him to list the objects in the first column. Next, circulate among the students the one-ounce weight, followed by the objects. After each student writes his estimate for each object, have volunteers help you weigh each one. Instruct each youngster to list the actual weights on his paper. Then prompt discussion to explore how students' estimates compare with the measurements.

| Item | Estimated Weight | Actual Weight |
|---|---|---|
| | | |
| | | |
| | | |

pam crane

197

## Capacity Comparison
**Skill: determining capacity**

Your young fairgoers won't want to miss this capacity exhibit! Obtain several nonbreakable liquid containers of various heights and widths. Letter them for easy identification. Place the containers on a table along with a pitcher of water, measuring cup, and supply of paper towels to clean up any spills.

To begin, ask students to imagine that they sell cider at a county fair and need to know how much cider each container can hold. Have each youngster silently predict the order of the containers from the least to greatest capacity and write his predicted sequence on provided paper. With students' help, use the measuring cup and water to determine the capacity of each container; write it on the board. Then, as students use this information to identify the correct sequence, arrange the containers in order. Point out that tall containers don't necessarily hold the most. Students are sure to agree that when it comes to capacity, appearances can be deceiving!

**APPLE CIDER**

## Pen Perimeters
**Skill: finding perimeter**

Students are bound to go hog-wild over this perimeter activity! Give each youngster a 12" x 18" sheet of white construction paper and four 1" x 18" construction paper strips. Confirm that she also has a ruler, scissors, crayons, and access to tape. Have her use the provided directions to make a three-dimensional pigpen and find its perimeter. Then, for more perimeter practice, have her head to the midway with the reproducible on page 200.

**Directions:**
1. Illustrate a pig in the middle of the paper.
2. To make four sides for the pen, trim the construction paper strips to create two pairs of identical whole-inch strips so that one pair is longer than the other.
3. Measure the strips. Write an addition sentence below the illustration to find the perimeter.
4. To form one long strip, lay the strips end to end and then tape the adjacent ends together, alternating the long and short strips.
5. Measure the length of the entire strip to check the perimeter.
6. Stand the strips to form a pen around the pig. Tape the free ends together; then tape the pen to the paper.

Misty

7 + 6 + 7 + 6 = 26 inches

Length

ribbon, inches

Weight

pig, pounds

Capacity

pitcher of cider, cups

## For Good Measure!
**Skill: identifying appropriate forms of measurement**

For the final event of this county fair, invite students to show what they know about forms of measurement. To do this, each student visually divides a vertically positioned sheet of drawing paper into three horizontal sections. He titles one section for each of the following: length, weight, and capacity. In the first section, he illustrates one or two things whose length can be measured. He does the same for weight and capacity. Then he labels each illustration and writes the most reasonable unit of measure. What a simple way to see how students' understanding measures up!

198

Name ______________________________________________

Measurement
Using nonstandard units

# Feeding Time!

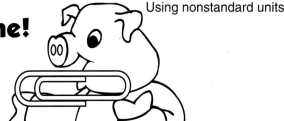

Estimate. Then use paper clips to measure.
Answer the questions.

a. Estimate. about ___ paper clips Measure. about ___ paper clips

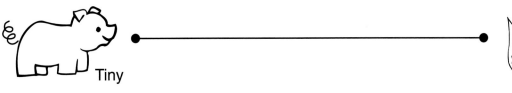

Tiny

b. Estimate. about ___ paper clips Measure. about ___ paper clips

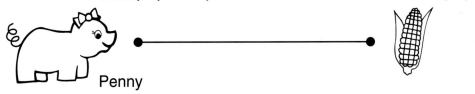

Penny

c. Estimate. about ___ paper clips Measure. about ___ paper clips

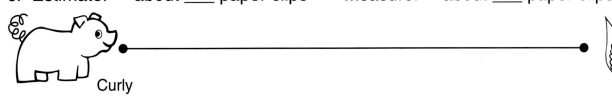

Curly

d. Estimate. about ___ paper clips Measure. about ___ paper clips

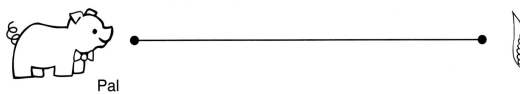

Pal

1. Which pig is farthest from the corn? ________________
2. Which pig is closest to the corn? ________________
3. What is the total distance for Curly and Pal? about ______ paper clips
4. What is the total distance for Penny, Tiny, and Pal? about ______ paper clips

**Bonus Box:** On the back of this sheet, draw an ear of corn that is about 3 paper clips long. Then list two things in the classroom that are about this long.



**Note to the teacher:** Each student will need six small paper clips to complete this activity.

Name_____

# Step Right Up!

For each game booth, measure the two sides in centimeters.
Write the lengths. Add to find the perimeter.
The first one has been done for you.

1. Perimeter _3 + 4 + 3 + 4 = 14 cm_

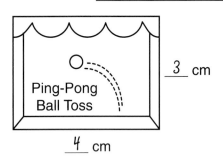

Ping-Pong
Ball Toss

_3_ cm

_4_ cm

2. Perimeter _____

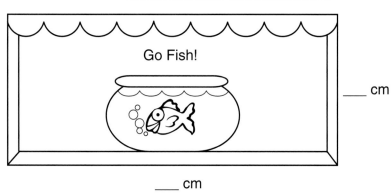

Go Fish!

___ cm

___ cm

3. Perimeter _____

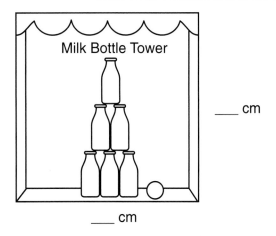

Milk Bottle Tower

___ cm

___ cm

4. Perimeter _____

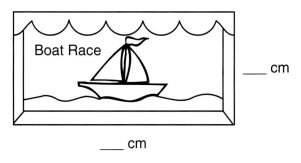

Boat Race

___ cm

___ cm

5. Perimeter _____

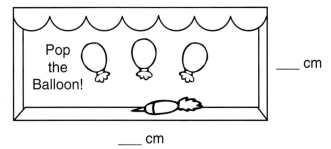

Pop
the
Balloon!

___ cm

___ cm

6. Perimeter _____

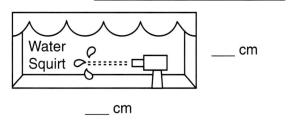

Water
Squirt

___ cm

___ cm

**Bonus Box:** On the back of this sheet, draw a booth 4 centimeters tall and 6 centimeters wide. Find the perimeter.

**Note to the teacher:** Use with "Pen Perimeters" on page 198. Each student will need a metric ruler to complete this activity.

# Stepping Ahead With Patterns

Use these ideas to pair up students' patterning know-how with their growing understanding of numbers. No doubt the mathematical possibilities will knock their socks off!

*ideas contributed by Starin Lewis, Phoenix, Arizona*

### Colorful Warm-Up
*Recording and continuing patterns*

Line up a colorful review of patterning skills! Rule a sheet of blank chart paper to make a grid with eight or more boxes per row. Display it within students' reach. To begin, connect six Unifix cubes to make a color pattern. After students identify the pattern, record it in the first row on the grid by coloring the appropriate boxes. Invite a student to continue the pattern for the rest of the row. Repeat the process with a desired number of patterns, leaving a blank grid row after each recorded pattern for ease of reading.

Next, divide students into small groups. Give each group a supply of various-colored manipulatives, crayons, and graph paper or prepared grids. Each group member, in turn, uses the manipulatives to make a six-item pattern. His group members identify the pattern; then each youngster records and extends it on his paper. Students will soon be recording patterns with flying colors!

How Many Socks?

1, ②
3, ④
5, ⑥
7, ⑧
9, ⑩

### Skip-Counting Savvy
*Using patterns to skip-count*

Introduce students to skip-counting with this simple class activity! Invite several youngsters who are wearing socks to stand at the front of the classroom. Then pose this question: How many socks are in the group? As you lead students in counting the socks individually, list the numbers on the board in pairs as shown. After the total is determined, circle the second number in each pair and challenge students to identify the number pattern *(twos)*. Explain that since each student has two socks, it would have been quicker to find the total by skip-counting. Lead the class in counting the students' socks by twos. For an added challenge, invite students to predict the sock total if every student in the class wears a pair of socks. Then skip-count to check.

Periodically pose other questions with skip-counting possibilities, such as "How many eyes are in our classroom?" and "How many fingers does our class have?" Students are sure to realize that number patterns come in handy!

201

## That's Odd!
### Identifying odd and even numbers

Help students get in step with odd and even numbers! Show students a pair of socks and a separate sock. Explain that you often have an odd sock, one without a partner. Suggest that this problem can help demonstrate a number pattern. Draw a two-column chart on the board. Label the first column "Odd" and the second "Even." Write "1" in the first column to represent a sock without a partner. With students' input, list the numbers for two, three, and four socks in the appropriate columns. Invite youngsters to share their observations about the developing number pattern.

To check their ideas, divide students into groups of five, six, or more. Have the students in each group pair off, as possible, to determine whether their group total is an odd or even number. Record each number on the chart. Whenever students need to determine odd or even, encourage them to check for partners!

## Patterns With a Beat
### Identifying odd and even numbers

Invite students to clap along as they chant this catchy verse. They'll remember the number patterns in no time at all!

Jennifer-Anne Creekmore, Kemp Elementary, Hampton, GA

> **Pattern Chant**
> 2, 4, 6, 8—
> Even numbers are so great!
> 3, 5, 7, 9—
> Odd numbers are divine!

## Chart Investigation
### Exploring patterns on a hundred chart

This hundred chart investigation will have students on the lookout for patterns! Give each student a copy of a hundred chart and divide students into five groups. Secretly assign each group a different color and number pattern (odds, evens, twos, fives, tens). Have the youngsters color their charts to show their group's pattern. Next, ask each group to display its charts and have a group member read several of the colored numbers aloud. After the remaining students identify the pattern, give the pattern recorders a round of applause!

## Amazing Changes
### Identifying number patterns

Spark curiosity with a pattern that appears right before students' eyes! In advance, decorate a large unlidded box. Program a blank white card for each of the numbers 1–4 and a colored card for each number 2–5; place the colored cards in the box. Post a two-row chart with ten boxes and label the rows as shown.

To begin, display the first white card and claim that you can change the number. After a student writes the number in the first row on the chart, drop the card into the box. Announce "Presto Chango!" and remove the number 2 with great fanfare. Have the student write this number below the first one. Repeat the process with the remaining cards, presenting each pairing in order. Then have students study the chart and identify the pattern. Plan to give repeat performances with different patterns.

| Before | 1 | 2 | 3 | 4 |
|--------|---|---|---|---|
| After  | 2 | 3 | 4 | 5 |

Name _____

# Hanging Out With Patterns

Read the patterns.
Color the socks to match.

  1. | AB |   2. | ABC |   3. | AAB |   4. | ABB |

Continue the patterns.

a.  1, 2, 1, 2, 1, _____, _____, _____, _____, _____

b.  3, 5, 7, 3, 5, 7, 3, _____, _____, _____, _____, _____

c.  4, 4, 6, 4, 4, 6, _____, _____, 6, _____, 4, _____

d.  2, 4, 4, 2, 4, 4, _____, 4, _____, _____, 4, _____

e.  3, 5, 3, 3, 5, 3, _____, _____, _____, 3, 5, _____

f.  1, 2, 2, 3, 1, 2, 2, 3, _____, 2, _____, 3, 1, _____, 2, 3

**Bonus Box:** On the back of this sheet, draw a striped sock. Color the stripes in an ABCC pattern.

# Making "Cents" of Rounding and Estimation

What does this unit have in store for students? A huge opportunity to stock up on rounding and estimation practice!

*ideas contributed by Laura Wagner, Raleigh, NC*

## Candy Count

**Skill: understanding estimation**

Sweeten students' understanding of the connection between rounding and estimating! In advance, place five to seven wrapped candies in each of several plastic snack bags so that there is at least one piece of candy per student. Show the bags to students and wonder aloud whether there is enough candy for the entire class. Suggest that since there are about five pieces in each bag, a quick way to estimate the total is to count the bags by fives. After students use this strategy, have volunteers determine an actual count. Point out that using a rounded number (five) helped ensure a reasonable estimate. Then offer each child a piece of candy.

As students enjoy their treats, explain that sometimes it is necessary to determine a precise number but other times an estimate will do. Have students brainstorm a list of situations in which estimation may be useful. Post the list in an accessible location and encourage students to add to it periodically.

### When Estimation May Be Useful

- deciding whether there's enough candy to share
- adding big numbers
- figuring out whether there's enough money to buy something
- determining about how much time is needed for homework
- figuring out about how long it will take to make cookies

## Well-Rounded Game

**Skill: rounding numbers to the nearest ten**

This whole-class game provides loads of rounding practice! To prepare, program two cards for each digit from 1 to 9. Shuffle the cards and stack them facedown. Give each child a handful of game markers and a sheet of paper. Have him visually divide the paper to make a 4 x 4 grid. Instruct him to randomly number the grid spaces with multiples of ten up to 100. Confirm that students understand when to round up or down.

Next, draw two cards from the stack. Use the numbers to write a two-digit number on the board and then place the cards in a discard pile. Invite a student to announce the displayed number rounded to the nearest ten. Instruct each student who has this number to place a marker on it. Continue play, reshuffling the cards as needed, until a student marks four numbers in a horizontal, vertical, or diagonal row and declares, "Round over!" After a win is confirmed, have students clear their grids for another round of play.

pam crane

$$\begin{array}{r} \$\,1.00 \\ +\ 3.00 \\ \hline \$4.00 \end{array}$$

## To Market, to Market
**Skill: rounding to estimate and compare sums**

Team up estimation and calculators to make this center a bargain of an idea! Gather several clean and empty nonbreakable food packages. Label each one with a price appropriate for rounding to the nearest dollar or ten dollars. Place the packages at a center along with paper, two calculators, and pencils. Arrange for students to visit the center in pairs.

Each student selects two items. He rounds each price and then adds the rounded prices on his paper. The students compare their sums and determine who has the greater total. Each student uses a calculator to find his actual total and check the comparison. Then the students select different items and repeat the process as time allows. (A student may select an item more than once.) Now that's a new angle on comparison shopping!

## Within Reason
**Skill: recognizing reasonable estimates**

Here's a valuable activity for helping students make reasonable estimates! Mount on a length of bulletin board paper several product pictures that you have cut from discarded catalogs or advertisements. Label each image with a price that is suitable for your students to round.

To begin, display the poster on the board. Direct students' attention to the prices of two selected items. Then write an estimated total (reasonable or unreasonable) beside the poster. Have each student add the rounded prices on provided paper. Next, instruct her to give a thumbs-up if she thinks the displayed estimate is reasonable or a thumbs-down if she believes it is unreasonable. Invite students to explain their thinking; determine the actual sum as a class. Repeat the process with different pairs of prices. For further reinforcement, have each student complete a copy of page 206.

## On a Budget
**Skill: rounding to estimate differences**

With this idea, students get the real deal on estimating differences. Give each student a book club catalog and a form similar to the one shown. The youngster writes a specified whole-dollar allowance in the first row of her form. She selects a book from her catalog that is within the allowance. She writes the actual and rounded prices, then subtracts the rounded price from her allowance to find the estimated difference. Invite volunteers to tell the class about their purchasing decisions and share their calculations. Point out that rounded numbers can make calculations easier. Then continue the activity with different allowances. Shop on!

| Allowance | Book Price | Rounded Price | Estimated Difference |
|---|---|---|---|
| $3.00 | $1.80 | $2.00 | $3.00 – $2.00 = $1.00 |
|  |  |  |  |
|  |  |  |  |
|  |  |  |  |
|  |  |  |  |

# Register Roundup

Look at each pair of price tags.
To estimate each total, round each price to the nearest ten dollars. Add.
Find the total closest to your estimate. Write it on the register.

| Totals | |
|---|---|
| $67 | $79 |
| $59 | $94 |
| $44 | $51 |

1.

$32
$12

$ ___ ___
+ ___
$ ___ ___

2.

$17
$62

$ ___ ___
+ ___
$ ___ ___

3.

$73
$21

$ ___ ___
+ ___
$ ___ ___

4.

$18
$49

$ ___ ___
+ ___
$ ___ ___

5.

$13
$38

$ ___ ___
+ ___
$ ___ ___

6.

$11
$48

$ ___ ___
+ ___
$ ___ ___

**Bonus Box:** Henry Hippo buys sneakers for $49 and slippers for $13. About how much does he spend in all? On the back of this sheet, round the prices to the nearest ten dollars and add to find the answer.

©The Education Center, Inc. • *THE MAILBOX* • *Primary* • Oct/Nov 2003 • Key p. 312

**Note to the teacher:** Use with "Within Reason" on page 205.

# Playing Up Math Facts

Looking for a kid-pleasing way to reinforce basic facts? Win students over with this collection of math games!

*ideas contributed by Laura Wagner, Raleigh, NC*

## Dandy Dominoes

**Skill:** addition or multiplication    **Players:** two

**Materials:** small gift bag containing a set of double-six dominoes (tiles with blank sections removed)

**Preparation:** Explain to students that two matching dominoes have the same number of dots in one of their sections. For example, 6–4 matches 1–4 because each has a section with four dots.

**Directions:**

1. Each player takes six dominoes at random and then stands them so that the dots are not visible to the other player. Player 1 takes an additional domino and lays it faceup on the playing surface.

2. Player 1 checks her dominoes for one that matches the displayed domino. If she doesn't have one, she takes a domino from the bag. If she has or gets a match, she uses the numbers represented on her domino to state an addition or multiplication fact; then she places her domino. If she has no match, her turn is over.

3. The next player takes a turn in a similar manner, trying to match a tile to a section at one end of the domino display as shown.

4. Alternate play continues. The winner is the first player to place all her dominoes or the player with fewer dominoes when no more matches can be made.

Ten minus six equals four.

## Take It Away!

**Skill:** subtraction    **Players:** two

**Materials:** 4 Ping-Pong balls, eight 8-oz. disposable cups, paper lunch bag, permanent marker

**Preparation:** Number the Ping-Pong balls from 5 to 8 and then place them in a paper lunch bag. Number the bottoms of the cups from 8 to 15.

**Directions:**

1. The players stand the cups in a row. Each player randomly takes a ball and drops it into a different cup. Each player, in turn, identifies the numbers on his cup and Ping-Pong ball and then announces the difference.

2. Both players return their balls to the bag. The player with the larger difference keeps his cup and the other player returns his. If the differences are the same, both players return their cups.

3. The players rearrange the cups and continue play. The first player to collect four cups wins.

# Clear the Cards

**Skill:** addition    **Players:** two to four
**Materials:** playing cards (tens, jokers, and face cards removed), pair of dice
**Directions:**

1. One player deals five cards faceup to each player, including himself. He stacks the remaining cards facedown.
2. To take a turn, a player rolls the dice and announces the sum. If possible, he places in a discard pile one or two cards that equal the sum (ace equals one). If he does not have an appropriate card, he draws a card from the deck. If possible, he plays the card as described. Otherwise, his turn is over.
3. Players alternate turns until one player discards all of his cards and is declared the winner.

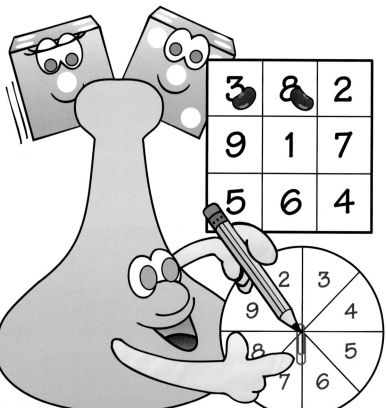

## Spin to Win!

**Skill:** addition or multiplication    **Players:** two
**Materials:** kidney beans, tagboard circle (spinner) visually divided into 8 sections numbered from 2 to 9, paper clip, pencil, two 3 x 3 grids, paper for keeping score
**Preparation:** Each player randomly labels his grid spaces with the numbers from 1 to 9.
**Directions:**

1. Each player places a bean on her top left grid space. Each player, in turn, uses the paper clip and a pencil to spin the spinner. She announces the sum (or product) of the number and the number marked on her grid.
2. The player who has the greater sum earns one point. If the sums are equal, each player earns one point.
3. Each player then places a bean on her next square and spins the spinner. Play continues, with players adding beans to move across the rest of the grid from left to right.
4. The top-scoring player wins.

## The Name of the Game

After students have become familiar with a variety of math games, why not have them create their own? Set out chosen gameboards for inspiration. Provide access to appropriate materials such as markers, dice, spinners, playing cards, blank cards, and tagboard sheets. Guide each student to create a basic facts game, encouraging him to test his game and revise it as needed. Then give him a copy of the game form on page 209. Have him write the name of his game in the top box and complete the rest of the form as indicated. After each student completes his game preparations, set aside time for students to try their classmates' games. Then collect the games. Each week, place two or more games and the corresponding forms at a math center. Play on!

pam crane

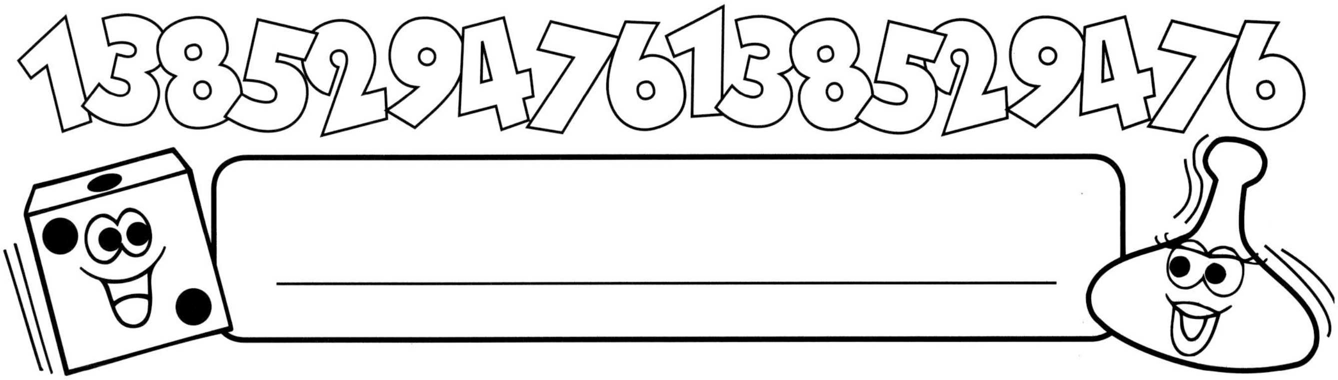

13852947613852947 6

_____

**Number of players:** _____

**Materials:** _____

_____

**How to play:** _____

_____

_____

_____

_____

_____

_____

_____

_____

By _____

# FAR-OUT CALCULATOR IDEAS

Propel students into a galaxy of cool calculations with these stellar suggestions!

*ideas contributed by Starin Lewis, Phoenix, AZ*

## What's Missing?
### *Exploring addition and subtraction*

Tap into your youngsters' reasoning skills with these puzzling equations! Write on the board an addition or subtraction sentence, substituting a box for the operation sign or one of the first two numbers. Encourage students to study the equation and silently guess what is missing. Have each youngster use a calculator to test his guess. If his guess is correct, he gives a thumbs-up sign. If it is not correct, he tries another guess. After an appropriate amount of time, ask a volunteer to complete the number sentence on the board. Then present a desired number of additional problems for students to solve in a similar manner.

**For an easier activity,** display complete number sentences on the board, some with correct answers and some with incorrect answers. Guide students in using their calculators to check them.

$$12 + \boxed{15} = 27$$

## Mystery Number
### *Completing multistep calculations*

Here's an intriguing idea for using calculators step-by-step. Secretly choose a number and write it on a piece of scrap paper. Identify a series of steps that can be performed on a calculator to result in this number. (See the example.) Then challenge students to determine the number, explaining that you will give four directions to help them figure it out. Announce each task, in turn, writing it on the board and allowing time for students to complete it. After inviting students to guess the number, have each youngster press the equal sign key on her calculator. Reveal the number you wrote earlier to confirm the correct answer. Challenge students to determine a few other secret numbers in a similar manner.

To follow up, ask each student to create a similar mystery number problem, writing the steps on the outside of a folded blank card and writing the number inside the card. Invite students to trade their prepared cards and challenge each other to determine the mystery numbers.

### Steps

A.    Start with 12.

B.   (+)   13

C.   (−)   10

D.   (−)   10

Use this class activity to help students feel right at home with calculators. Have each student write on a piece of scrap paper the number of people who live in his home, including himself. Then divide students into small groups. Ask the students in each group to add their numbers with calculators. After the group members agree on the total, instruct them to write it on a large blank card. Next, have a student from one group tape his group's card to the board. Write an addition symbol after it. As the remaining groups add their cards to the board, insert the appropriate symbols to create a horizontal addition problem. Invite students to guess the sum. Then slowly read aloud the problem and have them solve it with their calculators.

## Patterns Plus!
*Identifying patterns*

This partner game sets students' sights on number patterns. Each twosome needs one calculator and a sheet of paper. Partner 1 divides the paper into two columns. He titles the first column "2" and the second column "4." Partner 2 uses the calculator to add two plus two. She announces the sum, keeping it displayed on the calculator. Partner 1 writes the sum in the first column. Then he uses the calculator to add two more. He announces this sum, and Partner 2 writes it below the first sum. The partners continue taking turns adding and recording until they write at least ten sums. Next, they study the sums to identify a pattern. They write the pattern on the back of their paper. Then they repeat the activity with the number 4.

After each twosome completes its work, have the partners use their calculator to experiment with repeated addition problems for the numbers 2 and 4, such as 2 + 2 + 2 + 2 =. Encourage them to compare their results with the sums that they recorded earlier. Cool!

## Pleasing Purchases
*Adding money amounts*

When it's time to shop, a calculator can sure come in handy! Collect a supply of discarded sales circulars or catalogs. Set them out along with a supply of paper, scissors, and glue. Divide students into groups to share these resources and give each youngster a length of adding machine tape. Next, each student cuts a designated number of items from the ads or catalogs, being sure to cut out the prices as well. After she glues them on her paper, she writes the prices on her adding machine tape to set up a vertical addition problem. She uses a calculator to determine the sum and staples her resulting receipt to her paper. Now that's a bargain of a math idea!

$2.79
2.49
.99
+ 3.49

# Counting on the 100th Day of School!

Use these festive ideas to celebrate the 100th day of school, and math reinforcement will be a "shear" delight!

...80, 90, 100!

## Impressive Collections

*Representing 100 with concrete objects, skip-counting*

The 100th day of school calls for counting possibilities by the hundreds! A few days in advance, give each youngster a copy of the poem on page 214 and read it aloud. Guide students to brainstorm 100 similar items that they might find at home, such as paper clips or cereal pieces. Then have each youngster cut out his poem and glue it onto a personalized paper lunch bag. Ask him to use the bag to bring in a collection of 100 items.

On the designated day, have each student use a large sheet of construction paper to display his collection on his desk or another work surface. Invite students to walk along an established classroom path to view their classmates' collections. Next, instruct each student to arrange and count his items in sets of ten. Ask him to repeat the process with sets of five. So that's what 100 looks like!

Molly Peters
St. Lucie Elementary
Fort Pierce, FL

## Counting Sheep

*Using number order and number patterns*

Counting sheep has new meaning with this woolly hundred chart! Post a large piece of bulletin board paper within student reach. Copy the patterns on page 214 to make 100 sheep and distribute them to students. After the youngsters color the hats and cut out the cards, help them glue the sheep onto the paper in ten rows of ten. Then lead students in counting the sheep by tens.

To follow up, use a colorful marker to label the first sheep "1" and the last sheep "100." Number a selected sheep in each remaining row. Label several sticky notes with other numbers between 1 and 100. Give a volunteer a sticky note; then have her read the number aloud and adhere it to the appropriate sheep. Ask her to explain her strategy for determining the correct placement, such as counting back or using a number pattern. Invite the other students to identify different strategies. Continue with the remaining sticky notes in a similar manner. For additional reinforcement, arrange for the display to be a learning center option.

adapted from an idea by Sheli Funderburk
Grant Elementary
East Wenatchee, WA

# 100 Hearts
## *Representing 100*

This 100th day idea can double as a Valentine's Day display. With students' help, determine how the class will share the responsibility of using several templates to make 100 identical construction paper hearts. Once a plan is made, ask the youngsters to complete the task. Then use a similar plan to have students label the hearts with things or activities that they like. Have students glue the prepared hearts onto a jumbo heart-shaped wreath that you have cut from bulletin board paper. Display the wreath with a desired title for the 100th day and plan to update the title for Valentine's Day. Not only will the wreath represent 100, but it will also be an eye-catching reminder of the value of teamwork!

adapted from an idea by Alicia Nannetti
Milton Elementary
Milton, NY

# A Day to Celebrate!

There's no doubt about it—the 100th day of school is cause for celebration! To recognize the day in grand style, present each youngster with a copy of the badge on page 214 to color, cut out, and wear. Use one or more of the activities below to make math time extra special. Then, for a sweet finale, invite each youngster to prepare a snack by using a tube of decorating gel to label a cupcake or cookie "100."

- **…98, 99, 100!** Challenge groups of students to create posters for the day's events. The catch? Each poster needs to have 100 letters, words, or illustrations! *Counting to 100*

- **More or Less?** In each of four clear plastic containers, place a quantity of items that is more or less than 100. Letter each jar. Then have each child complete an estimation form similar to the one shown. Ask volunteers to count the items and announce the actual counts. *Estimating*

- **Tens Mystery** Program large blank cards by tens from 10 to 100. Randomly give the cards to ten students and ask them to line up in numerical order. Next, have the seated students cover their eyes. Silently signal one cardholder to step aside and conceal her number. Then ask the seated students to study the remaining cardholders and guess the missing number. To reveal the answer, have the chosen cardholder return to her position and display her number. Continue with different numbers and volunteers as time allows. *Using number patterns*

| 100th Day Estimates | | |
|---|---|---|
| Jar | Estimate | More or Less Than 100? |
| A | | |
| B | | |
| C | | |
| D | | |

## Poem and Patterns

Use the poem with "Impressive Collections" on page 212.

Use the badge with "A Day to Celebrate!" on page 213.

# Hooray for 100!

Check out the calendar.
What does it say?
It's almost time for the
    100th day!

Now take a look around
And try to find
100 things of just one kind.

Put the things in the bag—
Every last one.
Then bring them to school for
    counting fun!

©The Education Center, Inc. • *THE MAILBOX®* • *Primary* • Dec/Jan 2003–4

Use the sheep with "Counting Sheep" on page 212.

©The Education Center, Inc. • *THE MAILBOX®* • *Primary* • Dec/Jan 2003–4

# Tempting Multiplication

**Sweeten students' understanding of multiplication with these tantalizing ideas!**

*ideas contributed by Laura Wagner, Raleigh, NC*

## Group Solutions

### Skill: modeling multiplication with equal groups

Grouping manipulatives is an irresistible strategy for solving these problems! Divide students into small groups. Give each group five mini baking cups and a sheet of paper for each student. Also provide each group with a resealable plastic bag containing a large handful of kidney beans to represent jelly beans. To begin, pose a jelly bean–related problem that can be solved by grouping the manipulatives. For example, you might say, "There are three friends. Each friend has four jelly beans. How many jelly beans are there in all?" Have the students model the problem with their manipulatives and then write the solution.

Next, ask a volunteer to announce the correct answer. Guide students to identify the appropriate multiplication fact; have each youngster write it on his paper. Present additional problems for students to solve in a similar manner. To follow up, have each youngster complete a copy of page 217 and, if desired, give him a few jelly beans to enjoy.

## Picture a Product

### Skill: using pictures to solve multiplication problems

Help students get a clear picture of what it means to multiply. Give each youngster two 9" x 12" sheets of construction paper (one white and one light-colored), scissors, crayons, and glue. Use the directions below to help her create multiplication window scenes. Then have her trade projects with a classmate. Encourage each youngster to solve her classmate's problems mentally before opening the windows to check her answers. Now that's an idea worth looking into!

**Directions:**
1. Fold the sheet of colored paper in half twice (to 4½" x 6"). Fold it in half again (to 3" x 4½").
2. Make two cuts as shown, beginning at the folded edge and stopping about one inch from the opposite edge.
3. Unfold the paper once. To make windows, cut along the crease of the middle section only.
4. Completely unfold the paper. Glue it onto the white paper so that the windows are open.
5. In each window, illustrate groups of objects. Write the related multiplication fact.
6. Close each window. Write the corresponding multiplication problem on the flaps. Illustrate curtains.

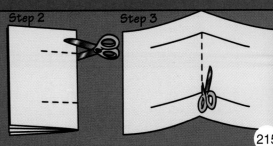

## Flavorful Facts
### Skill: relating addition to multiplication

Button up math skills with this delectable idea! Cut strips of Candy Button candies into various lengths to make a class supply of arrays that have three or four rows. (If desired, set aside additional candy for a later student treat.) Instruct each student to position his strip vertically. On scrap paper, have him add the number of candies in each row and then write the related multiplication fact. Ask volunteers to read aloud their number sentences.

For additional reinforcement, give each youngster a length of adding machine tape. Have him illustrate two or three candy button arrays, leaving a generous amount of space between them. Below each array, instruct him to write the appropriate addition and multiplication facts. Display students' work on a bulletin board titled "Mouthwatering Math."

Barbara J. Meigh
Old Bridge, NJ

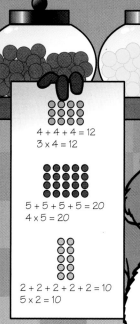

$$4 + 4 + 4 = 12$$
$$3 \times 4 = 12$$

$$5 + 5 + 5 + 5 = 20$$
$$4 \times 5 = 20$$

$$2 + 2 + 2 + 2 + 2 = 10$$
$$5 \times 2 = 10$$

## Color by Number
### Skill: modeling multiplication with arrays

This partner game provides an array of multiplication practice!

**Materials for two players:** two dice, crayons (including black), two 10 x 10 grids, a multiplication table for checking facts as needed

**Directions:**
1. To take a turn, a player rolls the dice. He uses a color other than black to color a corresponding grid array. For example, if he rolls a two and a four, he colors an array that is two spaces by four spaces or one that is four spaces by two spaces. Then he uses a black crayon or a pencil to label it with the appropriate multiplication fact.
   - If he rolls doubles, he may color the corresponding array or just one grid space.
   - If he rolls factors for an array that will not fit on his grid, his turn is over.
2. Players alternate turns. The game continues for an allotted time or until one player colors all of his grid spaces. The player who colors more spaces wins.

## Multiply to Win!
### Skill: reviewing multiplication facts

Here's a fact-review game that suits the whole class! Divide students into four teams. Give each team a multiplication table and a deck of playing cards (face cards and jokers removed). Have the team stack its cards facedown.

To begin, a member of each team takes its top two cards and shows them to her teammates (ace represents one). The team members work together to determine the product of the numbers, using their multiplication table to check their answer, if needed. Then each team, in turn, states its multiplication fact. Award the team with the greatest correct product one point. (If there is a tie, award each of those teams one point.) Play continues until all the cards have been drawn. The top-scoring team wins.

Name _____

# Candy Count

For each box, study the candies.
Fill in the blanks to tell about the groups.
Complete the multiplication sentence.

---

a.

____ groups of ____ = ____

____ x ____ = ____

b.
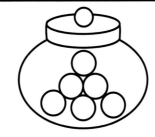

____ group of ____ = ____

____ x ____ = ____

c.
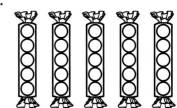

____ groups of ____ = ____

____ x ____ = ____

---

d.
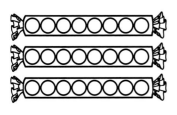

____ groups of ____ = ____

____ x ____ = ____

e.

____ groups of ____ = ____

____ x ____ = ____

f.
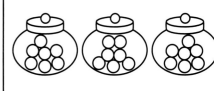

____ groups of ____ = ____

____ x ____ = ____

---

Look at each candy bar. Write the multiplication sentence for the array.

g.

____ x ____ = ____

h.
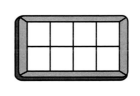

____ x ____ = ____

i.
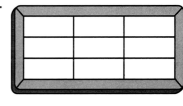

____ x ____ = ____

---

**Bonus Box:** Draw another candy bar on the back of this sheet. Write the multiplication sentence for the array.

## Exploring Probability

Unleash a better understanding of probability with these "paws-itively" kid-pleasing ideas!

*ideas contributed by Linda Masternak Justice, Kansas City, MO*

## Chances Are...

**Skill: understanding the likelihood of events**

Dig into the topic of probability with an exploration of "pet-acular" events. To prepare, use lengths of yarn to divide a bulletin board into four sections. Add the title "Pet Possibilities." Then label one section with each of these categories: "certain," "likely," "unlikely," and "impossible." To clarify the meaning of each term, read aloud each event shown and have students identify the word that describes the probability of the event.

Next, have each youngster illustrate a pet-related event of her choosing and write a caption for it. Ask her to share her work with the class and help her post it in the correct section of the board. After each youngster contributes to the display, prompt students to provide examples for any terms that are not represented.

**Events**

My cat will take a nap today. *(certain)*
A dog will bark at a stranger. *(likely)*
My old cat will chase a ball of yarn. *(unlikely)*
A fish will sit up and beg. *(impossible)*

Hi!

Impossible!

I heard a cat talk.

Name __Henry__

I predict that ___a cat___ will be rolled most often.

| Pet | Tally Marks |
|-----|-------------|
| cat | 卌 II |
| dog | III |
| hamster | I |

## Pet Predictions

**Skills: predicting and interpreting outcomes**

When it comes to improving prediction skills, this dice activity gives favorable odds! Give each child a copy of the die pattern on page 220. Guide students to notice that there are more dogs than cats and that there is only one hamster. Have each youngster color his pattern and cut it out. Tell him to fold the pattern on the thin lines and use tape to assemble his die.

Next, give each student a recording sheet similar to the one above and ask him to write his prediction in the provided space. At your signal, have each child roll his die and make a tally mark to record the outcome. Repeat this process until he has rolled a total of 20 times. Then poll students to determine which type of animal each youngster rolled most often. Prompt a class discussion to compare the results with students' predictions. What fur-raising fun!

# Pick a Pet!

**Skill: identifying possible outcomes**

With this partner activity, it's certain that learning fun is in the cards. On the board, list three types of pets, such as cats, rabbits, and dogs. Give each partner four paper rectangles the size of playing cards. Have him illustrate and label an example of a listed animal on each rectangle. (He does not need to illustrate the same animal on each one.) Ask the partners to combine their resulting cards. Guide the partners to consider the likelihood of randomly selecting a card that has a chosen pet or a pet with a characteristic such as feathers. On a provided sheet of paper, ask them to write an outcome that is certain, one that is likely, one that is unlikely, and one that is impossible.

Next, the partners list the numbers 1 to 20 on the back of their paper. Partner 1 scrambles the cards and spreads them facedown. Partner 2 randomly takes a card. After Partner 1 writes the name of the pet beside the appropriate number, Partner 2 mixes the card back in with the others. The partners switch roles and continue for a total of 20 trials. They compare the results with the outcomes that they identified earlier. Interesting!

# Taking a Spin

**Skill: conducting a probability experiment**

This spinner experiment is the cat's meow! Give each student a small paper clip and a copy of page 221. Demonstrate how to spin the spinner with a paper clip and pencil. Have each child follow the directions to complete his sheet. Then discuss the results as a class. Lead students to conclude that since the yarn section of the spinner is the largest, the spinner is most likely to stop on it. "Purr-fect" understanding is guaranteed!

# Doggy Bag

**Skill: identifying the probability of an event**

Here's a great way to help students bone up on determining probability! Each student traces a bone cutout (approximately 2" x 4") eight times on a 9" x 12" sheet of white paper. He uses two different crayons to color the bones so that there is an unequal number of bones for each color. Then he cuts out the bones.

On a chart similar to the one shown, the youngster writes the two colors. He indicates the probability of randomly selecting each color bone and draws an X in the appropriate box in the third column. Next, he places his bones in a small paper lunch bag. He takes one bone at random, makes a tally mark on his chart, and returns the bone to the bag. He repeats this process until he has 20 tally marks. Then he writes the totals and analyzes his data.

Name _Rex_

| Color | Probability | More Likely to Be Picked | Tally Marks | Total |
|-------|-------------|--------------------------|-------------|-------|
| green | _5_ chances out of 8 | X | III | |
| blue | _3_ chances out of 8 | | I | |

Name______________________________________________



# Toying With Probability

On which toy will Chester's spinner stop?

## Predict

Circle the toy on which the spinner is *most likely* to stop.

yarn mouse ball

Circle the toy on which the spinner is *least likely* to stop.

yarn mouse ball

## Test

Spin the spinner. If it stops on a line, spin again.
Color a box on the chart to show the type of toy.
Spin and color again until you have colored 20 boxes.

| | | | | | | | | | | | | | | | | | | | | |
|---|---|---|---|---|---|---|---|---|---|---|---|---|---|---|---|---|---|---|---|---|
|  | | | | | | | | | | | | | | | | | | | | |
|  | | | | | | | | | | | | | | | | | | | | |
|  | | | | | | | | | | | | | | | | | | | | |

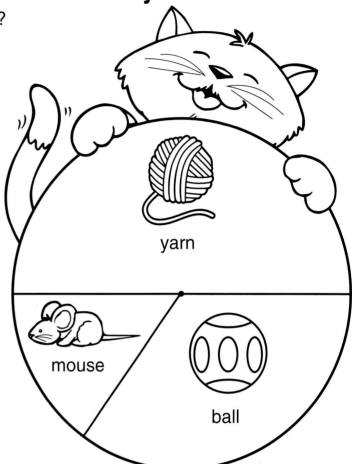

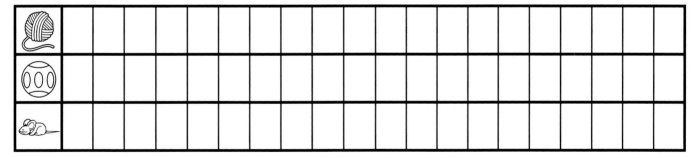

## Think

On which toy did the spinner stop most often? ______________________

Tell why you think this happened. ______________________

______________________________________________

**Bonus Box:** Choose two of the cat toys. On the back of this paper, draw a spinner that makes it *equally likely* for the spinner to stop on each toy. Test your spinner.



**Note to the teacher:** Use with "Taking a Spin" on page 219.

# Scoring With Multiplication and Division

When it comes to helping students meet the challenges of multiplication and division, these skill-boosting games are winners!

*ideas contributed by Starin Lewis, Phoenix, AZ*

## It's All Related

Students make the **connection between multiplication and division** during this fact-filled game!

**Preparation:** Establish teams of about five students each. Give each team an equal number of multiplication flash cards so that each student has at least one card. Have each team stack its cards facedown. For scorekeeping, write assigned team letters on the board.

**Directions:**

1. One player from the first team takes his team's top card. He reads the problem aloud and states the answer. If he is correct, his team earns one point. If he is not, his teammates supply the correct answer and no point is awarded.
2. The player states a related division fact for a second opportunity to earn a point.
3. One player from each remaining team takes a turn in a similar manner to complete the first round.
4. The game continues until all of the cards have been played. The top-scoring team wins.

## Just the Facts

Try this winning approach to **fact family** practice!

**Preparation:** Divide youngsters into teams of four (forming teams of three as needed). List chosen team names on the board for scorekeeping.

**Directions:**

1. Write two different digits on the board. Have the first player from Team 1 state a multiplication or division fact that includes the digits.
2. Write the fact on the board if it is correct and award the team one point. If it is not correct, write nothing.
3. Ask each remaining player on the team to use the digits to state a different fact from the same fact family. Award one point per fact. (For a team of three, have one player state two facts.)
4. When Team 1's turn is over, invite the next team to state any facts that Team 1 missed for one point per fact.
5. Erase the board and write two different digits to start a new round. Begin with the first player from Team 2 to play as described. Continue in this manner for a desired number of rounds. The team with the most points wins!

12 ÷ 3 = 4

12 ÷ 4 = 3

# Picture This!

With this game, players **represent facts with drawings** to get a clear picture of division.

**Preparation:** Sketch on the board the illustrations shown; guide students to identify the division facts represented. Divide students into an even number of pairs (or trios); then form groups with two pairs (or trios) in each group. Give each group a supply of drawing paper and 11 index cards. Post 11 chosen division facts. Have each group program one card for each fact and then shuffle the cards and stack them facedown.

**Directions:**

1. One player takes her group's top card; she keeps the fact from her original partner's view as she illustrates it. Then she displays her illustration. If her partner correctly identifies the fact represented, she keeps the card. Otherwise, she puts it in a discard pile.

2. The other pair in the group takes a turn in a similar manner.

3. Alternate play continues until the group uses all but one fact card. The pair with more cards wins. If there is a tie, one player from each pair in the group illustrates the remaining fact; the players display their illustrations for their partners at the same time. The pair with the partner who first identifies the fact wins the game.

# Three in a Row

Line up a review of **multiplication and division facts!**

**Preparation:** Draw a large 3 x 3 grid on the board and program the spaces with names of familiar book characters. Have each student color one side of a blank card green and the other side red. Divide the students into two teams.

**Directions:**

1. On the board, write an equation with either a correct or an incorrect answer. (To avoid later repetition, keep a running list of equations on a sheet of paper.)

2. Have each member of Team 1 display her card to judge the equation as true (green) or false (red). If most of the team members judge the equation correctly, draw an X in a team-selected space. If most of them do not, discuss the correct response. Change the answer on the board if it is incorrect.

3. Have Team 2 take a turn in a similar manner; use an O to indicate an earned space.

4. Alternate play continues until three spaces are marked in a horizontal, vertical, or diagonal row; the corresponding team earns one point.

5. Erase the Xs and Os to prepare for a new round. The team with more points after a desired number of rounds wins.

We'll take Ramona for the win!

Pam

4 x 6 = ~~10~~  24

6 x 3 = 18

21 ÷ 7 = ~~5~~  3

32 ÷ 4 = 8

20 ÷ 5 = ~~5~~  4

223

# It's Game Time!

Use the multiplication chart to complete each set of facts.
The first one has been done for you.

| x | 0 | 1 | 2 | 3 | 4 | 5 | 6 | 7 | 8 | 9 |
|---|---|---|---|---|---|---|---|---|---|---|
| 0 | 0 | 0 | 0 | 0 | 0 | 0 | 0 | 0 | 0 | 0 |
| 1 | 0 | 1 | 2 | 3 | 4 | 5 | 6 | 7 | 8 | 9 |
| 2 | 0 | 2 | 4 | 6 | 8 | 10 | 12 | 14 | 16 | 18 |
| 3 | 0 | 3 | 6 | 9 | 12 | 15 | 18 | 21 | 24 | 27 |
| 4 | 0 | 4 | 8 | 12 | 16 | 20 | 24 | 28 | 32 | 36 |
| 5 | 0 | 5 | 10 | 15 | 20 | 25 | 30 | 35 | 40 | 45 |
| 6 | 0 | 6 | 12 | 18 | 24 | 30 | 36 | 42 | 48 | 54 |
| 7 | 0 | 7 | 14 | 21 | 28 | 35 | 42 | 49 | 56 | 63 |
| 8 | 0 | 8 | 16 | 24 | 32 | 40 | 48 | 56 | 64 | 72 |
| 9 | 0 | 9 | 18 | 27 | 36 | 45 | 54 | 63 | 72 | 81 |

X ÷ X ÷ X ÷ X ÷

**Bonus Box:** Choose three products from the chart. For each product, write a multiplication fact and a related division fact on the back of this sheet.

A.  2 x 6 = __12__

 __12__ ÷ 2 = __6__

B.  10 x 3 = _____

 _____ ÷ 10 = ____

C.  5 x 3 = _____

 _____ ÷ 5 = _____

D.  5 x 9 = _____

 _____ ÷ 5 = _____

E.  6 x 4 = _____

 _____ ÷ 6 = ____

F.  4 x 9 = _____

 _____ ÷ 4 = ____

G.  6 x 7 = _____

 _____ ÷ 6 = _____

H.  7 x 8 = _____

 _____ ÷ 7 = _____

I.  3 x 9 = _____

 _____ ÷ 3 = _____

J.  5 x 6 = _____

 _____ ÷ 5 = _____

K.  8 x 9 = _____

 _____ ÷ 9 = _____

# High-Flying Fractions

Take students' understanding of fractions to new heights with the following ideas!

*ideas contributed by Starin Lewis, Phoenix, AZ*

## On the Whole
*Identifying equal parts of a whole*

Breeze into a study of fractions with this sky-high look at equal parts. Comment to students that fractions can be found in many places—even the sky. To demonstrate, draw a square kite on the board and divide it into four equal parts. Label each fractional part with students' help. Provide additional examples as appropriate; then have students make their own fraction kites.

To do this, each student needs a 12" x 18" sheet of blue construction paper, three four-inch paper squares in colors other than blue, scissors, and glue. With teacher assistance as needed, he folds one square in half, one square into thirds, and one square into fourths. He unfolds the squares and traces the fold lines. Next, he turns each square so that a corner is at the top and then labels each fractional part. After he positions the paper horizontally, he glues on the squares, leaving writing space above them. Then he writes the headings shown and draws kite tails. After students complete their projects, point out that the larger the denominator, the smaller the fractional part.

## Stamped Sets
*Identifying fractional parts of a set*

At this center, student-created sets earn a stamp of approval! Stock the center with a small rubber stamp, two different-colored stamp pads, paper, and pencils. A student folds her paper in half twice, unfolds it, and then traces the fold lines. In each resulting section, she uses both ink pads to stamp a desired number of images. Then she identifies the fractions for the colorful sets in each section.

## Fractional Stacks
*Modeling fractions*

Unifix cubes can make understanding fractions a snap! Pair students and give each twosome a sheet of paper, four cubes of one color, and four cubes of another color. To begin, announce a fraction. Have each twosome connect selected cubes to represent it and then hold up the resulting stack. Invite each of several partners to point out the designated fractional part in his stack. Repeat the process with a different fraction. To check understanding, instruct each twosome to illustrate three stacks of different cube combinations and label the illustrations with the fractional amounts.

225

## Please Stand Up!
*Representing fractions*

Students stand up to be counted during this fraction-identification activity! Have students sit on the floor in groups of five or less. Identify a characteristic that applies to at least one student in each group and pose a fraction-related question about it. (See the sample questions.) Ask each student who can answer "yes" to stand.

To represent his group's fraction, each student holds up the fingers on his left hand to show how many students are standing and the fingers on his right hand to show the total number of students. Then he positions his left hand above his right hand. After each student displays his response, invite each group to announce its fraction. Continue with a desired number of different questions. Now that's math practice that stands out from the rest!

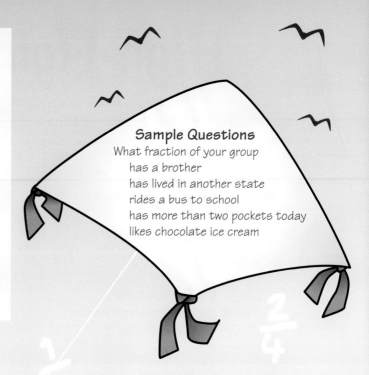

**Sample Questions**
What fraction of your group
   has a brother
   has lived in another state
   rides a bus to school
   has more than two pockets today
   likes chocolate ice cream

## Windy-Day Fractions
*Identifying fractional parts of a set*

The sky's the limit with this fraction display idea! To make a kite illustration, each student colors a 3 x 3 grid of one-inch squares in a two-color design (one color per square). She trims a 6" x 9" piece of white paper to make a cloud. She labels the cloud with the fractional amount of each grid color and then glues on her kite. Post students' work on a paper-covered bulletin board titled "Fractions in Flight!" Draw kite strings to complete the high-flying display.

## Pizza Problems
*Adding and subtracting fractions*

Serve up this tempting strategy for adding and subtracting fractions. Pair students and give each twosome two white paper plates, a sheet of paper, scissors, and crayons. The partners illustrate one plate to resemble a pizza. One partner folds the decorated plate in half three times, firmly creasing the folds. He unfolds the plate and cuts along the fold lines to make eight slices.

Next, have one partner write "$\frac{1}{8} + \frac{3}{8} =$" on his paper. Instruct the partners to solve the problem by arranging the appropriate number of pizza slices on their plate. After they write the sum, confirm the correct answer. Have students solve several addition problems in this manner; then help them use a similar process to subtract fractions. Lead them to realize that the denominators stay the same because the number of pizza slices that can fit on the plate does not change. What a mouthwatering way to solve problems!

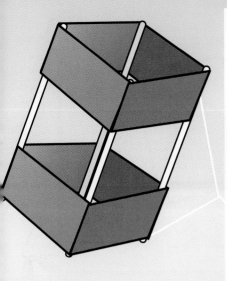

# Kite Comparison
*Comparing fractions with like denominators*

Here's a fraction game that's beyond compare! Give each student a copy of page 228 and ask him to color the correct fractional part for each kite. Have him cut out the cards and initial the back of each one for easy identification. Invite pairs of students to use the directions below to play.

**Directions:**
1. Each player shuffles his cards and stacks them facedown. He flips over his top card.
2. Players compare their cards. If the fractions are not equivalent, the player who has the larger fraction takes both cards. If they are equivalent, each player flips his next card. The player who has the larger fraction takes all of the cards played during the turn. (If there are no cards left to flip, each player takes his own cards.)
3. The game continues until there are no cards left in the stacks. The player with more cards wins.

# Fabulous Fraction Day
*Reviewing fractions*

Plan a special day to review fraction "fun-damentals!" To announce the event to students, copy a message similar to the one shown so that half of a class supply is on one color of paper and half is on another color. Cut the copies in half. Give each student two different-colored halves and ask her to tape them together to reveal the message. After students read it, clarify that they are encouraged to wear clothing that represents chosen fractions. Also suggest that each youngster bring in a parent-approved item that bears a fraction; name examples such as a canned food label or a measuring cup. On the designated day, use two or more of the ideas shown. To wrap up the celebration, give each student a serving of assorted small crackers and have her identify the fractional part of each variety.

Nancy L. Mullins—Gr. 3
Gordon Elementary School
Kingston, W

**Fraction Showcase:** After students present their items from home to the class, display the items by chosen categories.

**Fraction Fashion:** Have youngsters challenge their classmates to identify the fractions that their outfits represent.

**Letter by Letter:** For each of several spelling words, instruct students to determine the fractional parts of vowels and consonants.

**Picturing Fractions:** Invite each student to create a fraction-related illustration and write a caption to identify each fractional amount.

# Game Cards

Use with "Kite Comparison" on page 227.

$\dfrac{1}{8}$

$\dfrac{2}{8}$

$\dfrac{3}{8}$

$\dfrac{4}{8}$

$\dfrac{1}{8}$

$\dfrac{2}{8}$

$\dfrac{3}{8}$

$\dfrac{4}{8}$

$\dfrac{5}{8}$

$\dfrac{6}{8}$

$\dfrac{7}{8}$

Name _____

# Up, Up, and Away!

Look at each kite.
Count the parts. Write the denominator.
Color to show the fraction.

The **denominator** is the bottom number of a fraction.

a. $\frac{1}{\square}$

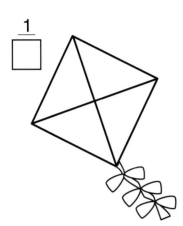

b. $\frac{1}{\square}$

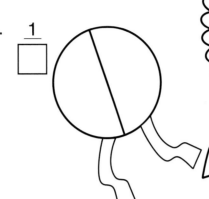

c. $\frac{1}{\square}$

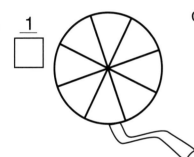

d. $\frac{1}{\square}$

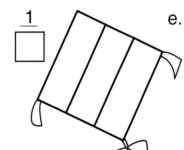

e. $\frac{2}{\square}$

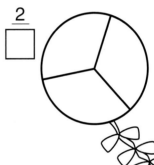

f. $\frac{2}{\square}$

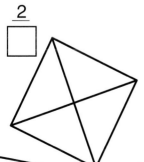

g. $\frac{3}{\square}$

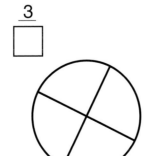

h. $\frac{4}{\square}$

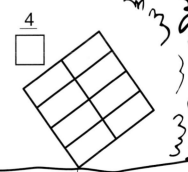

**Note to the teacher:** Use after students are familiar with identifying and writing fractions.

# Shoring Up Math Skills

Make a math review oceans of fun with these hands-on ideas and kid-pleasing skill sheets!

*ideas contributed by Leigh Anne Rhodes—Gr. 2, Victory Academy, Baton Rouge, LA*

## Sunny Solutions

*Completing basic addition and subtraction facts*

Students' addition and subtraction skills are bound to shine at this partner center. Prepare several eight-inch yellow construction paper circles (suns). Along the edge of each circle, write six basic facts, each with a missing addend or subtrahend. (See the illustration.) Place the circles and a generous supply of math links or interlocking cubes at a center stocked with paper.

A student pair selects a prepared circle. One student reads a chosen problem aloud, and each youngster writes it on his paper. Then the students use the manipulatives to determine the solution, arranging the final quantity of manipulatives beside the problem to resemble a ray of sunshine. After each student writes the answer on his paper, the twosome solves the remaining problems in a similar manner. What a bright way to practice basic facts!

## Clever Calculations

*Identifying equivalent forms of a number*

What's in a number? Lots of beach-themed possibilities! Label a separate blank card for each number from 12 through 20; place the cards in a sand pail. Invite a student to remove a card at random and read it aloud. Ask each youngster to use manipulatives to determine six different number combinations that equal the number, and have her list them on a sheet of paper.

After each student completes her work, compile a class list of the different combinations. Then ask each youngster to circle on her paper a chosen combination. On the back of her paper, have her illustrate and label a corresponding beach scene. For example, she might show four crabs riding surfboards, four crabs lying in the sun, and four crabs building a sand castle for 4 + 4 + 4. If desired, display students' illustrations on a wall with a poster bearing the featured number. Repeat the activity on each of several days for more picture-perfect math practice.

# Cube Comparisons

### Comparing numbers

Students see how their place-value skills stack up with this partner activity! For each pair of students, prepare eight number cards that are suitable for the youngsters' place-value skills. The students in each twosome also need a supply of interlocking cubes, one sheet of paper, and a book that they can stand between them to shield their work from their partner's view.

On a provided chart, the partners establish a place-value code, similar to the one shown, that corresponds with the colors of their cubes. They position their book and stack their cards facedown. Each student takes one card. He uses the code to model the number with stacks of cubes placed side by side. Then each partner displays his number card, and Partner 1 states which number is greater. The partners remove the book and compare their models to check the answer. They repeat the modeling and comparing process with the remaining cards, taking turns identifying the greater number.

# Sizable Sand Toys

*Estimating and measuring with nonstandard units*
Dig up "sand-sational" measurement practice with the ideas below!

- **Volume:** To establish a benchmark, display a sand pail labeled with the number of cubes it can hold. Set out other pails in various sizes and shapes; letter each one for easy reference. Challenge students to use the benchmark to make reasonable estimates of how many cubes each lettered pail can hold. Then have students determine the actual numbers.

- **Area and Perimeter:** Prepare several lettered sand-toy cutouts for students to share. Each student estimates how many cubes can be arranged on each cutout in a single layer; she writes the number on a recording sheet. She checks her estimate and writes the actual number. After she removes the cubes, she estimates and measures the perimeter of the cutout, writing the corresponding numbers on her recording sheet.

# Stripe Sequence

### Problem solving

This problem is a breeze for small groups to solve with manipulatives. Ask the students in each group to imagine that they design sails for a sailboat company. Explain that they need to determine how many different ways they can sequence three colors to create sails with exactly three horizontal stripes. Give each group a supply of manipulatives in three different colors. Ask the youngsters to use their manipulatives to model each possible sequence of stripes. After each group is satisfied with its work, invite the group members to explain their problem-solving strategy to the class and announce their answer. Guide students to realize that a systematic approach helps ensure that each possible sequence is identified. Then reveal that six different sequences of stripes are possible.

# It's All About Time!

Deliver timely learning fun with the following ideas!

## What a Day!

*Exploring time-related vocabulary*

Explore time morning, noon, and night! Display the day's schedule and review it with students. Then randomly name selected events; have students tell whether they are morning or afternoon activities.

Next, give each student a 6" x 18" strip of white paper. The youngster folds his paper in half twice. Then he unfolds his paper and traces the fold lines to establish four sections. In the first section, he writes "My Day," signs his name, and adds desired illustrations. He titles the remaining sections for the morning, afternoon, and evening as shown. He illustrates an activity in each section, labels it, and then writes the corresponding digital time. **For a more challenging activity,** have each student use a clock stamp to make a clockface in each section and then draw clock hands to show the time. My, how time flies!

| My Day | Morning | Afternoon | Evening |
|---|---|---|---|
| Alberto | Calendar Time 8:00 A.M. | Library 1:30 P.M. | TV 7:00 P.M. |

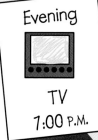
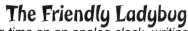

At ___11 o'clock___, the friendly ladybug talked to a grasshopper.

## The Friendly Ladybug

*Showing time on an analog clock, writing the time*

What better way to spark interest in time than with Eric Carle's popular tale *The Grouchy Ladybug*? After a first reading, invite students to use a demonstration clock to show when certain story events occur. Then point out that readers learn a lot about the grouchy ladybug's day, but they don't learn much about how the friendly ladybug passes the time. Announce that each student will share her ideas about the bug's activities in a booklet.

To make a booklet, each student cuts out three or more copies of the booklet page on page 234. She sandwiches them between two 4" x 6" white construction paper rectangles and then staples the stack along the left-hand edge. On each booklet page, she completes the sentence and adds an illustration. She also draws hands on the clockface and writes the digital time below it. After she completes each page, she titles the front cover and signs it. She uses provided arts-and-crafts materials to add a cover illustration. So that's what the friendly ladybug does!

Sister M. Francesca Santacroce—Gr. 1, Saint Michael's School, Hastings, NE

# Spot the Time!
### *Telling time to the half hour*

Cover time to the half hour with this class game! To prepare, each student needs a copy of the gameboard on page 234. He randomly labels the spots with different digital times to the hour and half hour. Then he colors the ladybug, leaving the spots white. He cuts it out and signs the back of it.

After each student prepares his gameboard, give him a handful of counters. To play one round, show a chosen time (hour or half hour) on a demonstration clock. Invite a student to read the clock; write the digital time on the board. If a student has the time on his gameboard, he marks it with a counter. If he does not, he waits for the next displayed time. Continue in this manner until one student marks all of his ladybug spots and calls out "Lucky Ladybug!" After confirming the times that this student marked, declare him the winner. To prepare for another round, have each youngster clear his gameboard and trade it with a neighboring classmate.

adapted from an idea by Linda Edwards
J. T. Barber Elementary School
New Bern, NC

# Springtime Clocks
### *Using a manipulative clock*

Students' time-telling skills are sure to blossom when they use these individual clocks. Have each student use the materials and steps below to make a flower clock. Then guide students to practice various time-related skills with their clocks. For example, announce a time and ask each student to show it on her clock. Or direct students' attention to the classroom clock and have them show the time it will be in 30 minutes. Ticktock!

**Materials for one flower clock:** 5" clockface pattern, 9" x 12" sheet of construction paper, brad, two ½" x 2½" tagboard strips, access to a hole puncher, scissors, glue

**Directions:**
1. Cut out the clockface. Glue it in the center of the construction paper.
2. Draw a blossom around the clockface. Cut it out.
3. Trim the tagboard strips to resemble clock hands (see the illustration). Hole-punch the straight end of each one.
4. Have an adult poke a hole in the center of the clockface. Use the brad to secure the clock hands.

# Booklet Page and Gameboard

Use the booklet page with "The Friendly Ladybug" on page 232.

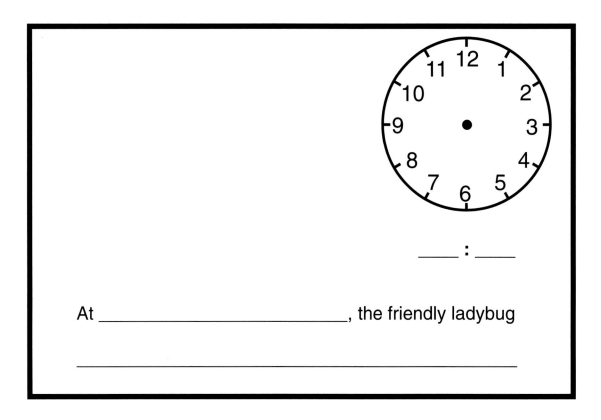

_____ : _____

At _____, the friendly ladybug

_____

Use the gameboard with "Spot the Time!" on page 233.

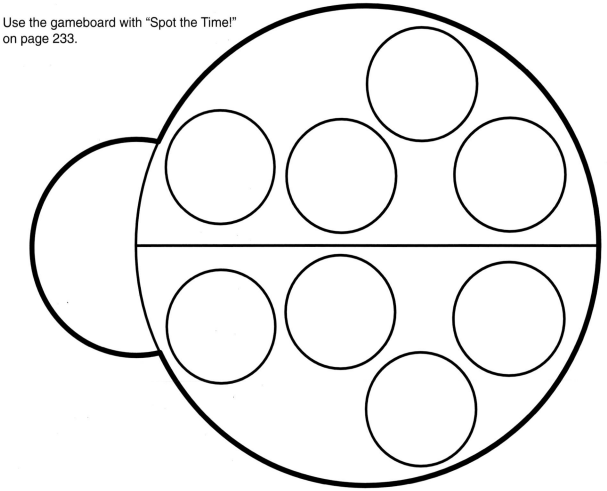

# SCIENCE UNITS

# On the Move!
## Exploring Force and Motion

Begin a study of force and motion at the playground! Use this kid-pleasing setting and the ideas below to familiarize your students with key concepts. Then move on to developing youngsters' investigative skills with the hands-on activities that follow.

*ideas contributed by Julie Hays—Primary Multi-Age, Alcoa Elementary, Alcoa, TN*

### A Moving Melody

Tune students in to the concepts of force and motion! Lead students in singing the provided song one or more times. Discuss each verse to help them understand that forces (pushes and pulls) make things move. Then encourage students to identify the words in the song that describe movements. What a toe-tapping strategy for building on youngsters' background knowledge!

### I'm a Little Playground
*(sung to the tune of "I'm a Little Teapot")*

I'm a little seesaw, long and low.
I move up and down; please help me go.
Take a seat on one end—push me down;
Watch me teeter above the ground.

I'm a little swing seat, small and strong.
I go back and forth; please ride along.
Just give me a good push—help me go;
Hard or easy, swing high or low.

I'm a little gray slide, smooth and bright.
I have a ladder; please hold on tight.
When you're at the top, just let go;
A force brings you down, fast or slow.

| Key Concepts | Playground Examples |
|---|---|
| Motion is moving from place to place. | A student makes a swing move back and forth. |
| Forces can make objects move. | A student throws a ball to a friend. |
| Pushes and pulls are forces. | One student pushes a wagon and another student pulls it. |
| Gravity is a force that pulls objects down. | A student goes down the slide. |
| The greater the force, the more something moves. | A student kicks a ball hard, and it rolls a long way. |

### The Swing of Things

Familiar playground experiences are a perfect tool for helping students understand the basics of force and motion! On a sheet of chart paper, list the concepts shown. In turn, read each statement aloud with students and then provide a playground example such as the one shown. Invite students to identify additional examples. If desired, continue the lesson outside with student demonstrations. Keep the concepts posted throughout your study to keep youngsters' learning on the move!

# Check Out These Moves!

How does force affect motion? Use the following investigations to help students find out! Post a list of movement-related terms—such as *fast, slow, back and forth,* or *up and down*—for student reference. To make an observation journal, instruct each youngster to staple three copies of the recording sheet (page 238) and several sheets of unlined paper inside a construction paper folder. Ask her to title and personalize the front cover.

For each investigation, have each student write the question on a duplicated journal page. After discussing the playground connection, group students and distribute the materials. Lead the youngsters through the procedure; then share the explanation (in italics). Encourage students to record later playground observations on their blank journal pages. They're sure to see recess in a new light!

## What are some ways to make things move?

**Playground connection:** Playing with a ball
**Materials for each student pair:** clay ball, length of string, shoebox lid
**Procedure:** Set the lid upside down on a work surface. Place the clay ball on it. Make the ball move in three ways: with a hand, the string, and the lid. Illustrate each movement and write what happened. Then answer the question. *(Pushing and pulling are ways to make things move. Gravity pulls things toward the ground.)*

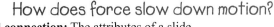

## How does force slow down motion?

**Playground connection:** The attributes of a slide
**Materials for each small group:** penny, shoebox lid, materials sized to cover the lid (felt, waxed paper, aluminum foil)
**Procedure:** Set the lid on a work surface so that the top is faceup. Place the felt on the lid and then set the penny on one end. Holding the felt in place, lift the end with the penny until the coin slides down. Illustrate and describe what happened. Remove the felt and repeat the process with the remaining materials. Then answer the question. *(Friction is a force that slows down or stops movement. When there is more friction, as with the felt, movement is slower.)*

## How do pushes and pulls change motion?

**Playground connection:** The movement of a tire swing
**Materials for each student pair:** length of string, crayon, ruler, heavy book
**Procedure:** Tie one end of the string to the ruler and one end to the crayon. Set the ruler near the edge of a desk or similar surface so that the crayon hangs freely. Place the book on the ruler. Push or pull the crayon to move it three ways: back and forth, side to side, and in a circle. Illustrate each movement, using an arrow to show the direction. Write to tell what happened; then answer the question. *(The way an object is pushed or pulled determines the direction in which it moves.)*

Name ______________________________



# A Movement Investigation

**Question:** ______________________________

______________________________

| Observation | Observation | Observation |
| --- | --- | --- |
| | | |

**What happened?**

______________________________

______________________________

______________________________

______________________________

**My Answer**

______________________________

______________________________

______________________________

______________________________

______________________________

______________________________

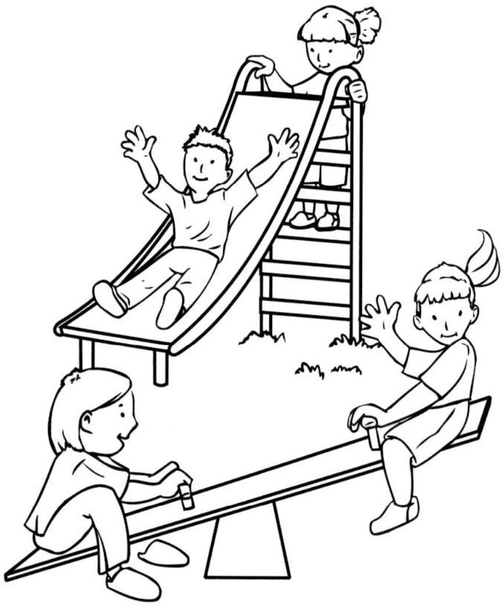





**Note to the teacher:** Use with "Check Out These Moves!" on page 237.

# Dive Right In!

## Learning About Sinking and Floating

These wet and wild science investigations are sure to create a splash of excitement!

### Fable to Fact
*Understanding water displacement*

Plunge into this watery demonstration of cause and effect! In advance, remove the label from a plastic water bottle. Adjust the water level so that the bottle is almost full and then mark it. Gather a supply of stones that fit into the bottle's opening. Also obtain a copy of the fable *The Crow and the Pitcher* such as *Professor Aesop's the Crow and the Pitcher* illustrated and interpreted by Stephanie Gwyn Brown.

To begin, show students the bottle. Tell them to imagine that a thirsty crow wants to drink the water, but his beak is too short to reach it. Invite students to suggest solutions. Then read the fable aloud, dropping rocks into the bottle to parallel the story's action. At the fable's conclusion, help students realize that the water level rises because the rocks push aside the water to make space for themselves. If appropriate for your students' level of understanding, explain that when some objects displace water, the water pushes back strongly enough to support them, causing them to float. Interesting!

Dawn Maucieri—Gr. 3
Signal Hill Elementary School
Dix Hills, NY

### Sink or Float?
*Making and testing predictions*

This buoyancy activity has students put their predictions to the test! Divide students into small groups. Give each group a large plastic bowl (or similar container) of water, student copies of the recording sheet (page 241), each object listed on the recording sheet, and paper towels for cleanup. Have students follow the steps below. After groups discuss their results and conclusions with the class, share the provided explanation.

**Steps:**
1. Predict whether the first object will sink or float. Record your prediction and discuss it in your group.
2. Have one group member place the object in the water, push it to the bottom of the bowl, and then let it go. Write "sink" or "float" to tell what happens.
3. Repeat the process to test the other objects.
4. Answer the questions.

**Explanation:** Factors such as size, weight, and material affect whether something sinks or floats. For example, light things usually float more easily than heavier things, wood or foam is more likely to float than solid metal or stone, and most hollow and waterproof objects stay afloat better than objects that absorb water.

| Sink | Float |
|------|-------|
| penny | sponge |
| cotton ball | pencil |
| rock | straw |
| paper clip | craft stick |

## Buoyant Boats

*Changing a material's properties*

When it comes to helping students understand buoyancy, this idea rises to the top! Prepare a class supply of 1½-inch clay balls plus one extra. Set out several large bowls (or similar containers) of water. Explain to students that *buoyancy* is the ability to float. Then display a clay ball and ask students to tell whether they think it is buoyant. Gently drop the ball into a container of water to demonstrate that it sinks.

Next, suggest that shaping the clay into a boat will help it stay afloat. To investigate this possibility, pair students. Give each youngster a clay ball and a copy of the recording sheet below. The partners in each twosome shape one ball into a boat, place it in water, and record what happens. They repeat the process with another ball. Then each partner writes an explanation at the bottom of his recording sheet. (If neither of their boats float, have the partners observe a classmate's boat that does.) After each twosome completes the investigation, lead students to conclude that a clay boat floats if it displaces more water than a clay ball. For a later extension, have students make various types of clay boats and determine which ones hold the most pennies without sinking.

---

Name _____

# Make It Float!

**Step 1**

Shape one clay ball into a boat.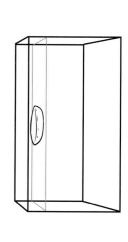
On the back of this paper, draw the boat near the top.

Does the boat float? Yes _____ No _____

**Step 2**

Shape another clay ball into a boat.
On the back of this paper, draw the boat near the bottom.

Does the boat float? Yes _____ No _____

Clay balls sink, but some clay boats float.
Explain why. _____

©The Education Center, Inc. • *THE MAILBOX*® • *Primary* • Feb/Mar 2004

Name_____

# Sink or Float?

Will each object sink or float?
Draw an **X** to show your prediction.
Test your prediction.
Write what happens.

| Object | Prediction | | Results |
| | Sink | Float | |
|---|---|---|---|
| penny | | | |
| sponge | | | |
| cotton ball | | | |
| pencil | | | |
| straw | | | |
| craft stick | | | |
| rock | | | |
| paper clip | | | |

Think about the objects that sink. How are they alike? _____

_____

Think about the objects that float. How are they alike? _____

_____

**Note to the teacher:** Use with "Sink or Float?" on page 239.

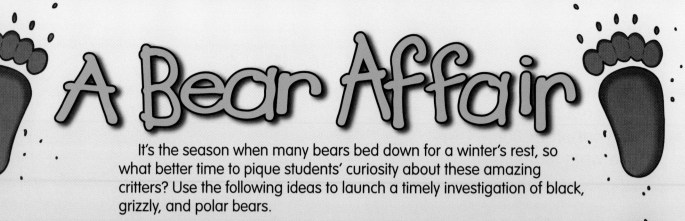

# A Bear Affair

It's the season when many bears bed down for a winter's rest, so what better time to pique students' curiosity about these amazing critters? Use the following ideas to launch a timely investigation of black, grizzly, and polar bears.

*ideas contributed by Starin Lewis, Phoenix, AZ*

## What a Group!
### Identifying characteristics of mammals

Launch your study by prompting students to bear in mind the characteristics of mammals. First, draw a large circle on the board and label it "Mammals." Ask each student to do the same on a sheet of drawing paper, leaving a generous amount of space at the top of his paper. Then guide youngsters to recall the characteristics of mammals. As you list each characteristic in the circle, have each youngster note it on his paper.

Next, announce that students will learn about one group of mammals. To give a hint about which group, add four paws to the circle as shown; challenge students to guess which type of animal the illustration will represent. Continue with additional features, as illustrated, to reveal that the bear family is the new topic of study. Have each youngster complete his drawing in a similar manner and lightly color it. Then ask volunteers to tell the class additional information they know about bears. After this intriguing introduction, you can bet students will be eager to learn more!

Mammals
1. have fur or hair
2. don't hatch from eggs
3. are warm-blooded
4. drink their mothers' milk

## Family Resemblance
### Understanding that offspring are similar to their parents

Students' understanding of a bear's life cycle is sure to grow with this activity! Ask students to brainstorm similarities and differences between human babies and adults. Then tell students that bear cubs grow and change just as babies do. Comment that newborn cubs are smaller than newborn babies. Explain that when cubs are first born, their eyes are closed, they have no teeth, and they have little or no fur. Then give each youngster a copy of page 245. Encourage her to use the illustration and what she knows about bears to complete her paper. After each youngster finishes her work, prompt a class discussion to check students' answers. The family resemblance will become clear!

242

## Lines for Bear Roles

<u>Black Bears</u>
- We live in forests.
- We rest in trees or on the ground.
- In the winter, we may make dens near trees or under bushes.

<u>Grizzly Bears</u>
- We live near mountains.
- We sleep on grass and pine needles.
- In the winter, we may dig dens in hillsides.

<u>Polar Bears</u>
- We live near the Arctic Ocean.
- We sleep in holes that we dig in the snow.
- In the winter, female polar bears make dens in the snow. Most male polar bears do not stay in dens.

# Bears at Rest
### Recognizing how bears take shelter

Everyone needs a resting place, even a bear! Most of the time, bears have temporary resting places. During the winter when food is scarce, some bears settle into dens for a long sleep. Bears are not true hibernators, though, since they may wake up on warm days or when danger is present. Share this information with students. Then divide them into three groups. Assign a different type of bear to each group and give each student a copy of the appropriate lines on this page.

Next, each student makes two construction paper bear ears and tapes them to a chenille stem. He curves the stem, making a headband to wear. (He keeps it in place with a bobby pin if necessary.) The students in each group rehearse their lines, acting them out as desired. Then they announce their type of bear and present their lines to the class. Bravo for bears!

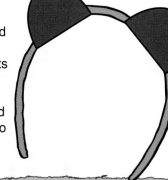

# Home Territory
### Matching bears to their habitats

Take your study of bears on location with this unique habitat project! Tell students that in addition to shelter, bears need food, water, and space. Explain that a place that provides these things is called a *habitat*. On a map, help students locate the habitat of polar bears (the Arctic) and many grizzly bears (Alaska and western Canada). Comment that black bears live in forests throughout North America. Then give each youngster a copy of page 246, a 12" x 18" sheet of white paper, crayons, scissors, and glue. Help her use the directions below to complete her project.

**Project directions:**
1. Read the sentence boxes. Fill in the blanks.
2. Color the pictures as shown. Cut out the patterns.
3. Fold the white paper in half. Cut the top layer into three equal flaps as shown.
4. Trace the den pattern near the edge of each flap. Cut out the tracings.
5. Glue the correct sentences under each flap and the correct bear in each den.
6. Label each flap. Add crayon details.

Polar Bears

Black Bears

Grizzly Bears

## Cool Adaptations
### Understanding adaptations

With its frigid temperatures, it's no surprise that the Arctic is home to few animals. Polar bears are right at home in this frosty world though. Tell students that adaptations make polar bears well suited for Arctic life. Share the provided information and, if possible, display a realistic picture of a polar bear in its natural habitat. To follow up, each student positions a 9" x 12" construction paper folder so that the fold is at the top. On the front of the folder, he uses desired arts-and-crafts materials to illustrate a polar bear in its habitat. The youngster writes a paragraph about polar bear adaptations and then staples his writing inside the folder. Cool!

### Polar Bear Adaptations

- double-layered fur for warmth
- black skin that absorbs heat from the sun
- thick layer of fat for warmth
- webbed toes that are good for swimming
- pads and fur on their feet that make it easier to walk on ice

### Bear Body Parts and Uses

snout *(good sense of smell for finding food)*
claws *(digging for roots, picking fruits, and catching animals)*
paws *(catching fish or turning over rocks)*
sharp front teeth *(biting and tearing meat)*
flat back teeth *(grinding plants and roots)*

## Hungry As a Bear!
### Identifying how bears find and gather food

Bears have huge appetites and eat almost all of the time. How do they find and gather their food? That's what students learn with this thought-provoking activity. To begin, tell students that bears eat foods such as meat, plants, fruits, roots, and honey. Add that some bears catch fish or eat insects that live under rocks. On the board, write the body parts listed on this page. Then have each youngster discuss with a classmate how the body parts might be helpful to a hungry bear. Invite students to tell the class their ideas; use the information shown to guide the discussion. If desired, ask your school media specialist to provide grade-appropriate nonfiction books, and have students research the diets of specific types of bears. Interesting!

## The Bear Facts
### Recalling factual information

Invite students to "paws" and reflect on what they've learned with this nifty booklet project. Each student uses a template to make two construction paper paw-shaped covers and four white pages. He staples the pages between the covers and glues construction paper claws to the front cover as shown. After he titles his resulting booklet, he labels the first page "Bears" and each remaining page with a different type of bear. On each page, he writes and illustrates information about the corresponding topic. The result will be a "beary" handy resource!

The Bear Facts

Nigel

# All in the Family

Read each word or group of words.
Decide whether it tells about a cub, a mother bear, or both.
Use the code to write the correct letter on the pawprint.

**Code**
**C** = cub
**M** = mother bear
**B** = both

1. small eyes

2. round ears

3. about 500 pounds

4. claws

5. not very heavy

6. grows quickly

7. short, strong legs

8. short tail

9. long, shaggy fur

10. almost helpless

Write a sentence to answer each question.

a. What is one way that a cub and its mother are the same?_____

_____

b. What is one way that a cub changes as it grows? _____

_____

**Note to the teacher:** Use with "Family Resemblance" on page 242.

245

## Patterns
Use with "Home Territory" on page 243.

**sentence boxes**

A. _____ bears live in one of the coldest places. They live close to the Arctic Ocean. Ice covers the water for most of the year. Sometimes _____ bears sit on chunks of ice in the ocean!

B. _____ bears live in the woods in North America. They use trees and bushes for shelter. Some _____ bears live near campsites. Sometimes they look in garbage cans for food!

C. Most _____ bears live in Alaska and western Canada. They live where there are mountains and open spaces. They do not like to live near people. There are about 200 _____ bears in Yellowstone National Park.

black bear

grizzly bear

polar bear

den

246     

# Science Fair Success

Use these suggestions from our science-savvy subscribers to plan an event that gets results!

## Choice Topics

Generate interest in choosing science fair topics! Explain that an experiment begins with a question. Then, to spark students' questions, take a class walk around school grounds or make a variety of nonfiction books available. Comment on intriguing details to model thoughtful observation. Later, guide students to use their observations to form questions; compile the questions into an ongoing list. When it's time for a student to choose a science fair topic, he'll have lots of inspiration!

adapted from an idea by Sungja S. Collins
Fulton, MS

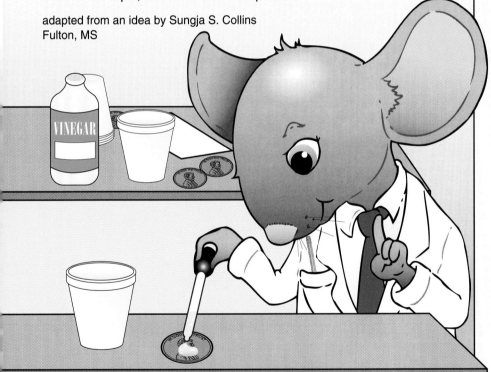

## A Family Affair

Prepare students and parents for an upcoming science fair with this hands-on event! To get ready, designate one or more work areas for each experiment on page 248. Stock each area with the required materials, pencils, paper towels (for cleanup), and copies of the experiment sheet. Begin the scheduled event by reviewing science fair expectations and other relevant information with parents and students. Then invite each student to conduct the experiments with his family member(s). To conclude the event, gather the participants and ask volunteers to share their results. What a nifty way to increase anticipation for a science fair!

Kathy Kopp

## Experiment or Not?

Here's a suggestion to help students distinguish between experiments and nonexperimental projects. Explain that projects such as models or displays share information, while experiments are tests designed to find out something. For each project listed below, have each student give a thumbs-up or thumbs-down to signal whether it is an experiment. Encourage students to recall this experience as they put their science fair ideas to the test!

Kathy Kopp
Lecanto Primary School
Hernando, FL

**Are These Experiments?**
- Model of a solar system *(no)*
- Testing a magnet's strength *(yes)*
- Model showing how a volcano erupts *(no)*
- Finding out how plants are affected by the amount of sunlight they receive *(yes)*
- Figuring out how wand shape affects bubble shape *(yes)*
- Report on electricity *(no)*

## Step by Step

Help students step up to the challenge of planning for experimental projects! Program a copy of the checklist on page 249 with the appropriate dates. Make one copy for your reference and ask each student to keep a copy in a provided folder. In addition to having a handy time-management tool, the youngster will have a pride-boosting strategy for tracking her progress!

Cynthia Holcomb, San Angelo, TX

# Experiment Sheets

Use with "A Family Affair" on page 247.

## Penny Drop

**Question:** How many pennies can be dropped into a cup of water before the water spills over?

**Hypothesis:** _____ pennies can be dropped into the cup.

**Materials:** 3 oz. paper cups, water, about 30 pennies

**Procedure:**
1. Fill a cup to the brim with water.
2. Drop in pennies until water spills.
3. Count the pennies in the cup.

**Results:** On the back of this paper, write what happened.

## Drop by Drop

**Question:** How many drops of water fit on a penny before the water spills over?

**Hypothesis:** _____ drops fit on a penny.

**Materials:** eyedroppers, cups of water, pennies

**Procedure:**
1. Take a penny. Dry it if necessary.
2. Fill the eyedropper with water.
3. Drop water onto the penny, counting each drop. Stop when the water spills over.

**Results:** On the back of this paper, write what happened.

## Shiny Pennies

**Question:** Which cleans pennies better: water and salt or vinegar and salt?

**Hypothesis:** _____ cleans pennies better.

**Materials:** white vinegar, water, salt, 3 oz. paper cups, spoon, dirty pennies

**Procedure:**
1. Use two cups. Pour vinegar in one cup and the same amount of water in the other cup. Use the spoon to add the same amount of salt to each cup.
2. Drop a penny into each cup. Count to 30 slowly.
3. Remove the pennies. Wipe them.

**Results:** On the back of this paper, write what happened.

## Paper Bridge

**Question:** Which type of paper bridge holds more weight: a flat bridge or an accordion-folded bridge?

**Hypothesis:** A(n) _____ bridge holds more weight.

**Materials:** pennies, 9" x 12" sheets of construction paper, small foam cups

**Procedure:**
1. To make a flat bridge, lay a sheet of paper across two cups.
2. Carefully stand a cup on the bridge. Drop pennies into it until the bridge falls. Count the pennies in the cup.
3. Repeat with a sheet of paper that you have accordion-folded into eight or nine sections.

**Results:** On the back of this paper, write what happened.

Name _____

# Step by Step

Start at the bottom.
Check the box after you complete the step.

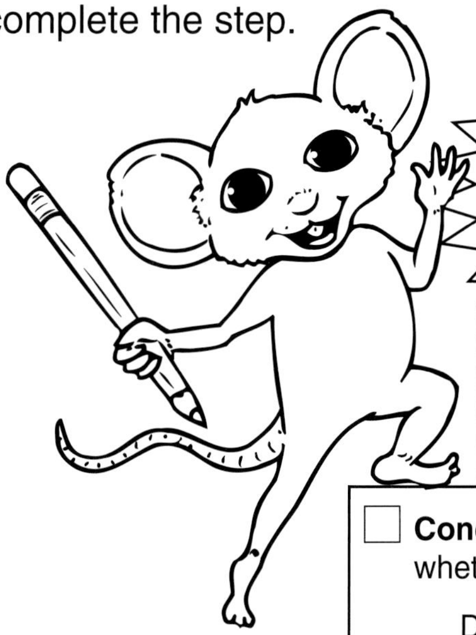

Science Fair!

Date: _____

☐ **Display:** Make a display to share your work.

Due: _____

☐ **Conclusion:** Answer your question. Tell whether your hypothesis was correct.

Due: _____

☐ **Results:** To tell what happened, write a report or make a chart or graph.

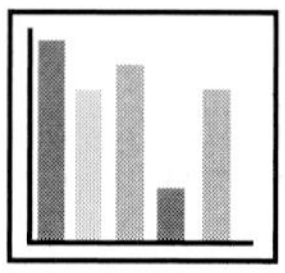

Due: _____

☐ **Experiment:** Do the experiment. Repeat it at least two times.

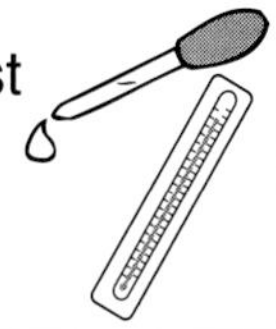

Due: _____

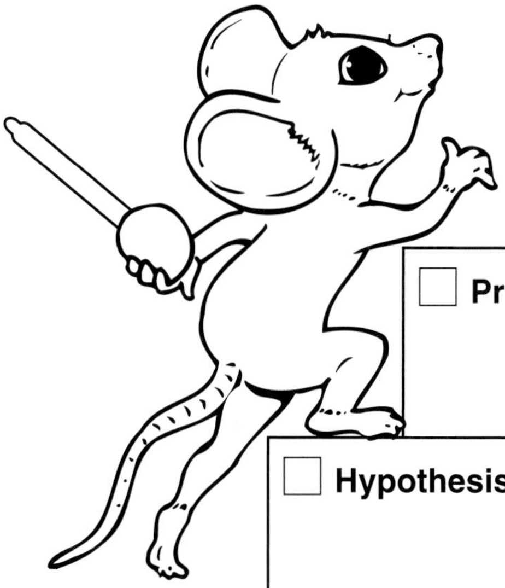

☐ **Procedure:** List the steps for your experiment.

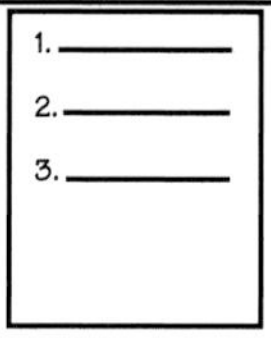

1. _____
2. _____
3. _____

Due: _____

☐ **Hypothesis:** Predict your results.

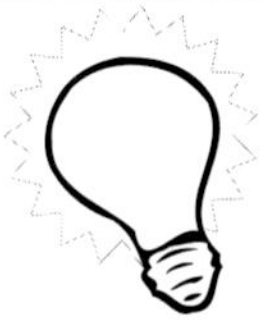

Due: _____

☐ **Research:** Gather information about your topic.

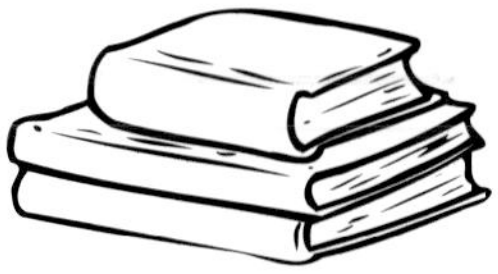

Due: _____

☐ **Question:** Decide what you want to find out.

Due: _____

# Right at Home!

## An Investigation of Plant and Animal Communities

Explore the connection among plants, animals, and their environments with this look at four North American biomes!

*ideas contributed by Stacie Stone Davis*
*Bloomfield Elementary School, Bloomfield, NY*

The **tundra** is windy and cold, and it has little rain or snow. Part of the soil is always frozen, so there are no trees. Small plants with shallow roots grow best.

## Communities Beyond Compare

*Recognizing that plants and animals live in various environments*

Students take note of different plant and animal communities with this ongoing project! To begin, ask students to picture a desert in their minds; invite them to describe their images. Then have students visualize and describe a forest. Lead students to conclude that the settings are different, but they each provide shelter for certain plants and animals. Explain that students will learn about four plant and animal communities. To make a learning log, give each student the listed materials and then guide him through the directions shown. Throughout your study, periodically set aside time for each youngster to write or illustrate an entry in his log. Now that's a simple way to home in on student learning!

### Learning Log

**Materials for one learning log:** 12" x 18" sheet of construction paper, 2 sheets of white paper, scissors, crayons, markers, access to a glue stick

**Directions:**
1. Position the construction paper horizontally. Fold it in half and then unfold it.
2. Fold in each side to meet at the crease. Unfold the paper to reveal four sections.
3. Cut each sheet of white paper in half vertically to make a total of four strips.
4. Use a marker to title one strip for each of the following: desert, forest, prairie, tundra.
5. Glue one strip in each section of the construction paper.
6. Close the resulting learning log. Title and personalize the front of it as desired.

## Where in North America?

*Using a map key, understanding adaptations*

Put plant and animal communities on the map! Give each student a copy of the map on page 252. Explain that it shows the general location of four plant and animal communities. Then announce a chosen biome and have each student find it on her map. As she colors it by the key, share the corresponding information from "Biomes at a Glance" in the boxes above and on page 251. Invite students to speculate on characteristics that help plants or animals survive in the described area. For example, students may conclude that animals with thick fur may be suited to life in the tundra. Continue with the remaining biomes in a similar manner. Then, for easy reference, have each student cut out her completed map and glue it onto the back of her learning log (see "Communities Beyond Compare" on this page).

A **desert** gets less than ten inches of rain each year. Deserts may be hot or cold during the day, but even a hot desert may be cold at night. Some deserts are sandy and others are rocky.

A **prairie** is warm in the summer and cool in the winter. It is covered with grass and shrubs but few trees. A prairie does not get enough rain for most kinds of trees.

Some **forests** are in areas that have warm, wet summers and cool winters. Most of the trees in these forests have leaves that change color in the fall.

## Looks Like Rain!

*Understanding that plants and animals live in various climates*

What a difference the climate makes! That's what students discover with this graphing activity. Tell students that the climate influences where plants and animals live. An area that usually has little rain, for example, would not make a good home for plants that cannot store water. Point out that the exact amount of precipitation an area has varies from year to year. Next, give each student a copy of page 253. Comment that the activity focuses on precipitation, but climate also includes temperature, wind, and sunlight. Have each youngster follow the directions to complete his sheet. Then discuss the answers to check students' understanding.

## Amazing Adaptations

*Matching plants and animals to environments*

What helps some plants and animals fit in certain environments? Adaptations! Explain to students that some animals change, or adapt, to become better suited for their environments. Post the code shown and ask students to tell what they recall about each biome. Then give each student a copy of page 254. Read the first box with students and guide them to identify the biome for which the plant or animal life is best adapted. Have each youngster use the code to label the box. Repeat the process with the remaining boxes and then invite each student to color the illustrations.

To compile the information into a minibooklet, each youngster cuts out her boxes. She horizontally positions a 12" x 18" sheet of construction paper and then folds it into four sections (4½" x 12"). Next, she unfolds the paper, cuts along the creases to make four strips, and folds each strip in half to 4½" x 6". She labels a folded strip for each biome and then glues the two corresponding boxes inside. She uses a hole puncher and yarn to fasten the resulting pages together as shown. What a handy resource for each of your budding ecologists!

### Code

D = desert
F = forest
P = prairie
T = tundra

# Map

Use with "Where in North America?" on page 250.

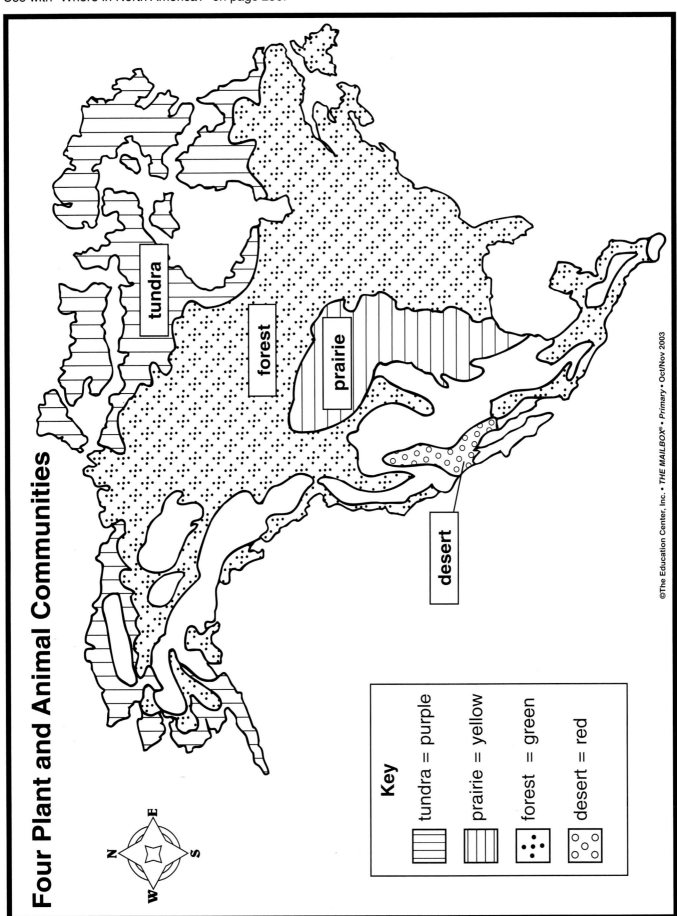

## Four Plant and Animal Communities

tundra

forest

prairie

desert

**Key**

tundra = purple
prairie = yellow
forest = green
desert = red

N
E
S
W

Name _____

# Measuring Up!

Help the animals show how much rain or snow fell.
Read the box below. Then color the graph.

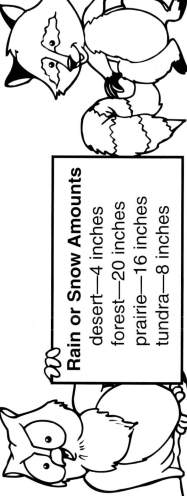

**Rain or Snow Amounts**
desert—4 inches
forest—20 inches
prairie—16 inches
tundra—8 inches

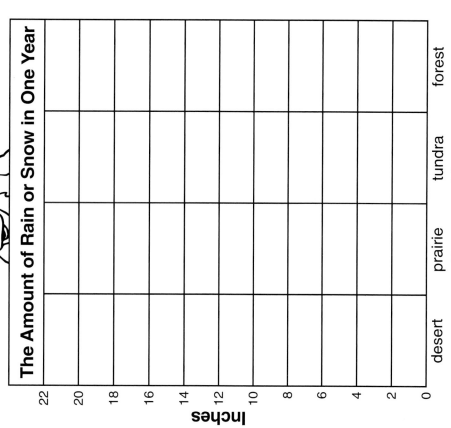

## The Amount of Rain or Snow in One Year

| Inches | | | | |
|---|---|---|---|---|
| 22 | | | | |
| 20 | | | | |
| 18 | | | | |
| 16 | | | | |
| 14 | | | | |
| 12 | | | | |
| 10 | | | | |
| 8 | | | | |
| 6 | | | | |
| 4 | | | | |
| 2 | | | | |
| 0 | desert | prairie | tundra | forest |

**Communities**

Now use the graph to answer the questions.

1. Which two places had the smallest amount of rain

   or snow? _____

2. Which two places had the most rain or snow? _____

   _____

3. Kangaroo rats do not need to drink water. Where

   do you think you would find them? _____

4. If a plant needs a lot of water, where might it grow

   best? _____

©The Education Center, Inc. • *THE MAILBOX*® • *Primary* • Oct/Nov 2003 • Key p. 313

**Note to the teacher:** Use with "Looks Like Rain!" on page 251.

253

# Booklet Boxes

Use with "Amazing Adaptations" on page 251.

An Arctic fox has thick fur to keep warm. Its fur turns white in the winter to blend in with the snow.

A jackrabbit does not drink much. It gets water from the plants it eats. It has long ears that keep it cool.

Mosses and lichens grow close to the ground. This helps shelter them from strong winds.

Some animals that live here have teeth that grow all the time. They eat tough grass that wears down teeth.

Some squirrels that live here make their homes in trees. They store acorns to eat in the winter.

Each cactus stores water in its leaves or stem. Its waxy stem helps the cactus hold the water.

Grasses are common here. Grass grows from the bottom of its stem. If an animal eats the top of it, it will grow back.

Many trees here have leaves that turn colors and fall off in autumn. Some other trees have needles that can grow in the winter.

# A "Sun-sational" Star

**Brighten science time with this dazzling investigation of the sun!**

### Bright Facts
*Identifying characteristics of the sun*

Bring sun-related facts to light with this nifty project! Give each student a copy of page 257. Have him color his triangles yellow and then cut them out. Explain that all but one of the phrases tells about the sun; ask him to set aside the phrase that he does not think is a characteristic of the sun. Next, encourage students to remember the phrases as you read aloud *The Sun: Our Nearest Star* by Franklyn M. Branley or another chosen sun book. At the book's conclusion, allow time for students to reconsider the phrases they set aside and make any desired changes. Then reveal that the phrase "biggest star" does not describe the sun. Comment that the sun only appears to be the biggest star because it is the closest one to Earth.

To showcase the seven identified characteristics, each youngster arranges his corresponding triangles along the outer edge of an eight-inch yellow construction paper circle. He adjusts the sequence of triangles as needed so that none of the phrases is completely upside down. He glues each triangle in place and then adds a happy face to his resulting sun. Cool!

> Imagine if Earth were the size of this candy.

### Dazzling Diameter
*Investigating the sun's size*

The sun isn't the biggest star, but it's huge in comparison to Earth. To help students understand how Earth measures up, divide them into two or three groups and ask each group to sit in an open area on the floor. Give each group a piece of scrap paper, a narrow 55-inch-long strip of paper, a ball of yarn, and one-half cup of M&M's candies (reserve extra candies for a later student snack). Instruct each group to lay its strip on the floor. Have the group members make a yarn circle to represent the sun, using the strip as its diameter.

Next, ask each group to imagine that Earth is the size of one candy. Have the group members discuss among themselves how many Earths would fit across the sun and then write a group prediction. To check their prediction, ask the youngsters to arrange the candies side by side on their strip and then count them. After each group completes its work, reveal that it would take about 109 Earths to equal the sun's diameter. Amazing!

Laurie Gibbons, Huntsville, AL

255

## Just Another Star?
*Understanding the sun's importance*

The sun is an ordinary star with extraordinary importance! Have students brainstorm a list of reasons that the sun is important, using the information shown to guide their responses. Next, have each youngster title a half sheet of paper "The Sun." Referring to the brainstormed list, each student writes a poem by listing four phrases that tell about the sun. Then she staples her writing to a sheet of construction paper and illustrates it as desired. Display students' poetic tributes on a bulletin board titled "Hooray for the Sun!"

The Sun
Keeping Earth warm
Giving us light
Helping plants grow
Nearest star

**Why the Sun Is Important**

The sun gives off heat and light.

Green plants need sunlight to make food; people and animals need the plants.

The weather depends on the sun.

Without the sun, there would be no life on Earth.

## Round and Round
*Understanding day and night*

If the sun never stops shining, why is it dark at night? Pose this question to students and welcome their responses. Then spin a toy top; explain that Earth rotates similarly, taking 24 hours for each rotation. Adhere a sticky dot to one side of the top to represent a point on Earth. Next, dim the lights and give a volunteer a flashlight (sun) to shine. Hold the top in the light and slowly turn it. Then have students share their observations. Clarify that when it is night on one side of Earth, it is day on the other side. To check students' understanding, ask each youngster to imagine that an alien has asked him what causes day and night. Have him write a letter to the creature to share the information. Far out!

## Stellar Timepiece
*Observing shadows, collecting data*

This timely investigation explores the connection between shadows and the sun's position in the sky. Early on a sunny morning, explain to students that long ago people used shadows to tell time. Invite students to share their ideas about how shadows could be used in this way. Next, divide students into pairs and go outside to a blacktopped surface. In each twosome, Partner 1 stands as Partner 2 traces her shadow with chalk. Then Partner 1 labels the shadow with the time, measures its length, and writes the information on a provided recording sheet. At about two-hour intervals, arrange for the partners to repeat the tracing and recording process in the same location. After each twosome studies its data, discuss with students how the length and position of the shadows change over time.

Laurie Gibbons, Huntsville, AL

256

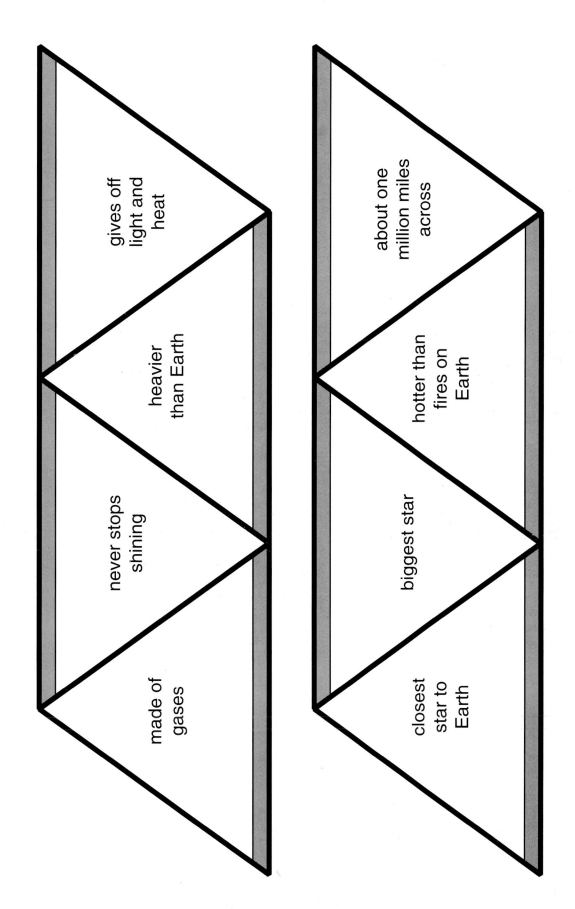

gives off light and heat

heavier than Earth

never stops shining

made of gases

about one million miles across

hotter than fires on Earth

biggest star

closest star to Earth

# In Full Bloom

## An Investigation of Flowering Plants

Flowering plants grow almost everywhere. In fact, most plants have flowers. Explore the world of flowering plants with the following ideas and cultivate students' science skills in the process!

*ideas contributed by Starin Lewis, Phoenix, AZ*

### Upon a Closer Look...

*Recording observations, identifying plant parts*

Count on students' observation skills to blossom with this introductory activity! In advance, purchase a few lilies, tulips, or other cut flowers that have both pistils and stamens. Ask students to imagine that they are botanists who need to observe the flowers closely so they can describe them to others. Next, divide students into groups so that each group has a flower. Invite students to tell what they notice about their flowers, including details about color, shape, and size. Then, in each group, have one person carefully remove a few petals from the group's flower to expose the inside of it. Give each group at least one magnifying glass, and allow time for each group member to examine the flower. After volunteers share their observations with the class, use the provided diagram to identify the four featured plant parts; list the names of the parts on the board.

To follow up, each youngster folds a sheet of drawing paper in half. On one half, she illustrates her group's flower and labels the listed parts. On the other half, she describes her observations. Students are sure to agree that there's more to a flower than what first meets the eye!

### Parts With Purpose

*Recognizing the functions of plant parts*

From the tips of its stamens to the ends of its roots, the various parts of a flowering plant play important roles in its survival. Ask students to share their ideas about the functions of familiar plant parts such as petals, stems, and roots. Then comment that the powdery grains of pollen on a flower's stamen are so small that about 50 of them would fit on the head of a pin. Explain that even though the pollen grains are tiny, they play a big role in the creation of new flowers. To further explore the functions of several plant parts, have each student complete a copy of page 261. Fascinating!

## Collecting Samples
*Sorting parts of flowering plants*

This partner game helps students sort out the connection between blossoms and fruits. Tell students that a fruit is the part of a flowering plant that holds seeds. Give examples such as strawberries, oranges, and apples. Guide students to understand that apples grow from apple blossoms. Next, give each youngster a copy of the game cards on page 262. Prompt discussion to compare and contrast the different plant parts. Have each youngster cut out his cards and sign the back of each one. Then pair students and give each twosome a sheet of paper for keeping score. Explain that the goal of the game is to collect sets of cards; a set is three cards with the same type of part from different plants, such as the cards with apple seeds, orange seeds, and strawberry seeds.

To play one round, the partners shuffle their cards together. Player 1 deals four cards to his partner and four to himself. He stacks the rest of the cards facedown. If a player has a set, he places it aside, earns one point, and takes three more cards. Player 2 draws a card and then decides whether to keep it or discard it. If he keeps it, he discards another card from his hand. Player 1 takes a turn in a similar manner. Alternate play continues with each player replacing any cards he sets aside until no cards are left in the deck. The player who makes more sets during a designated number of rounds wins.

## Plant Food Recipe
*Identifying how plants produce food*

What sets green plants apart from all other living things? They make their own food! Share this information with students. Then explain that the green pigment in a plant's leaves is called chlorophyll, and it helps the plant use sunlight to make food. Tell students that (1) a plant absorbs sunlight and takes in air through its green leaves, (2) the plant takes in water through its roots, and (3) it uses energy from the sun to change the water and part of the air into sugar. To check understanding, have students name the four things that plants need to make food *(chlorophyll, air, water, and sunlight)*.

Next, have each youngster prepare a recipe card for a flowering plant. To do this, she cuts the top of a large blank index card as shown to make a tab and then titles the tab. She lists the four ingredients for photosynthesis and summarizes the process in a recipe-like format. Then she illustrates her work as desired. Now that's a sweet science idea!

### Perfect Plant Food

Ingredients: chlorophyll, air, water, sunlight

Steps:
1. Take a cup of sunshine and some chlorophyll.
2. Add air.
3. Add just the right amount of water.
4. Combine to make sugar. Enjoy!

259

## Welcome Visitors

*Understanding that flowers are part of a system*

People aren't the only ones who appreciate flowers. Blooms are important to insects and birds too! A flower's scent and bright color signal that the flower has nectar, a sweet liquid that some insects and birds drink. When a bee or another creature drinks the nectar, pollen may stick to it and then get brushed off onto another flower later. Share this information with students, pointing out that pollen transfer is necessary for seeds to form. To enhance understanding, read aloud *The Reason for a Flower* by Ruth Heller.

Next, each student folds up the bottom 2½" of a horizontally positioned 9" x 12" sheet of drawing paper and then unfolds it. Above the fold line, he creates a simple illustration to represent the pollination process. Below the fold line, he writes an explanation. So that's why bees and flowers are important to each other!

A bee sees a colorful flower. It flies over to get some nectar. Pollen gets stuck all over the bee! Then the bee lands on another flower. Some of the pollen comes off. Later, seeds will form.

### Life Cycle

- A seed takes in water.
- The seed sprouts and grows a root.
- The plant gets bigger and grows flower buds.
- The flowers blossom. Insects or birds pollinate them.
- The flowers die, and the seeds scatter.

## Round and Round

*Summarizing a flower's life cycle*

The story of a flower comes full circle with this crafty project! Use the provided information to familiarize students with the flower's life cycle. Next, on a 9" x 12" sheet of light-colored construction paper, each youngster traces a blossom template that has five large petals. Then she cuts out the tracing. She draws an arrow on a three-inch circle pointing from the center toward the edge. She uses a brad to secure the center of the circle to her blossom. She summarizes the life cycle of a flower in her own words, writing about each stage in sequence on a separate petal. Then she glues on a construction paper stem and leaves. The result will be a nifty reminder of how a tiny, dull seed may become a large, beautiful flower!

## Garden Variety Show

*Researching a topic, planning a presentation*

This culminating activity puts plants in the spotlight! Ask students to imagine that they are the stars of a TV garden show and need to plan a classroom performance for a designated date. Then pair students. Have each twosome use provided resources to research an assigned type of flowering plant, including how to care for it. Ask the partners to use their research and desired arts-and-crafts materials to prepare a brief presentation, such as a how-to segment or a skit. For added fun, post a TV-style listing of the presentation times. Rave reviews are guaranteed!

Name _____

# Take Note!

Read. Study the pictures.
Fill in the blanks.

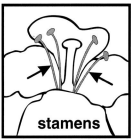
**stamens**

1. The _____ holds up the flower. It takes water from the roots to the leaves.

2. A green _____ grows from the stem. It helps make food for the plant.

3. The _____ hold the flower in the ground.

4. The _____ is in the middle of the flower. Seeds grow inside it.

5. The _____ make pollen. They are thin like thread.

6. The _____ are bright colors. They attract some insects and birds.

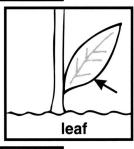
**leaf**

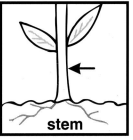
**stem**

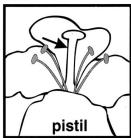
**pistil**

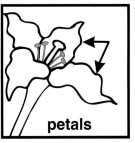
**petals**

Now follow the directions below.

• Find the plant part that has seeds inside. Use a green crayon to trace the box.

• Find the plant parts that make pollen. Use a yellow crayon to trace the box.

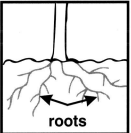
**roots**

# Game Cards

Use with "Collecting Samples" on page 259.

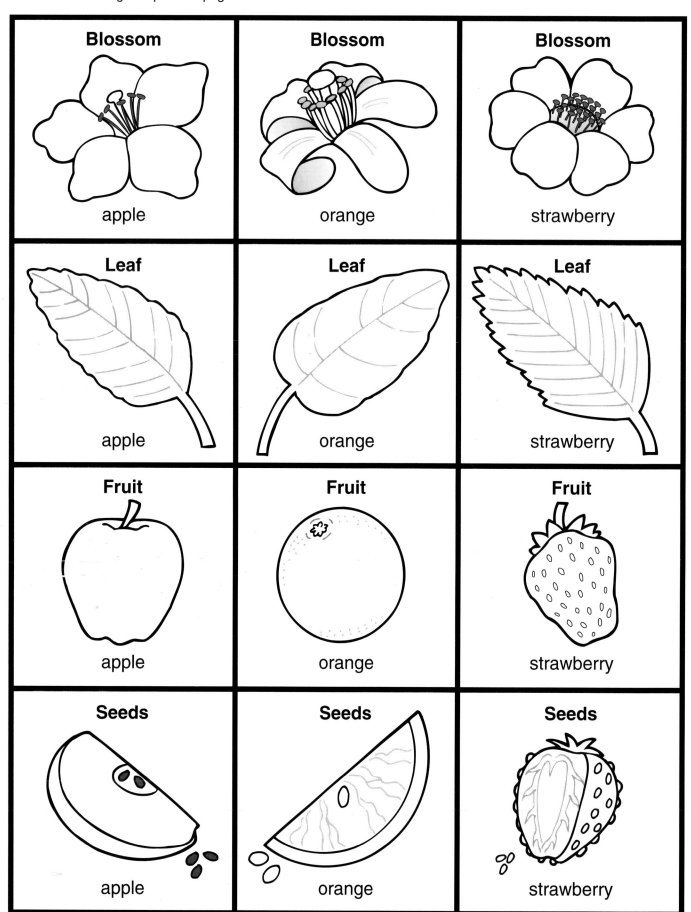

| Blossom | Blossom | Blossom |
| apple | orange | strawberry |
| **Leaf** | **Leaf** | **Leaf** |
| apple | orange | strawberry |
| **Fruit** | **Fruit** | **Fruit** |
| apple | orange | strawberry |
| **Seeds** | **Seeds** | **Seeds** |
| apple | orange | strawberry |

# SEASONAL UNITS

# 'Tis the Season for... Crayons!

## SCIENCE
## What's the Matter?

Help students gain a solid understanding of matter! Explain that the crayon-making process involves two forms of matter: liquids and solids. Review with students the attributes of each form. (A liquid flows and has a fixed volume; its shape changes to match its container. A solid has a fixed shape and volume.) Then use the provided information to summarize the crayon-making process, asking students to identify the form of matter after each step. So that's how crayons are made!

### Crayon-Making Process

1. Heated paraffin (a kind of wax) and powdered pigments (materials that give color) are mixed. The mixture can be poured easily. *liquid*
2. The mixture is poured into crayon molds. *liquid*
3. Water cools the mixture and it hardens. *solid*
4. The resulting crayons are pushed out of the molds. *solid*
5. Damaged crayons are remelted in a kettle. *liquid*
6. Perfect crayons are labeled and sorted into boxes. *solid*

## LITERATURE
## Helpful Crayons

Crayons and creativity go hand in hand! Read aloud *Harold and the Purple Crayon* by Crockett Johnson. Remind students that whenever Harold needs something, he simply draws it. Invite students to brainstorm different scenarios in which things would be needed. Then have each student develop her version of a chosen scenario. To do this, she visually divides a sheet of white paper into quarters and chooses one crayon. She imitates the book's art style to illustrate each section with herself as the main character. She adds captions and then mounts her paper onto a sheet of construction paper. Showcase students' colorful work on a bulletin board titled "[Your name]'s Class and the Crayons."

It was the first day of school, so I drew a new pencil.

I needed a teacher, so I drew Ms. Rhodes.

I got hungry, and I drew my lunch.

Then I drew a friend to play with at recess.

## MATH
## Class Colors

How do your students' favorite crayon colors compare with the Crayola company's most popular hues? Find out with this graphing idea! Prepare a poster-size grid that has one row for each of the eight basic crayon colors and an appropriate number of columns to accommodate student votes. Label the grid and title it "Favorite Crayon Colors." Display the poster within students' reach and place a supply of crayons nearby. Invite each student to cast his vote by coloring the appropriate space with the corresponding crayon. When the graph is complete, announce that the Crayola company identifies blue as its most popular crayon color and red as its second most popular. Guide students to analyze their data and compare it with this information.

## VOCABULARY
# Meaningful Names

Boost students' vocabularies with an exploration of crayon names! Obtain several crayons that have image-evoking names (see the suggestions). In turn, announce each crayon name without showing students the crayon. Have students guess each color and explain their reasoning; then reveal the crayon.

Next, set out a dictionary and crayons in a variety of hues. To make a color-word reference, a youngster folds a sheet of white paper in half twice (to 2¾" x 8½"). She trims one end to resemble a crayon tip and then unfolds the paper. Using both sides of the paper, she colors one crayon tip for each of these colors: blue, brown, green, orange, pink, purple, red, and yellow. She labels each color. Then she lists variations of it, referring to the crayons and dictionary as needed. Finally, she writes an original crayon name for each color and circles it. What a vivid collection of words!

pink
carnation
pink

cotton
candy

strawberry
ice cream

purple

mulberry

violet

grape

red

brick red

scarlet

fireball

yellow

banana
mania

dandelion

sunshine

You're looking
blue today!

Seeing Red

## WRITING
# In Black and White

Help students add color to their writing! Discuss with students common color-related expressions, such as seeing red and green with envy. Set out red, pink, blue, and green crayons. Then have each child complete a copy of page 276.

To follow up, ask each child to think about a time when she was sad, jealous, angry, or happy. Instruct her to incorporate the appropriate color-related phrase into a paragraph about the occasion. Then have her copy her edited writing onto one or more 3" x 8½" strips of paper. To publish her work, the youngster folds a 9" x 12" sheet of construction paper in half lengthwise. She trims one short end to resemble a crayon tip. She staples her writing inside, titles the resulting booklet, and adds desired crayon details.

Brighten your classroom with student-made crayon buddies! See page 6 for simple directions.

## MATH
# Crayons by the Batch

At the Crayola crayon factory, machines make about 2,500 crayons in three to five minutes. Share this information with students. Then, to enhance understanding of the production rate, ask students to imagine that they're crayon makers. Explain that each child will use tally marks to represent the crayons he makes.

To begin, have each child write on provided paper how many crayons he thinks he will "make" in one minute. At your signal, have him quickly draw tally marks for one minute. Then ask him to count them, suggesting that he circle sets of tally marks to ensure accurate counting. Prompt students to compare their totals and estimates. If desired, instruct each youngster to multiply his total with a calculator to determine an approximate number for three, four, or five minutes. Now that's a lot of crayons!

# 'Tis the Season for... Squirrels!

This cross-curricular collection of ideas features some of the season's most familiar critters—squirrels!

*ideas contributed by Laura Wagner*
*Raleigh, NC*

## SCIENCE
### Forest Acrobat

What makes tree squirrels well suited for forest life? That's what students find out with this intriguing look at adaptations! First, explain that tree squirrels live in trees, while ground squirrels, such as chipmunks and prairie dogs, live in burrows. Then display realistic pictures of tree squirrels or share a relevant picture book, such as *Nuts to You!* by Lois Ehlert. As students study the pictures, refer to the provided information to prompt discussion about how a squirrel's features help it survive in its habitat.

Next, each student summarizes on a half sheet of writing paper what she knows about squirrel adaptations. She staples her writing to a 6" x 9" piece of construction paper. Then she draws a squirrel face on a four-inch construction paper circle and cuts a squirrel tail from a 6" x 9" piece of construction paper. She uses construction paper scraps to make paws and ears; then she assembles the squirrel on her paper as shown. No wonder tree squirrels are nicknamed acrobats!

Tree Squirrels
Some squirrels live in the forest. They are really good at climbing trees. They have sharp claws that help them. When a squirrel leaps from branch to branch, it uses its tail to balance.

Olivia

### A tree squirrel has
- strong front teeth and jaw muscles that help it gnaw hard foods
- sharp claws that help it climb trees
- back toes that can bend to grip branches
- a flexible body that moves easily among treetops
- a large bushy tail that helps it balance, protects it from the weather, and gives signals
- a good sense of smell that helps it find hidden food

## WORD STUDY
### Gathering Blends

While squirrels are busy stashing acorns this fall, get your students busy sorting acorns with this consonant blend idea. Label a blank card for each of the following: "flying," "ground," "tree." Program several acorn cutouts with words for each of the initial blends. Display the cards and guide students to realize that they name types of squirrels. (Clarify that flying squirrels seem to fly, but they actually glide from branch to branch.) Point out that each word begins with a blend, and have students brainstorm other words with these blends. Then place the cutouts and cards at a center stocked with paper and pencils. Have students visit the center in pairs.

To use the center, one student arranges the cards as column headings. Then both students sort the acorns by reading each one and placing it below the appropriate heading. After all of the acorns are sorted, each youngster writes the groups of words and presents his paper for teacher approval.

grow

ground

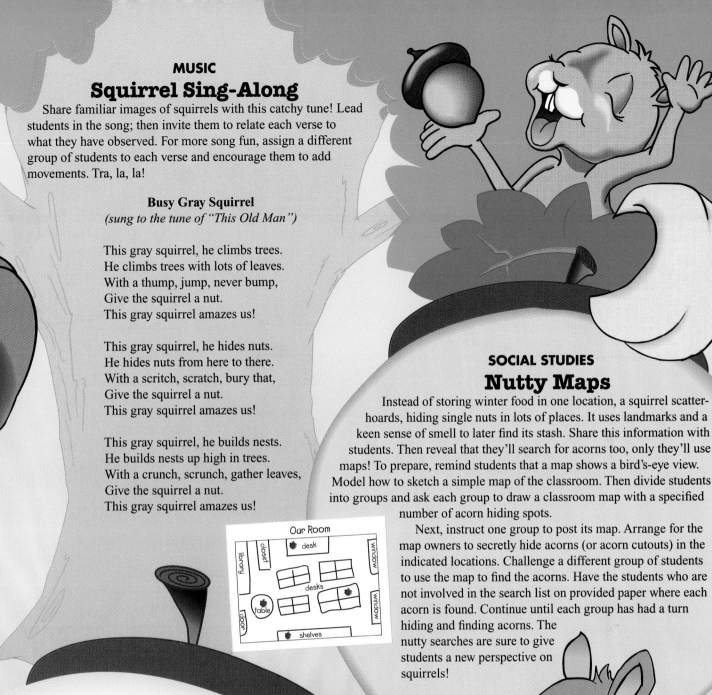

## MUSIC
# Squirrel Sing-Along

Share familiar images of squirrels with this catchy tune! Lead students in the song; then invite them to relate each verse to what they have observed. For more song fun, assign a different group of students to each verse and encourage them to add movements. Tra, la, la!

### Busy Gray Squirrel
*(sung to the tune of "This Old Man")*

This gray squirrel, he climbs trees.
He climbs trees with lots of leaves.
With a thump, jump, never bump,
Give the squirrel a nut.
This gray squirrel amazes us!

This gray squirrel, he hides nuts.
He hides nuts from here to there.
With a scritch, scratch, bury that,
Give the squirrel a nut.
This gray squirrel amazes us!

This gray squirrel, he builds nests.
He builds nests up high in trees.
With a crunch, scrunch, gather leaves,
Give the squirrel a nut.
This gray squirrel amazes us!

## SOCIAL STUDIES
# Nutty Maps

Instead of storing winter food in one location, a squirrel scatter-hoards, hiding single nuts in lots of places. It uses landmarks and a keen sense of smell to later find its stash. Share this information with students. Then reveal that they'll search for acorns too, only they'll use maps! To prepare, remind students that a map shows a bird's-eye view. Model how to sketch a simple map of the classroom. Then divide students into groups and ask each group to draw a classroom map with a specified number of acorn hiding spots.

Next, instruct one group to post its map. Arrange for the map owners to secretly hide acorns (or acorn cutouts) in the indicated locations. Challenge a different group of students to use the map to find the acorns. Have the students who are not involved in the search list on provided paper where each acorn is found. Continue until each group has had a turn hiding and finding acorns. The nutty searches are sure to give students a new perspective on squirrels!

## WRITING
# On the Go

Climb, jump, scamper, scurry, and glide! Squirrels can do all this and more! Focus on the squirrel's lively nature with this writing activity, and explore vivid verbs in the process. Have students brainstorm a list of action verbs that describe various squirrel behaviors. Then ask each student to imagine watching one or more squirrels through a window. To capture the scene, she incorporates listed verbs into a descriptive paragraph. She staples her writing inside a construction paper folder. Then she uses provided arts-and-crafts materials to illustrate the front of the folder to resemble the window scene. Showcase students' completed work on a bulletin board so that the folders can open, and title the display "Squirrel Sightings."

# 'Tis the Season for... Snow!

Bring snow onto the scene with this cool collection of cross-curricular activities!

*ideas contributed by Laura Wagner, Raleigh, NC*

### SCIENCE
## A Wintry Cycle

Where does snow come from? Count on your students to know after this frosty look at the water cycle. Give each student a copy of the picture cards on page 278. Ask him to refer to them as you summarize the water cycle. Explain that (1) the heat from the sun causes water to evaporate; (2) the water vapor condenses into water droplets, which form clouds; (3) if it is cold enough, ice crystals form and snow falls; and (4) when the snow melts, it continues the cycle. Use the vocabulary words on the picture cards to check students' understanding. Then have each student use the materials and the directions shown to make a wintry model of the water cycle. Encourage him to take his model home and use it to tell his family where snow comes from. Let it snow!

**Materials for one model:** 9" paper plate, copy of the picture cards on page 278, 4 Popsicle sticks, crayons, scissors, tape, glue

Step 3

**Steps:**
1. Cut the outer rim from the paper plate and then discard it.
2. Label the resulting circle "Let It Snow!" Draw clockwise arrows along the edge.
3. Tape the Popsicle sticks onto the back of the circle as shown.
4. Color the picture cards and then cut them out.
5. With the project right side up, glue the picture cards onto the Popsicle sticks in the correct sequence.

### PHONICS
## Snowball Word Sort

This cool word sort is bound to help students catch on to the *ow* vowel pattern! Write "snow" and "plow" on the board and point out that *ow* makes two sounds. Draw a box around each word. Nearby, randomly list the other *ow* words shown; have volunteers read them aloud. Next, each student traces her hand on construction paper to make two mitten shapes. She cuts out each tracing and labels one "snow" and the other "plow." She cuts 12 circles (snowballs) from construction paper squares. She labels each snowball with a different listed word. Then she sorts the snowballs onto her mittens by vowel sound. After students are satisfied with their work, announce the correct groupings and have students make any needed corrections. Ask each student to store her mittens and snowballs in a resealable plastic bag for later practice.

| Snow | Plow |
|------|------|
| blow | chow |
| grow | cow |
| mow | how |
| show | now |
| slow | pow |
| throw | wow |

## CHARACTER EDUCATION
# One of a Kind

No two snowflakes are exactly alike! Tell students this amazing fact and explain that Wilson Bentley was so intrigued by snowflakes that he spent years studying them. If desired, read aloud the award-winning biography *Snowflake Bentley* by Jacqueline Briggs Martin to share additional details. Suggest that people, like snowflakes, are unique. Provide examples of distinguishing characteristics, such as interests, hobbies, and talents. Then recognize each student's uniqueness with this snowy mobile project.

To make a mobile, a student folds a coffee filter in half three times and then makes desired cuts (see the example). After he unfolds the resulting snowflake, he tapes a length of string to it. He personalizes one side of a blank card as desired and identifies two or more of his distinguishing characteristics on the other side. He assembles his mobile as shown. Suspend students' mobiles from the ceiling to create a blizzard of appreciation for classmates' special qualities!

kids sledding
pretty yards
snow forts
no school

slippery roads
people shoveling
snow
cancellations
no school

## WRITING
# Frightful or Delightful?

Snow can be a source of great fun, but it can also be downright inconvenient! Use this writing activity to explore ways that snow affects people's lives. Post a two-column chart that you have labeled with a happy and an unhappy snowpal as shown. Guide students to brainstorm positive and negative outcomes of snowstorms. Write the information in the corresponding columns, pointing out that some outcomes may be listed in both columns. To follow up, have each youngster write about selected outcomes on story paper. Ask her to add her opinion of the wintry precipitation and illustrate her work. Display students' thought-provoking papers on a bulletin board titled "Frightful or Delightful?"

## PROBLEM SOLVING
# "Snow" Problem

Line up problem-solving practice with Frosty look-alikes! Give each student a copy of the snowpals on page 278 and have her cut them out. Read the provided clues aloud, pausing after each one to have students arrange their snowpals as indicated. Reread the clues and ask students to check their work. Then use the identifying shape on each card to announce the correct sequence. For additional reinforcement, repeat the activity with different snowpal sequences, modifying the difficulty of the clues to match your students' abilities.

### Clues
1. The first snowpal has square buttons and a hat.
2. The last snowpal has a scarf.
3. The snowpal holding a shovel is before the snowpal holding a broom.
4. The next to the last snowpal has round buttons.
5. The fourth snowpal has round eyes.

(Correct sequence: ■, □, ▲, ●, △, ○)

269

# 'Tis the Season for... Presidents!

Make Presidents' Day more meaningful for students with this tribute to two memorable leaders and the powerful role of American presidents.

*ideas contributed by Leigh Anne Rhodes*
*Victory Academy, Baton Rouge, LA*

## MATH
### A "Cent-sational" Introduction

This idea is right on the money for launching a Presidents' Day study. Direct students' attention to a February calendar and point out that the holiday is on the third Monday. Explain that the holiday now honors all U.S. presidents but that it was established to recognize the birthdays of George Washington and Abraham Lincoln, two of the most admired leaders. Comment that the United States has also honored the presidents in other ways, such as establishing memorials and minting coins with their images. Have each youngster examine a provided penny and quarter. Confirm that he knows which president is depicted on each coin and each coin's value.

Next, give each student a copy of page 279 and, if desired, several imitation quarters and pennies to use as manipulatives. Help students use a classroom calendar to answer the questions. Then have them follow your directions to complete their papers and gain more valuable math practice.

### George Washington
- Was the first U.S. president
- Is sometimes called the father of his country
- Was a farmer, soldier, and general
- Chose the site of the nation's current capital
- Helped plan the U.S. government

### Abraham Lincoln
- Was the 16th U.S. president
- Was nicknamed "Honest Abe"
- Was a lawyer
- Loved to read
- Helped end slavery

## SOCIAL STUDIES
### Two Legendary Leaders

Use this simple class activity to build on what students know about Presidents Washington and Lincoln. Draw a cherry tree and a log cabin on the board. Explain that the tree represents the legend about the first president's honesty and the log cabin symbolizes Lincoln's humble birthplace. Invite students to tell the class any other details they know about the presidents.

To follow up, have each student illustrate each symbol on a different side of a blank card. Then announce a fact about one of the two presidents without revealing his name (see the listed suggestions). Ask each student to hold up her card to signal which president she thinks the fact is about. After scanning students' cards, reveal the correct answer and elaborate on it as appropriate. Explore several other facts in a similar manner. Then have each youngster sign her card. Collect the cards for safekeeping, and plan to repeat the activity to check students' learning.

## VOCABULARY
# In a Few Words

Admired, brave, and powerful are fitting descriptions for Presidents Washington and Lincoln, and this activity helps students understand why. Write the word *admired* on the board. Use the word in a sentence about each leader and have students use context clues and their prior knowledge to define it. Explore the words *brave* and *powerful* in a similar manner. Then instruct each youngster to feature the words in a patriotic booklet.

To do this, the student stacks two 9" x 12" sheets of white construction paper. He holds them vertically and slides the top sheet upward about one inch. He folds the papers forward to create four graduated layers and staples the stack near the fold. He labels and colors the resulting tabs as shown. On each page, he defines the corresponding word and uses it in an original sentence about either president. Then he adds a booklet title and illustrations.

## WRITING
# Making a Difference

What a difference a president can make! Comment to students that presidents are often remembered for their achievements. Discuss with students the influence of chosen accomplishments from the distant or recent past, such as George Washington helping to plan the U.S. government or John F. Kennedy establishing the Peace Corps. If desired, arrange for students to research other examples.

After students are familiar with several historic achievements, have each youngster write on provided paper a paragraph about one way that a chosen president made a difference. Ask her to write a second paragraph about a wish that she has for the country or world. Instruct her to mount her writing on a sheet of construction paper and illustrate it as desired. Showcase students' work on a patriotic bulletin board titled "Achievements and Dreams."

Making a Difference
When Abraham Lincoln was president, there was a war. He was a good leader because he helped end slavery. He made America a better place to live.
My wish for America is that there would be no more pollution. We need clean land and water. We need safe places to live. That's why my dream is important.

Michele

## SPEAKING
# Speaking of the President...

Imagine being the president! That's what students do with this speaking activity. Remind students that a president's responsibilities often include giving speeches. Have students brainstorm a list of speechmaking tips, such as speaking clearly and at an appropriate pace. Then announce that each student will give a speech to the class. The topic? What his life would be like if he were president! Lead a class discussion to help students imagine being in this role, including details such as living in the White House, traveling frequently, and making important decisions. If desired, share *If I Were President* by Catherine Stier to spark additional thoughts. After each youngster writes his speech, have him practice it with the speaking tips in mind and then present it to the class. So that's what it's like to be the president!

# 'Tis the Season for... Bees!

Buzz into spring with this swarm of bee-related activities!

ideas by Laurie Gibbons, Huntsville, AL

Use the beeswax from "What's the Buzz?" for a gift idea on page 306.

## ART
### What's the Buzz?

Begin your study with this "bee-dazzling" display idea. In advance, purchase a sheet of beeswax (available in arts-and-crafts stores). Pass the beeswax among students without revealing what it is called; explain that it is a hint about the next topic of study. After students identify the material and guess that they'll be learning about bees, set out the beeswax with yellow paper and brown crayons (papers removed).

Next, arrange for each student to use the provided materials to do a crayon rubbing on the beeswax. As a student waits for his turn, he uses a copy of the pattern on page 307 to make a construction paper hive. He adds bees to the hive with markers or other arts-and-crafts supplies. Then he glues his hive atop his crayon rubbing and trims the excess paper. Post students' artwork on a bulletin board titled "What's the Buzz About Bees?" Throughout your study, encourage youngsters to use blank cards and provided nonfiction books to add facts to the display.

Bees fan their wings to keep hives cool.

Three types of honeybees live in a hive: drones, workers, and a queen.

## MATH
### Honeycomb Hexagons

If worker bees had a favorite shape, surely it would be the hexagon. After all, they build thousands of six-sided cells! Use this booklet project to have students "build" their own hexagons. First, draw a hexagon on the board and explain that each cell of a honeycomb has six sides and corners. Confirm that students know the name of the shape. Then have each student cut out one copy of the booklet cover and four copies of the booklet page on page 280. (For a more challenging activity, have her use seven copies of the booklet page.) Ask her to sign and color her cover and then staple it atop her pages.

After each student assembles her booklet, divide students into small groups. Give each group crayons and these pattern blocks: two trapezoids, three rhombuses, and six triangles. Post labeled illustrations of the shapes for student reference. Challenge each group to identify four pattern block combinations that form a hexagon. When a group identifies a combination, each student records it on a page in his booklet by coloring tracings of the pattern blocks in the provided space and completing the caption. What a honey of an idea!

I made this hexagon with

6 triangles.

272

## SOCIAL STUDIES
### A Sweet Search

What do a dancing bee and a map have in common? Entertain students' responses to this question; then reveal that both things communicate locations. Tell students that sometimes bees dance to let other bees know where to find flowers whose nectar they can use to make honey. Explain that different dances signal whether the flowers are nearby or far away.

To follow up, divide students into an even number of small groups. Give each group crayons, a sheet of paper, and a different color or type of flower cutout. Instruct the group members to draw a classroom map and then illustrate their flower on it in a chosen hiding place. Next, pair the groups. Designate the members of one group in each pair as scouts. Have the other group leave the classroom while the scouts hide their flower. When the students return, they use their partners' map to locate the hidden flower. Then the groups switch roles and repeat the process. For a fun extension, serve each student Honeycomb cereal as he completes a copy of page 281.

**The Wild Flower Garden Map**

**Down there!**

## SCIENCE
### Important Insects

Even though bees are known for their painful stings, they are among the most useful insects. They produce honey as well as beeswax, which is used to make candles, lipstick, shoe polish, and many other products. Plus, many crops depend on bees for pollination. Share this information with students; then have each youngster bring in one item (or an illustration of an item) that was produced with the help of bees. Give each student an identical white paper hexagon. Ask each youngster to illustrate and label his item on his hexagon. After students color their hexagons yellow, arrange the shapes on a wall to resemble a honeycomb and title the display as desired.

**honey graham crackers**

**Honey Graham Crackers**

## LANGUAGE ARTS
### Haiku From the Hive

Sweeten students' interest in poetry with this culminating project. Use the display from "What's the Buzz?" on page 272 to review what students know about bees. Familiarize students with the format of haiku (three lines of five, seven, and five syllables); then have each youngster pen a bee-related haiku on provided paper. To showcase her work, the student writes her edited poem on a yellow construction paper bee cutout similar to the one shown, writing on alternating stripes. She uses a black crayon to color her bee and glues on two construction paper antennae. To make wings, she rounds the corners of a 3" x 12" strip of waxed paper. She pinches the center of the strip and tapes it to the back of her bee.

**Busy honeybees**
**Work very hard in the hive**
**Making sweet honey.**

# 'Tis the Season for...
# Watermelon!

This sweet collection of cross-curricular
ideas is just ripe for the picking!

*ideas contributed by Julie Hays—Gr. 1*
*Foothills Elementary School, Maryville, TN*

## LANGUAGE ARTS
### Watermelon Pockets

What kind of melon is about 93 percent water? Why, watermelon, of course! Share this information with students, pointing out that the two words that form the compound word *watermelon* help convey its meaning. Next, help each student use the directions shown to make a watermelon pocket. Ask her to label a provided paper strip for each listed word and then store it in her prepared pocket. Later, have her form compound words with her strips, rearranging the strips as needed to form at least ten words and listing each one on a sheet of paper. For additional reinforcement, announce the meanings of chosen compound words and ask students to form the words. Now that's skill practice fresh off the vine!

### How to Make a Watermelon Pocket

1. Fold a 9" x 12" sheet of green paper into thirds (to 4" x 9"). Round the ends.
2. Position the paper with the flap on top (see the illustration). Color green stripes to resemble a melon.
3. Unfold the paper and position it vertically. Trim about half an inch from the bottom.
4. Trace the bottom section on red paper. Cut out the tracing and trim it to resemble watermelon flesh. Use a black crayon to add seeds.
5. Fold up the bottom section and glue the sides in place. Glue on the watermelon flesh.

### Words

| | |
|---|---|
| coat | rain |
| day | shine |
| drop | sun |
| fall | tan |
| light | time |
| melon | water |

100 > 40

## MATH
### In Comparison

Most watermelons weigh between five and 40 pounds, but some tip the scales at 100 pounds or more. One record-breaking melon weighed in at a whopping 262 pounds! Use these weighty facts to put a creative spin on comparing numbers. First, cut a triangle from a white paper plate to represent an inequality sign. Trace two edges as shown and color the triangle to resemble a watermelon slice. Then program a blank card for each of these numbers: 5, 40, 100, 262. Next, tape two cards to the board, leaving space between them. Use the information above to explain how the numbers relate to watermelons. Invite a student to tape the prepared inequality sign in place to compare the numbers; ask a different student to read aloud the resulting math expression. Display different pairs of cards to provide practice as needed. Then have each student complete a copy of page 282.

274

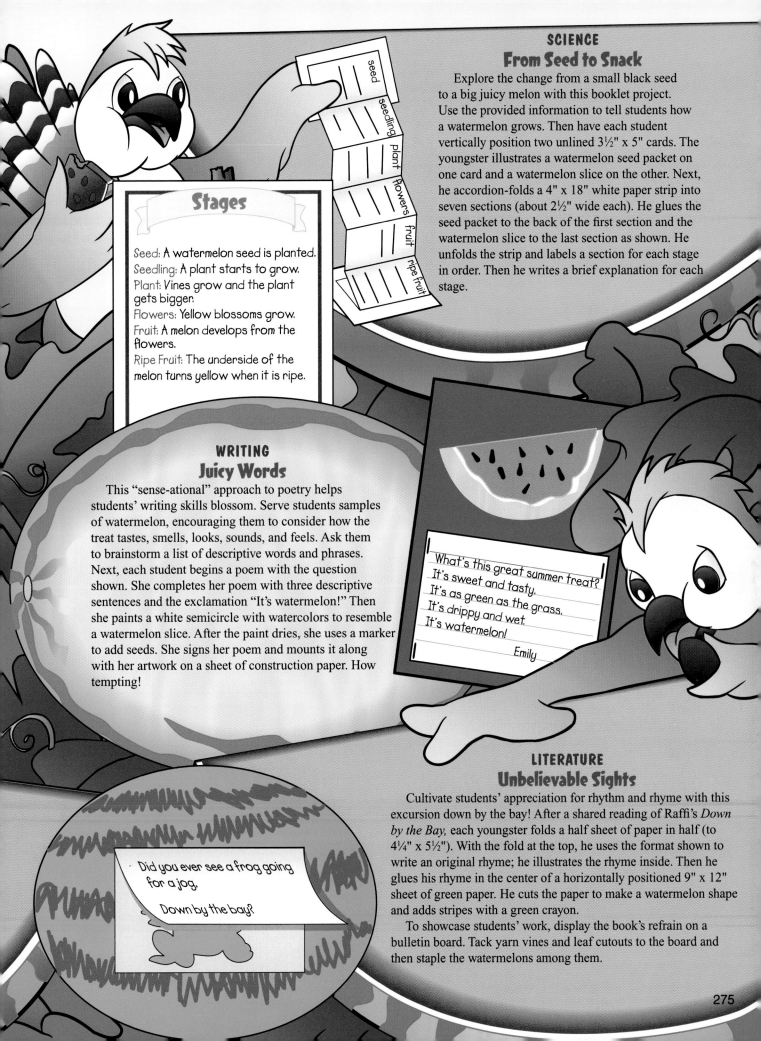

## Stages

Seed: A watermelon seed is planted.
Seedling: A plant starts to grow.
Plant: Vines grow and the plant gets bigger.
Flowers: Yellow blossoms grow.
Fruit: A melon develops from the flowers.
Ripe Fruit: The underside of the melon turns yellow when it is ripe.

seed
seedling
plant
flowers
fruit
ripe fruit

## SCIENCE
## From Seed to Snack

Explore the change from a small black seed to a big juicy melon with this booklet project. Use the provided information to tell students how a watermelon grows. Then have each student vertically position two unlined 3½" x 5" cards. The youngster illustrates a watermelon seed packet on one card and a watermelon slice on the other. Next, he accordion-folds a 4" x 18" white paper strip into seven sections (about 2½" wide each). He glues the seed packet to the back of the first section and the watermelon slice to the last section as shown. He unfolds the strip and labels a section for each stage in order. Then he writes a brief explanation for each stage.

## WRITING
## Juicy Words

This "sense-ational" approach to poetry helps students' writing skills blossom. Serve students samples of watermelon, encouraging them to consider how the treat tastes, smells, looks, sounds, and feels. Ask them to brainstorm a list of descriptive words and phrases. Next, each student begins a poem with the question shown. She completes her poem with three descriptive sentences and the exclamation "It's watermelon!" Then she paints a white semicircle with watercolors to resemble a watermelon slice. After the paint dries, she uses a marker to add seeds. She signs her poem and mounts it along with her artwork on a sheet of construction paper. How tempting!

What's this great summer treat?
It's sweet and tasty.
It's as green as the grass.
It's drippy and wet.
It's watermelon!

Emily

## LITERATURE
## Unbelievable Sights

Cultivate students' appreciation for rhythm and rhyme with this excursion down by the bay! After a shared reading of Raffi's *Down by the Bay*, each youngster folds a half sheet of paper in half (to 4¼" x 5½"). With the fold at the top, he uses the format shown to write an original rhyme; he illustrates the rhyme inside. Then he glues his rhyme in the center of a horizontally positioned 9" x 12" sheet of green paper. He cuts the paper to make a watermelon shape and adds stripes with a green crayon.

To showcase students' work, display the book's refrain on a bulletin board. Tack yarn vines and leaf cutouts to the board and then staple the watermelons among them.

Did you ever see a frog going for a jog,
Down by the bay?

# Colorful Feelings

Read. Look at each underlined name.
Choose the phrase that best tells how the
person may feel.
Color the crayon tip with the matching color.
Write the correct feeling word on the crayon.

### Color Phrases

| | | | |
|---|---|---|---|
| sees red | = angry | feels blue | = sad |
| tickled pink | = happy | green with envy | = jealous |

1. <u>Sue's</u> brother breaks her toy after she tells him to be careful.

2. <u>Jack</u> gets a brand-new bike.

3. <u>Tia</u> wants a doll just like Pam's.

4. <u>Bobby's</u> best friend moves away.

5. <u>Carlos</u> gets a surprise gift.

6. Ann gets the dress that <u>Maria</u> wants.

7. <u>Jill</u> loses her favorite baseball card.

8. <u>David's</u> sister turns the TV off during his favorite show.

**Bonus Box:** Reread sentence 1 and your answer. On the back of this sheet, write a sentence to tell another way that Sue may feel. Explain your answer.

©The Education Center, Inc. • THE MAILBOX® • Primary • Aug/Sept 2003 • Key p. 313

# Nuts About Facts

Write the fact family for each set of numbers.

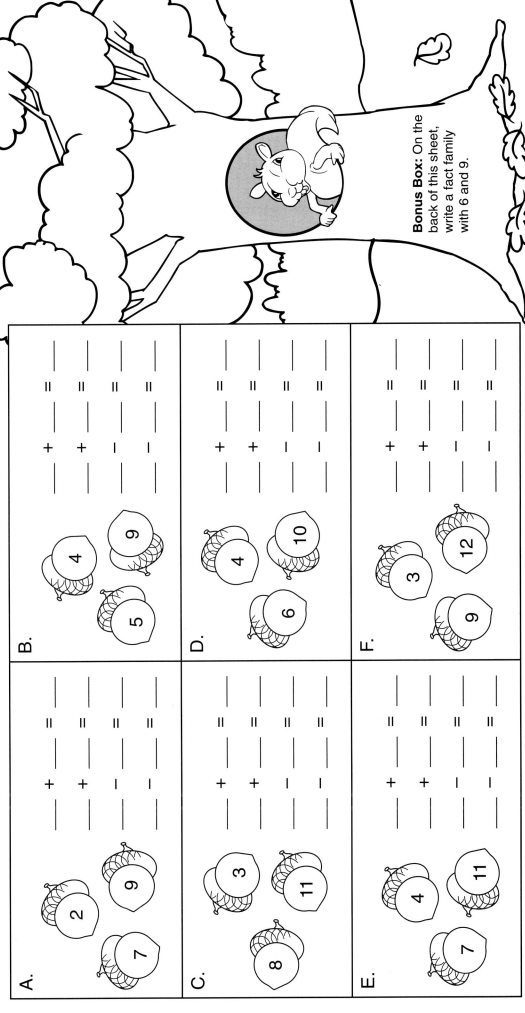

**A.** 7 2 9

___ + ___ = ___
___ + ___ = ___
___ − ___ = ___
___ − ___ = ___

**B.** 4 5 9

___ + ___ = ___
___ + ___ = ___
___ − ___ = ___
___ − ___ = ___

**C.** 3 8 11

___ + ___ = ___
___ + ___ = ___
___ − ___ = ___
___ − ___ = ___

**D.** 4 6 10

___ + ___ = ___
___ + ___ = ___
___ − ___ = ___
___ − ___ = ___

**E.** 4 7 11

___ + ___ = ___
___ + ___ = ___
___ − ___ = ___
___ − ___ = ___

**F.** 3 9 12

___ + ___ = ___
___ + ___ = ___
___ − ___ = ___
___ − ___ = ___

**Bonus Box:** On the back of this sheet, write a fact family with 6 and 9.

©The Education Center, Inc. • *THE MAILBOX® • Primary • Oct/Nov 2003 • Key p. 313

**Note to the teacher:** To modify this activity, make one copy and white-out the numbers on the acorns; program the acorns with different numbers and then make student copies. Or, to give youngsters extra support, write the correct numbers on selected blanks before making student copies.

# Picture Cards and Snowpals

Use the picture cards with "A Wintry Cycle" on page 268 and
the snowpals with " 'Snow' Problem" on page 269.

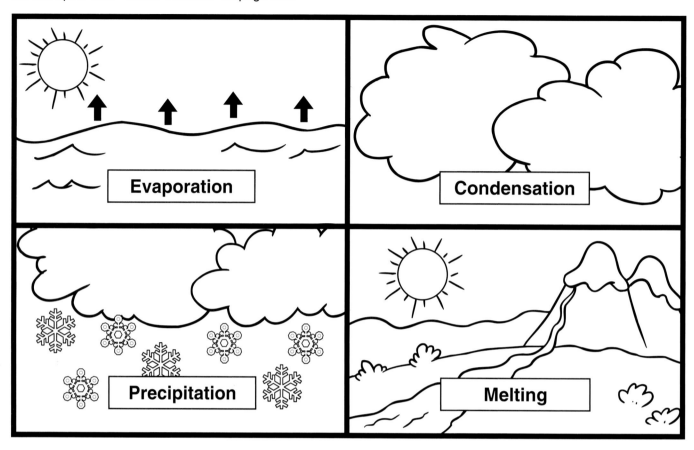

Evaporation

Condensation

Precipitation

Melting

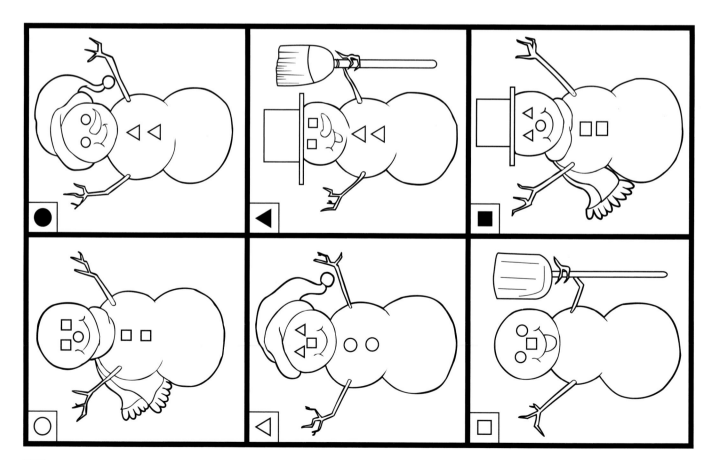

Name _____

# Party Plans

It's almost time for a Presidents' Day party!
Look at a February calendar.
Answer the questions below.

Let's Celebrate!

1. George Washington was born on February 22. What
   day is that? _____

2. Abraham Lincoln was born on February 12. What day
   is that? _____

3. Presidents' Day is the third Monday. What is the date?
   _____

Only quarters and pennies may be used to buy party
supplies.
Follow your teacher's directions to show the fewest
coins needed for each item.

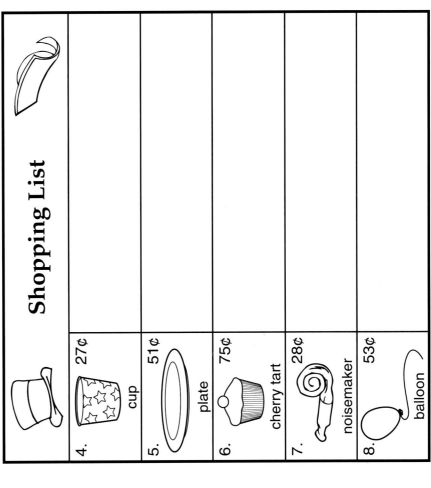

## Shopping List

| | |
|---|---|
| 4. 27¢ cup | |
| 5. 51¢ plate | |
| 6. 75¢ cherry tart | |
| 7. 28¢ noisemaker | |
| 8. 53¢ balloon | |

©The Education Center, Inc. • THE MAILBOX® • Primary • Feb/Mar 2004 • Key p. 313

**Note to the teacher:** Use with "A 'Cent-sational' Introduction" on page 270. To show the needed coins, have students draw large and small circles to represent quarters and pennies and then label each circle with the correct value. Or ask more advanced students to write money equations.

# Booklet Cover and Page

Use with "Honeycomb Hexagons" on page 272.

## Honeycomb Hexagons

Name _____

I made this hexagon with

_____

_____

_____

# Busy Bees

Mr. Brown is a beekeeper.
Study the map of his farm. Answer the questions.

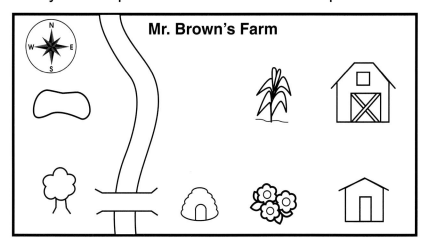

Map Key

= pond    = garden
= orchard    = field
= bridge    = barn
= river    = house
= hive

1. What is north of the house? _____

2. What is south of the garden? _____

3. What is west of the bridge? _____

4. A bee leaves the hive and flies east. What is the first place that it will come to?
   _____

5. A bee flies from the garden to the field. In what
   direction does it go?
   _____

6. A bee in the orchard flies to the pond.
   In what direction does it go?
   _____

7. A bee flies from the house to the barn.
   In what direction does it go?
   _____

8. A bee in the hive wants to get nectar from
   the orchard. In what direction should it go?
   _____

Name ____________________

Watermelon
Comparing numbers

# Melon Math

Cut. Read each pair of numbers.
Glue a watermelon slice to compare them.

| | | |
|---|---|---|
| 1. 204 ☐ 200 | 2. 562 ☐ 560 | 3. 729 ☐ 731 |
| 4. 845 ☐ 846 | 5. 978 ☐ 976 | 6. 653 ☐ 654 |
| 7. 390 ☐ 392 | 8. 457 ☐ 455 | 9. 612 ☐ 610 |
| 10. 871 ☐ 872 | | |

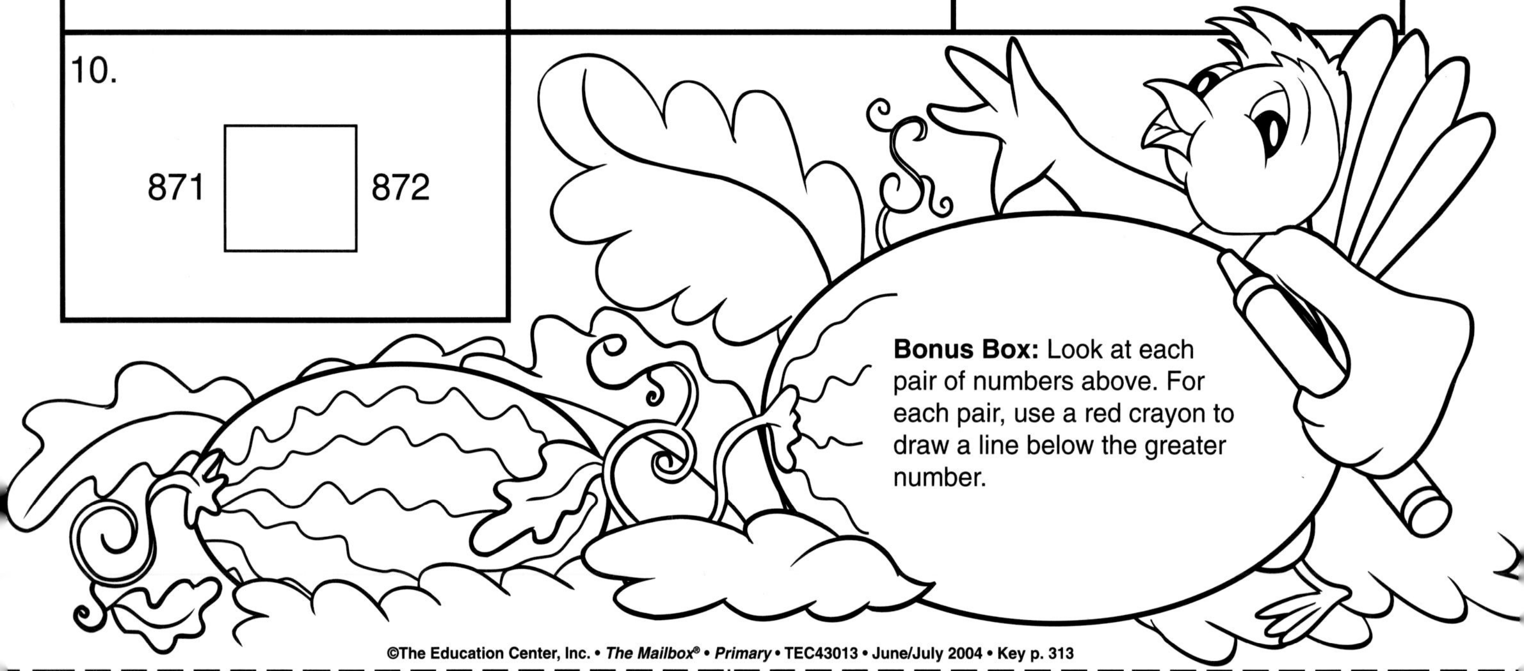

**Bonus Box:** Look at each pair of numbers above. For each pair, use a red crayon to draw a line below the greater number.



 **Note to the teacher:** Use with "In Comparison" on page 274.

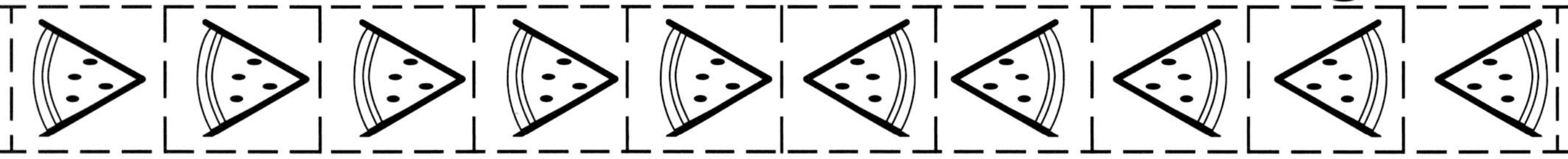

# SOCIAL STUDIES UNITS

# Economics in

Bank on this collection of ideas to help students make "cents" of basic economics concepts, from wants and needs to producers and consumers.

## Necessary or Not?

*Distinguishing between wants and needs*

Begin your study of economics with this valuable classification activity. List these two groups of words on the board: *sandwiches, tent, sweater* and *book, shampoo, backpack.* Explain that the items are for a fishing trip, and challenge students to determine how you grouped them. Lead youngsters to realize that the items are grouped into needs (things a person must have to live) and wants (things that are not necessary). Point out that food, shelter, and clothing are basic needs.

To follow up, each student draws a line down the center of a horizontally positioned 9" x 12" sheet of white paper. Leaving a few inches at the top of his paper blank, he titles one column "Needs" and one column "Wants." He lists three or more items for each category. Then he illustrates a provided head-and-shoulders cutout to make a self-likeness. He glues his cutout and two construction paper hands to his paper as shown. After each student completes his work, invite your budding consumers to share their ideas about the influence of wants and needs on purchasing decisions.

adapted from an idea by Sister Santa Teresa—Gr. 2
Holy Innocents School
Philadelphia, PA

| Needs | Wants |
| --- | --- |
| food | CD player |
| warm clothes | computer |
| house | skateboard |

## Workplace Mural

*Exploring different types of work*

At this display, satisfying needs and wants is the talk of the town! To begin, divide students into small groups. Have the students in each group illustrate an assigned workplace on provided paper and then cut it out. (Or, if desired, give each group a snapshot of a local workplace.) Instruct the youngsters to label an index card with the name of their workplace and write a sentence to explain its role in meeting people's needs or wants. Post each completed illustration with the corresponding card on a paper-covered bulletin board. To complete the scene, arrange for students to add background details with desired arts-and-crafts materials. The result will be a handy reference for use throughout your economics study!

Laura Knarr—Gr. 3, St. Charles School, Lima, OH

284

# the Community

## Spending Savvy
*Distinguishing between goods and services*

Cash in on this introduction to goods and services. Divide students into small groups and give each group a large sheet of paper. On the board, write the businesses listed below. Ask the students in each group to divide their paper into two columns. Have them list the businesses in the first column. Instruct them to write in the second column one thing that they might pay for at each business.

After each group announces its purchases to the class, comment that only two types of purchases were possible: goods or services. Clarify that a good is something that is made or grown and then sold, and a service is work that is done for others. Then have students code each of their purchases with a *G* for good or an *S* for service. For additional reinforcement, encourage youngsters to identify goods and services when they go on errands with their families.

| Businesses | Purchases |
|---|---|
| pet shop | dog food |
| doctor's office | |
| grocery store | |
| bakery | |
| car wash | |
| bicycle repair shop | |

## Dual Roles
*Understanding the roles of producers and consumers*

This look at producers and consumers is sure to spark your students' imaginations! Ask students to suppose that they own businesses that make and sell things. Invite them to brainstorm goods that their companies could produce. Comment that students would be consumers as well as producers since they would make purchases for their businesses.

To explore these two roles, give each youngster a 6" x 18" strip of white paper. The youngster folds in the ends of her paper to meet in the middle and then unfolds her paper to reveal three sections. She labels the first section "Consumer" and the third section "Producer." In the second section, she writes the name of her business and illustrates the goods that her company produces. She lists her purchases in the first section and her company's goods in the third section. Then she refolds her project and illustrates her business on the front of it.

## On the Town
*Classifying purchases*

After students are familiar with goods and services, use this booklet project to take them around town. To begin, each student cuts out the two booklet strips from a copy of page 286. He glues the strips together where indicated to form one long strip. Then he signs his name. He reads each spending scenario and writes the appropriate word in each blank. To complete his booklet, he colors the illustrations and accordion-folds his strip. Nifty!

285

# Booklet Strips

Use with "On the Town" on page 285.

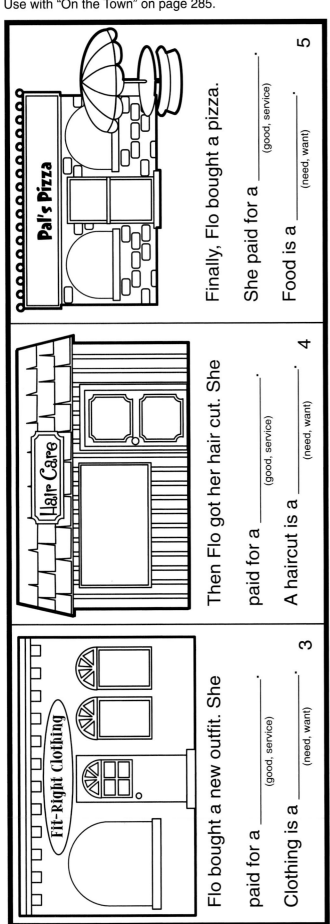

**Pal's Pizza**

Finally, Flo bought a pizza.

She paid for a _____ .
(good, service)

Food is a _____ .
(need, want)

5

**Hair Care**

Then Flo got her hair cut. She

paid for a _____ .
(good, service)

A haircut is a _____ .
(need, want)

4

**Fit-Right Clothing**

Flo bought a new outfit. She

paid for a _____ .
(good, service)

Clothing is a _____ .
(need, want)

3

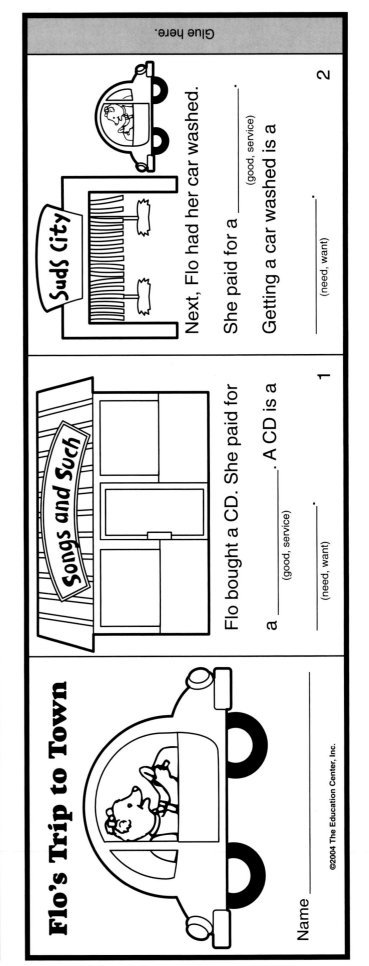

Glue here.

**Suds City**

Next, Flo had her car washed.

She paid for a _____ .
(good, service)

Getting a car washed is a

_____ .
(need, want)

2

**Songs and Such**

Flo bought a CD. She paid for

a _____ . A CD is a
(good, service)

_____ .
(need, want)

1

# Flo's Trip to Town

Name _____

# Towns, States, and Beyond!

Use the following activities to take students on location and help them recognize their place in the world!

## Community Comparison
*Comparing rural and urban communities*

Focus on community settings with this picture-perfect comparison! Ask volunteers to define *community* in their own words. Remind students that a community may be in a city, the country, or in a suburb. Wonder aloud how the communities in city and country settings compare. To find out, each youngster makes a large Venn diagram in the center of a 12" x 18" sheet of white construction paper. He labels one circle "country" and the other circle "city."

Guide students to identify characteristics of the two types of communities and have them write the details on their diagrams. Then ask each youngster to divide his paper into two sections as shown. Have him illustrate a country scene and a city scene on the corresponding parts of his paper. The similarities and differences will become clear!

Nancy Jonas—Gr. 2, Lincoln Elementary, La Porte, IN

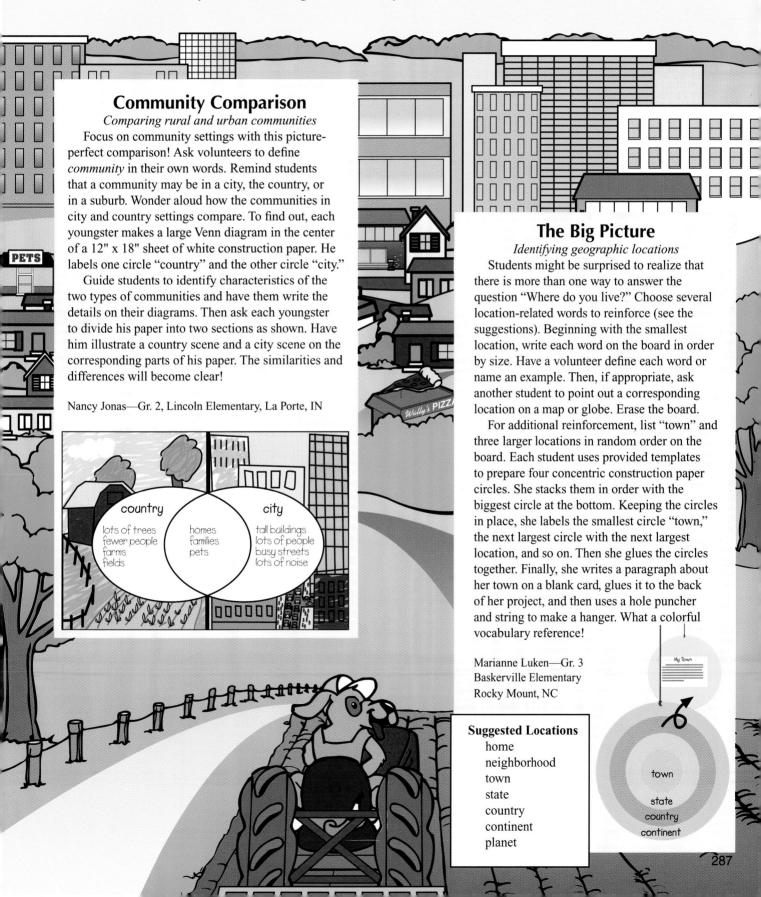

country | city
lots of trees / fewer people / farms / fields | homes / families / pets | tall buildings / lots of people / busy streets / lots of noise

## The Big Picture
*Identifying geographic locations*

Students might be surprised to realize that there is more than one way to answer the question "Where do you live?" Choose several location-related words to reinforce (see the suggestions). Beginning with the smallest location, write each word on the board in order by size. Have a volunteer define each word or name an example. Then, if appropriate, ask another student to point out a corresponding location on a map or globe. Erase the board.

For additional reinforcement, list "town" and three larger locations in random order on the board. Each student uses provided templates to prepare four concentric construction paper circles. She stacks them in order with the biggest circle at the bottom. Keeping the circles in place, she labels the smallest circle "town," the next largest circle with the next largest location, and so on. Then she glues the circles together. Finally, she writes a paragraph about her town on a blank card, glues it to the back of her project, and then uses a hole puncher and string to make a hanger. What a colorful vocabulary reference!

Marianne Luken—Gr. 3
Baskerville Elementary
Rocky Mount, NC

### Suggested Locations
home
neighborhood
town
state
country
continent
planet

My Town

town
state
country
continent

287

# Where, Oh Where?

*Exploring location in global terms*

This unique address book gives students a global perspective! Give each youngster the listed materials and help him use the directions to make a booklet. He'll soon be right at home with explaining where he lives!

**Materials for one booklet:**

copy of the boxes below and on page 289 (or selected boxes to modify the activity, as desired)

4½" x 6" construction paper rectangle (for front cover)

6" x 9" construction paper rectangle (for back cover)

scrap of white construction paper

sheet of white paper

crayons

scissors

stapler

glue

**Directions:**

1. Complete the sentences and cut out the boxes.
2. Fold the sheet of white paper in half twice. Unfold it, and then cut it into quarters using the creases as a guide.
3. Vertically position the larger rectangle on a work surface. To make a booklet, staple the smaller rectangle and quarter sheets of paper to the bottom of it as shown.
4. Trim the top of the booklet to resemble a roof. Make two cuts in the front cover to create a door similar to the one shown. Fold back the resulting flap.
5. On the back of the front cover, glue a piece of white construction paper to cover the doorway.
6. Close the booklet and illustrate yourself in the doorway. Add crayon details to the cover.
7. Sequence the boxes, beginning with the smallest location. Glue them in the booklet, using the front and back of the pages.
8. Illustrate your neighborhood on any blank pages.

Cindy Fingerlin—Gr. 3, Arleth School, Parlin, NJ

Step 3

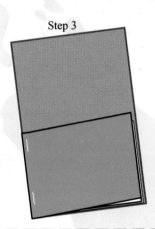

- - - - - - - - - - - - - - - - - - - - - - - - - - - - - - - - - - - - - - - - - - - - - - - - - - - - - - - - - - - - - - - -

## Booklet Boxes

Use with "Where, Oh Where?" on this page.

| **Continent** | **Planet** |
|---|---|
| My country is on the continent of _____. | I live on the planet _____. |
| There are ____ continents. | It has land, oceans, and seas. |

## Home

My name is _____

_____. My

home is near _____.

Home, Sweet Home

©2003 The Education Center, Inc.

## Neighborhood

I live on _____

_____. In my neighborhood,

I see _____

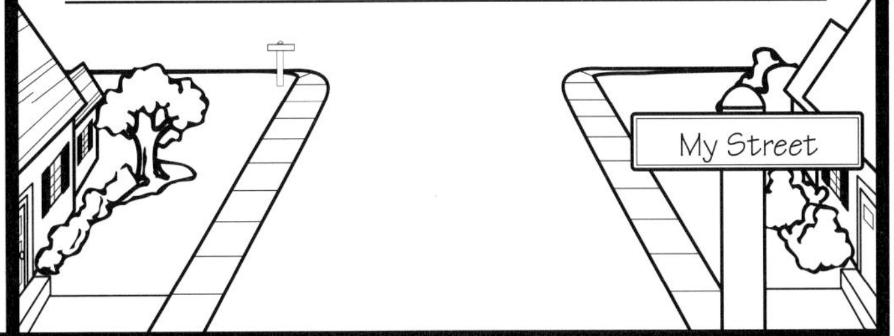

_____.

My Street

## Town

I live in the town of _____

_____.

My town is _____.

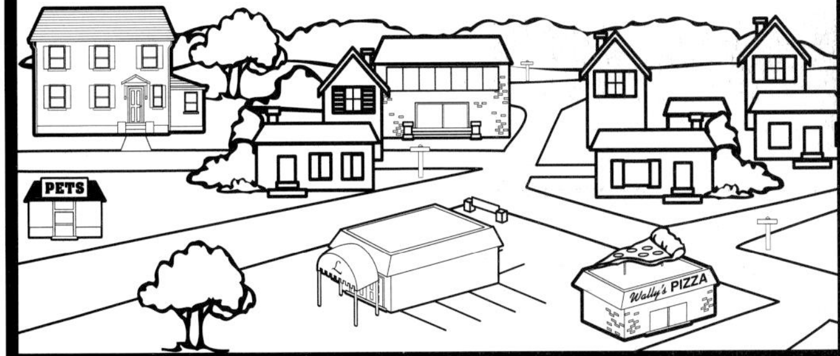

PETS

Wally's PIZZA

## The City, Suburbs, or Country?

My town is in the _____.

My town has _____

_____.

## State

I live in the state of _____

_____.

The capital of my state is _____

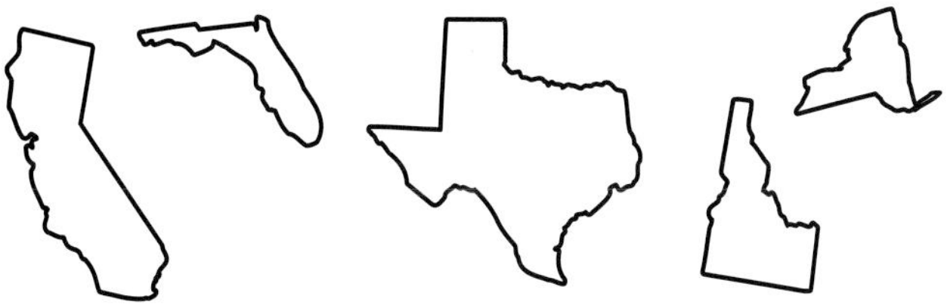

_____.

## Country

My state is in the country of _____

_____.

It has _____ states.

# Get the Message?

## Exploring Communication Through Time

Tune in to a variety of social studies skills with this look at communication past, present, and future!

*ideas contributed by Starin Lewis, Phoenix, AZ*

## Timely Signals

***Using the terms*** past, present, ***and*** future

Set the stage for clear communication with a review of timely vocabulary! Write the words *past, present,* and *future* on the board. Ask students to tell in their own words what each term means. To check understanding, have volunteers use the words in sentences. Next, name a listed communication method and have each student categorize it as past, present, or future by giving a signal—tapping his desk if it is commonly used now, gesturing behind him if it is mainly from long ago, and pointing forward if it's not yet common. Ask a student who responded correctly to name the correct term. Then encourage youngsters to tell the class any relevant information they know. Continue with the rest of the list to get students thinking (and talking!) about communication.

### Ways to Communicate

feather pen and ink *(past)*
telephone with no buttons or dials *(past)*
television *(present)*
cordless phone *(present)*
radio *(present)*
teleputer, a computer and television combined *(future)*
smoke signals *(past)*
mobile phone in a glove *(future)*
Pony Express *(past)*
email *(present)*

## Winged Messengers

***Exploring changes in communication***

This partner activity is bound to be a vivid reminder that communication has changed a lot! Tell students that long ago some messages were sent by trained pigeons. A person would roll up a message and tie it to a pigeon's back or leg; the bird would return after delivering it. Use the following activity to represent this form of communication. To begin, pair students and give each pair a copy of the pigeon on page 292 and a length of string. Each twosome cuts out the pigeon and glues it onto a folded sheet of paper. Partner 1 unfolds the paper and writes a question inside. Each partner takes one end of the string. The partners move apart until the string is taut; then Partner 2 sits on the floor. Partner 1 folds the paper over the string and angles the string so that the paper slides down to Partner 2. This student unfolds the paper, reads the question, and writes a response. She stands (as her partner sits) and uses the established method to send her response.

After each student sends and receives a few messages, have youngsters brainstorm the benefits and challenges of using real pigeons for communication. Then ask them to compare this form of communication with today's methods, from snail mail to email!

## Mail Call!

***Distinguishing between communication then and now***

Through snow, rain, heat, and gloom of night, mail has been delivered for years! Use this activity to explore how the delivery system has changed over time. Have students recall what they know about today's postal service. Explain that around 140 years ago, horseback riders used a relay system called the Pony Express to deliver mail between Missouri and California. Then give each student a copy of page 293.

Each youngster colors the illustrations. He cuts out his strips, stamp, and envelope. Then he titles the blank side of his envelope "USPS" (United States Postal Service), signs the top left-hand corner, and glues on the stamp. He decides whether each strip tells about the Pony Express or USPS and sorts the strips into these categories. When students' sorting is complete, review the categories as a class and have students check their work. Then instruct each youngster to glue his strips onto the correct sides of his envelope. Now that's a first-class look at communication!

## Dots and Dashes

***Recognizing an invention's significance***

What better way to teach students about the telegraph than by having them use Morse code? On the board, write a one-word message with the code on page 292. Explain to students that you have written a message in code. Then give each youngster a copy of the code and have him decode the word. Remark that the code was used with the telegraph that Samuel Morse and his partner developed in the early 1800s. Explain that messages were sent over a wire and the code was recorded at the receiving end with dots and dashes.

Next, give every two students a length of adding machine tape. In turn, each youngster asks his partner a question that requires a brief response. His partner uses Morse code to write his answer on the adding machine tape, leaving extra space between letters for easier decoding. He draws a vertical line to mark the end of his response. After each twosome has a few exchanges, discuss with students the impact of the telegraph. Point out that telegraphs were a popular way to quickly share news, and Morse code was used for emergency communication until recent years. Impressive!

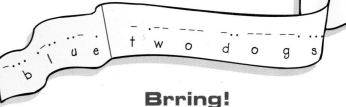

## Brring!

***Explaining the significance of an inventor's accomplishment***

Thanks to Alexander Graham Bell, it's possible to talk with people thousands of miles away. Tell students that when Bell invented the telephone, it was the first time sound was sent over wires. Ask students to imagine what people's lives would be like without telephones. Have each youngster write a paragraph to share her ideas and then mount it on a slightly larger piece of construction paper. Showcase students' writing on a bulletin board titled "Thank You, Mr. Bell!" Decorate the display with student-made illustrations of various types of telephones.

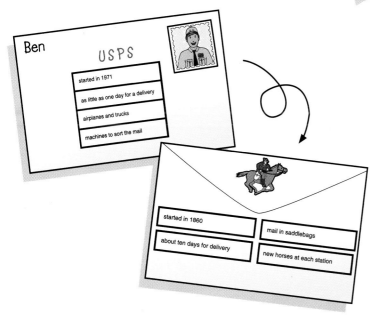

291

## Pigeon Pattern
Use with "Winged Messengers" on page 290.

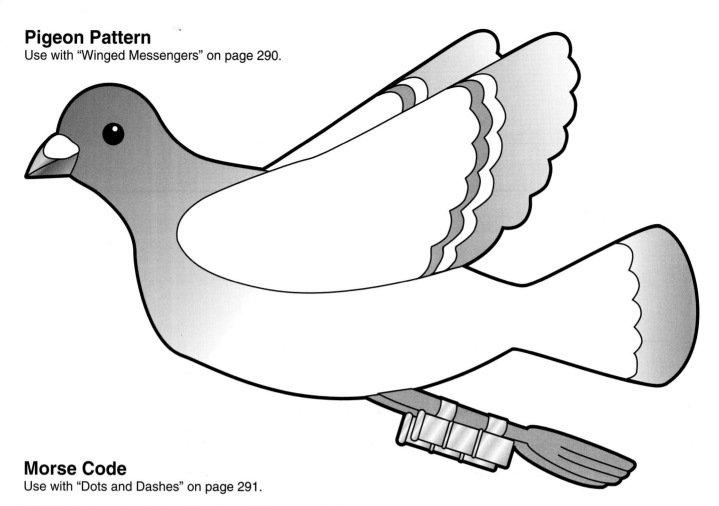

## Morse Code
Use with "Dots and Dashes" on page 291.

| Morse Code | | |
|---|---|---|
| A •— | J •——— | S ••• |
| B —••• | K —•— | T — |
| C —•—• | L •—•• | U ••— |
| D —•• | M —— | V •••— |
| E • | N —• | W •—— |
| F ••—• | O ——— | X —••— |
| G ——• | P •——• | Y —•—— |
| H •••• | Q ——•— | Z ——•• |
| I •• | R •—• | |

| about ten days for delivery | airplanes and trucks |
| --- | --- |
| started in 1971 | mail in saddlebags |
| new horses at each station | started in 1860 |
| as little as one day for a delivery | machines to sort the mail |

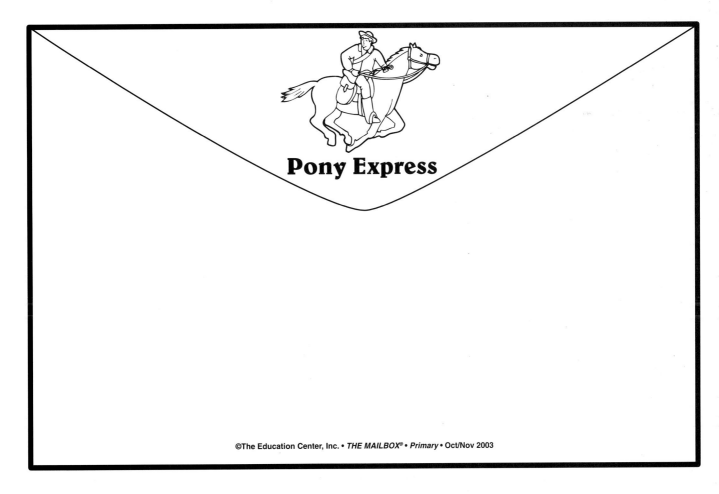

**Pony Express**

# Hooray for the USA!
## Investigating Historic Landmarks
With summer vacation approaching, there's no better time for a cross-country tour of several famous American sites!

*ideas contributed by Laura Wagner, Raleigh, NC*

 Mount Rushmore

### Mount Rushmore Facts
- The monument honors George Washington, Thomas Jefferson, Theodore Roosevelt, and Abraham Lincoln.
- The faces are 60 feet tall.
- About 400 workers helped build the monument.
- To shape the rock, workers were strapped into chairs and lowered down the mountain.

### Grand Canyon Facts
- The canyon is the biggest in the world (277 miles long and 18 miles wide at some points).
- The layers of rock are various colors. They seem to change tones as the sun moves.
- Animals such as beavers, elk, mountain lions, and snakes live in the area.
- Some tourists hike, ride mules, or ride rafts in the canyon.

Grand Canyon

## Grand Canyon Greetings
Begin your sensational tour at the awe-inspiring Grand Canyon! Ask a volunteer to find on a map the state where the canyon is located (Arizona). Explain that the canyon was formed over millions of years by the Colorado River cutting through layers of rocks. Share the facts shown and illustrations from selected books about the canyon. Next, each child imagines that she is sending a postcard from the Grand Canyon to a loved one. She illustrates the canyon on one side of a large blank index card. On the other side, she writes a message that includes descriptive or factual details about the landmark. "Send-sational!"

Dear Grandma,
I am at the Grand Canyon in Arizona. Some of the rocks are red and brown. They look like they change color during the day. It's awesome!
Love,
Ayanna

## Mount Rushmore Heroes
This exploration of Mount Rushmore helps students put names with faces and historic facts. Display an illustration of the South Dakota monument and explain that it is a tribute to four of the most popular American presidents. Identify each president and share the facts listed above. Then pair students. Give each twosome a quarter sheet of paper with the name of a featured president, telling the students not to reveal the name. On the blank side of the paper, have the twosome use provided references to write a "Who Am I?" riddle with three clues about the president. Check the clues. Then arrange for each twosome to read its riddle to another student pair and challenge the youngsters to solve it. What a rock-solid review of presidents!

Theodore (Teddy) Roosevelt

I was the 26th U.S. president.

I was the youngest president.

A type of stuffed animal was named after me.

Who am I?

## Statue of Liberty Symbols

Set students' sights on Lady Liberty! Display pictures of this gift from France and use the provided information to explain how the statue symbolizes freedom. Tell students that long ago many immigrants passed the statue in New York as they entered the country. Guide youngsters to imagine how the immigrants might have felt when they saw the 305-foot figure.

Next, have each student write about the statue on a 4" x 6" index card, including why it is an important landmark. Then ask her to staple her writing to a 6" x 9" piece of construction paper and add patriotic decorations. Display students' completed work on a bulletin board titled "Lady Liberty." Youngsters are sure to agree that the statue was a monumental gift!

Statue of Liberty

Kerry

The statue was a huge present from France. The statue shows everyone that Americans believe in being free. My favorite part is the torch. I like it because it means lighting the way to freedom.

**Statue of Liberty Facts**
- The statue welcomes people to the United States.
- The seven spikes on the crown represent the light of liberty shining on the seven seas and continents.
- The torch stands for lighting the way to freedom.
- The tablet shows the date of the Declaration of Independence.

Washington, DC

## Wow! Washington, DC!

Conclude your tour with a look at four important landmarks in the U.S. capital. Confirm that students can locate the city on a map. Then give each student a copy of page 296. Read each set of facts with students and help them identify the corresponding picture. Have each student embellish his fact cards with crayon details and then cut out all of the cards. Ask him to glue each fact card onto one side of a construction paper rectangle (about 3" x 4½") and the matching picture card on the other side. The resulting souvenirs will help him keep the facts in mind!

## What a Trip!

These travel booklets will be lasting reminders of your landmark tour. To prepare, copy page 297 to make seven booklet pages and one picture strip for each student. Prompt a class discussion to help students recall details about each featured landmark. To make his booklet, each youngster cuts out his pages and pictures. He staples the pages inside a 3" x 5" construction paper folder and glues a picture onto each one. He labels each page with the corresponding landmark and location. Then he writes an interesting fact about the landmark. On the front cover, he writes a title, adds an illustration of himself traveling, and signs his name.

My Landmark Tour

Hector

# Fact and Picture Cards

Use with "Wow! Washington, DC!" on page 295.

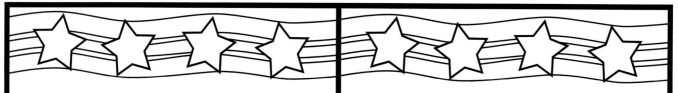

## Jefferson Memorial

- Built to remember Thomas Jefferson (third U.S. president)
- Honors his belief in freedom
- Has a dome just as his home does

## Lincoln Memorial

- Built to remember Abraham Lincoln (16th U.S. president)
- Honors his work to end slavery
- Has a 19-foot statue of Lincoln in a chair

## Washington Monument

- Built to remember George Washington (first U.S. president)
- Honors him as the Father of the Country
- Is about 555 feet tall and has a pointed top

## White House

- Has been a home to each president except George Washington
- Is where the president works
- Has 132 rooms, including a bowling alley

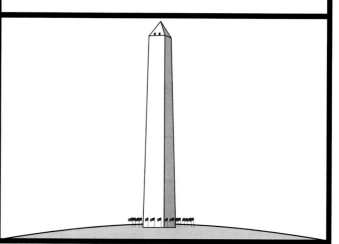

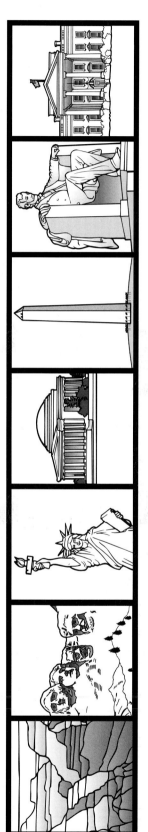

(landmark)

(location)

Interesting fact:

(landmark)

(location)

Interesting fact:

(landmark)

(location)

Interesting fact:

(landmark)

(location)

Interesting fact:

# At the Top of the World

## Learning About Mountains

This intriguing look at mountains is sure to take your students' understanding of geography to new heights!

*ideas contributed by Stacie Stone Davis, Lima, NY*

### Mountain Mix-Up

*Prompting prior knowledge, using a map*

"Peak" your students' interest in mountains with a letter-perfect introduction. In advance, program a blank card for each letter in the word *mountain*. Secure the cards to the board in random order. To begin, challenge students to unscramble the letters to find out what topic they'll be studying next. Allow time for each youngster to use scrap paper for this purpose. Then entertain students' guesses and guide them as needed. After the topic is identified and the word is correctly spelled, invite students to share their ideas about the distinction between *mountains* and *hills*. Clarify that mountains and hills are both landforms that are higher than their surroundings but that mountains are much higher than hills.

Next, divide students into groups. Give each group a grade-appropriate atlas or a U.S. map that shows mountains. Then have students locate various mountains. Wow! Some mountain ranges are long!

### Information in Place

*Using a graphic organizer*

Showcase a range of knowledge at this ongoing display! Cover a large, easily accessible bulletin board with white paper and title it "Mountains." Draw three mountains and label them as shown. Have each student prepare an individual version of the graphic organizer on a sheet of paper. On his first two mountains, encourage him to jot down what he already knows about mountains and what he would like to learn about them. Invite students to share what they wrote; compile their thoughts on the appropriate parts of the display.

Throughout your study, have students add information to their papers. Periodically enlist students' help to incorporate their learning into the display. To complete the mountain scenes, encourage youngsters to add colorful details to the display and their papers.

---

## Mountains

**Know**

Some have snow.
They're tall.
People ski on them.
They are fun to climb.

**Want to Know**

How are they made?
How many are there?
Why do they have snow in the summer?
Why are they different shapes?

**Learned**

Many mountains are more than two miles high.
Mountains are made in different ways.
The higher you go, the colder it gets.

## Amazing Changes
*Understanding how landforms change*

Mountains are growing and changing all of the time! After sharing this information with students, explain that mountains build up so slowly that people do not see the changes happening. Then give each youngster a copy of page 300. Read with students the information about a fold mountain. For clarification, lay a dish towel on a table top, place a hand on either end of the towel, and then slowly push the ends inward to create one or more folds and ridges. After a few volunteers repeat the demonstration, set the towel aside for other students to experiment with later. Then read and discuss the information about block, dome, and volcanic mountains.

To complete her project, each student colors the mountain patterns and cuts them out. She signs her name on the cover, colors the cover illustration, and cuts out the booklet pages. She uses context clues to match each mountain pattern with the appropriate information and then glues the patterns in place. She stacks her pages behind her cover and staples the stack at the bottom of a 6" x 9" construction paper rectangle as shown. She cuts the paper to resemble a mountain. Then she glues on a snowy peak that she fashions from construction paper.

## In the Region
*Investigating mountain regions*

What's it like in the mountains? That's what students explore with this discussion activity. Program a large blank card for each sentence shown, omitting the information in the parentheses. Draw a T chart on the board and label one column "True" and the other column "False." Remind students that different habitats influence people, plants, and animals in different ways.

After dividing students into small groups, display a card and read it aloud. Allow time for each group to decide whether the statement is true or false. At your signal, ask each student to give a thumbs-up (true) or thumbs-down (false) to indicate his group's answer. Invite a student from each group to share the group's reasoning. Then tape the card in the correct column and share the provided information. Continue with the remaining cards in a similar manner.

## True or False?

- It is hotter at the top of a mountain.
  *(False. It is colder, so mountain climbers should dress warmly.)*

- Millions of people vacation in mountain regions.
  *(True. Many local people work in tourism.)*

- All animals have a hard time walking on rocky mountains.
  *(False. Mountain goats have adapted with hooves.)*

- It is easy for farmers to grow plants on mountains.
  *(False. The soil is thin and rocky.)*

- Many mountain animals have thick fur.
  *(True. They have adapted to the cold.)*

- Trees grow all over mountains.
  *(False. Some parts of some mountains are too cold.)*

How Are Mountains Made?

Name _____

**Fold Mountain**

The earth has layers of rock. Sometimes the layers push up and fold over. This makes a mountain with a pointed top.

**Block Mountain**

Sometimes the rocks deep in the earth move and make cracks called faults. The rock near the cracks pushes up. It makes a mountain with a flat top.

**Dome Mountain**

In some places, magma fills a hole that is deep in the earth. As more magma gathers, it pushes up rock. The rock makes a mountain with a round top.

**Volcanic Mountain**

Sometimes magma pushes through cracks in the earth. Then it cools, hardens, and piles up. This makes a mountain that has a cone shape.

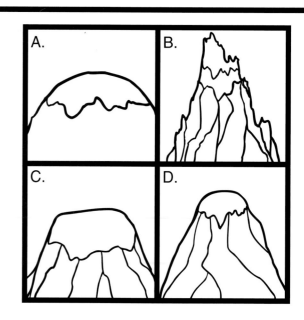

A.

B.

C.

D.

# TEACHER RESOURCE UNITS

# Get Acquainted With _____

name _____

| Family Members | Hobby | Best Memory |
|---|---|---|
| | | |

| Favorite Animal | Funniest Memory | Favorite Place |
|---|---|---|
| | | |

302

©2003 The Education Center, Inc.

**Note to the teacher:** Use with "Get Acquainted!" on page 304.

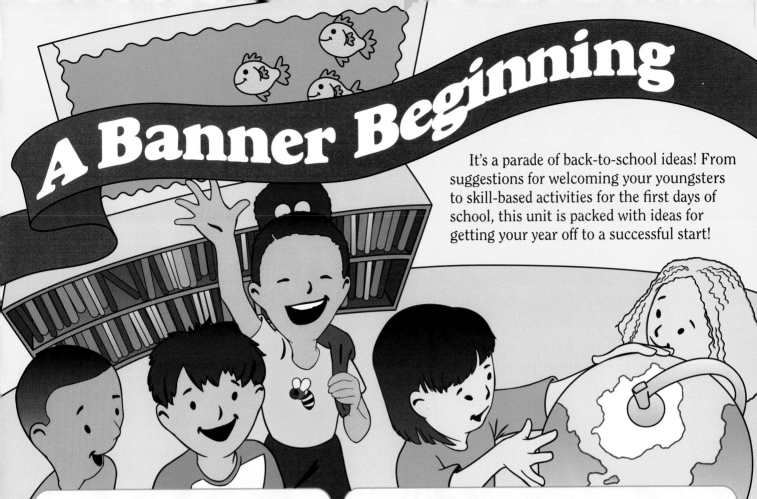

# A Banner Beginning

It's a parade of back-to-school ideas! From suggestions for welcoming your youngsters to skill-based activities for the first days of school, this unit is packed with ideas for getting your year off to a successful start!

## First-Day Fun

Greet students with a back-to-school version of a welcome wagon! Line a toy wagon, basket, or another large open container with colorful tissue paper; then label it with a welcoming sign. Place inside several school-themed books, such as *First Day Jitters* by Julie Danneberg and *Never Ride Your Elephant to School* by Doug Johnson. Add desired student supplies including blank nametags and novelty pencils. Use bulletin board paper to prepare a banner for students to sign and decorate. Roll it up and tuck it among the supplies.

On the first day of school, direct students' attention to the festive display with a great deal of fanfare. Distribute the supplies and have each student prepare a nametag. Then set aside time for students to complete the banner and enjoy the reading selections. Hooray for school!

Heather Leverett
Nashville, TN

## Meaningful Gift Bags

These unique gift bags double as an introduction to your classroom. For each child, personalize a paper lunch bag. Inside place several items that represent school-themed messages (see the suggestions). Fold over the top of the bag and then seal it with a decorative sticker. Before students arrive, place each youngster's bag and a copy of the provided poem on his desk.

Tell students that each bag contains items that represent details about being in your class. Invite each youngster to open his bag, examine the contents, and silently guess each item's significance. Prompt a class discussion to explore students' ideas; then reveal the intended meaning of each item. What a motivating welcome!

Leann Schwartz—Gr. 2
Ossian Elementary
Ossian, IN

### Poem
Our banner year begins right here
With nifty bags of new school gear.
Look inside and try to guess
Why each item means success!

### Gift-Bag Items
**Bookmark:** We'll read lots of great books.
**Notepaper:** We'll have fun writing.
**Pencil with an eraser:** We'll make mistakes, and that's okay.
**Stickers:** We'll stick together by helping each other.
**Roll of Smarties candy:** We'll learn a lot!

## Name Scramble

Use word-building practice to help students learn their classmates' names forward and backward! Give each student a mini chalkboard, a piece of chalk, and an eraser. Secretly choose a student's first or last name. On the board, write the letters of his name in scrambled order. Challenge each student to use selected letters to write the smallest possible word, pointing out that there might be multiple words with the same number of letters.

At your signal, have each youngster hold up his chalkboard. Ask one or more students to read their words aloud; write them on the board. Continue with increasingly larger words until all of the letters are used and the name is spelled. Repeat the activity with a few names each day until every youngster's name has been featured.

Michelle Rosengrant—Gr. 1, Wingate Elementary School, Wingate, PA

## What a Summer!

Organizing information is the key to this summer survey. Suggest that whether students stayed home or traveled, they did many different things this summer. Name several possible activities, including commonplace pastimes. Ask each student to list five of her vacation activities on provided paper. Then have volunteers read their completed lists. Wonder aloud whether each student listed more indoor or outdoor activities. Guide students to realize that organizing the data would help them find out.

Next, post a two-row chart similar to the one shown. Label one row "Indoor" and one row "Outdoor." Ask each student to use *I* (indoor) and *O* (outdoor) to code her listed activities. Have her place a personalized sticky note on the chart to show which type of activity she listed more often. Then help students interpret the displayed data. For fun extension activities, have students use different categories to analyze their data.

adapted from an idea by Rhonda Cratty—Gr. 3, Sierra School, Arvada, CO

| Summer Activities | | | | |
|---|---|---|---|---|
| Indoor | Erin | Paul | Carlos | Kerry |
| Outdoor | Sam | Thomas | Pam | Mike |
| | Susie | Peter | Nate | |

## Get Acquainted!

**Topics**
family members
hobby
best memory
favorite animal
funniest memory
favorite place

What's the topic of this activity? Getting acquainted! Cover a cube-shaped box with light-colored paper and label one side for each topic shown. To begin, sit with students in a circle on the floor. Roll the cube. Then read the topic aloud and briefly respond to it. Have each student take a turn in a similar manner. To follow up, give each youngster a copy of page 302. Ask her to write and illustrate a response in each section. Display students' resulting introductions below the title "Meet [teacher's name]'s Class!"

adapted from an idea by VaReane Heese—Gr. 2, Springfield Elementary, Springfield, NE

## A Classy Book

Give each student a turn in the spotlight! To prepare, establish a "Student of the Day" schedule. On a child's designated day, invite her to show the class three items or pictures that are important to her and explain their significance. At the conclusion of the student's sharing time, title a sheet of giant writing paper with the youngster's name. Then have students help you write a summary of the presentation. Use metal rings to secure the paper between poster board covers and then title the resulting book "Our Class Directory." As other students are honored, insert their pages into the book in alphabetical order. Count on students to read this classy book again and again!

Deborah Patrick—Gr. 2, Park Forest Elementary, State College, PA

## Piece by Piece

This puzzle activity generates interest in the year ahead! In advance, write "grade" and the number of your grade level on a length of bulletin board paper. Decorate the resulting banner with words and simple illustrations related to upcoming activities or units. Then cut the banner into a class supply of puzzle-shaped pieces, plus a few extra for any late enrollees.

To begin, distribute the puzzle pieces and ask students to predict what the puzzle will spell. Then help the youngsters use pushpins to assemble the puzzle on a bulletin board. Invite students to tell what they think the assembled puzzle reveals about the year. Redirect and elaborate on their ideas as appropriate. Plenty of enthusiasm for school is sure to be the result!

Jeremy Engebretson—Gr. 3, Groveland Elementary, Wayzata, MN

## Very Busy Students

Here's an ongoing booklet project that helps students realize how much they do (and learn!) at school. On the first day of a full week of school, read aloud *The Very Hungry Caterpillar* by Eric Carle. Point out that the caterpillar's food-filled week helps him grow and change. Predict that with all that students will do at school, they'll grow and change too!

Next, each student staples five sheets of story paper inside a 9" x 12" construction paper folder. He titles his resulting booklet "The Very Busy [ordinal number] Grader." He uses a format similar to the one shown to complete a page each day. At the week's end, he takes the booklet home to share with his family. Repeat the activity periodically to track students' work and progress. Busy, busy students!

Rebekah A. Kreyling—Gr. 1, Our Redeemer Lutheran School, Fords, NJ

# Great Gift Ideas

These tokens of appreciation are perfect for recognizing volunteers, student teachers, and other special adults!

## All Aglow!

Warm hearts with candles that are as cute as can "bee"! To make one, vertically position a 3" x 8" strip of beeswax (available in arts-and-crafts stores) on a piece of waxed paper. Lay a four-inch length of candlewick across one end of the beeswax as shown. Press it in place. Roll up the beeswax from the end with the wick. Then press the loose end to secure it.

Use the pattern on page 307 to make a construction paper hive. Illustrate it with bees; then glue the hive to a larger piece of black construction paper. Trim the excess from the outer edges and make two vertical cuts in the black paper as shown. Thread a length of ribbon through the cuts and tie it to secure the candle. Embellish a homemade card with a desired message (page 307), and the gift will be ready to present!

Laurie Gibbons, Huntsville, AL

## Pen Posy

A pen is tucked into this desktop decoration! To begin, use dots of paint to decorate two identical construction paper blossoms. After the paint dries, tape one end of a chenille stem to the back of one blossom. Glue the blossoms together, paint side out. Place the stem atop an upside down pen (cap on) so that the blossom is slightly above the pen. Cut the stem above the pen cap and secure it with floral tape. Next, use a permanent marker to collect student signatures on a large terra-cotta flower pot. (Or, for an individual gift, have a student use paint to decorate a small flower pot.) Label the rim with the intended recipient's name. Place a snug-fitting piece of foam in the flower pot, stand the flower in it, and then glue Spanish moss on the foam. Too cute!

Gayle Lormand—Gr. 1
Richard Elementary, Church Point, LA

## Helping Hand

Here's a simple way to thank a volunteer. Purchase a light-colored oven mitt that is made with material that can be easily written on. Have each youngster sign the mitt with a permanent marker. Write the message shown on a decorative recipe card and attach it to the mitt with ribbon. How handy!

Cindy Barber
Fredonia, WI

Thanks for the helping hand!

Use the hive with "What's the Buzz?" on page 272 and "All Aglow!" on page 306.

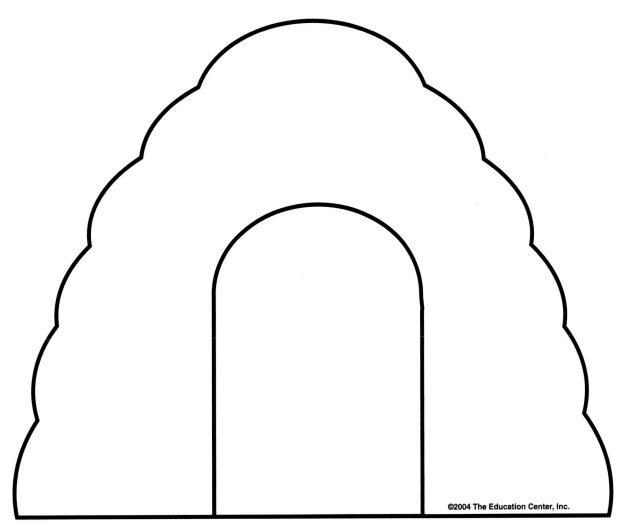

# A "Marble-ous" End!

**When it comes to closing out the school year, these activities aim to please!**

A is for the apple butter we made in September.

## The Year From A to Z

Here's a way for students to remember the school year to the letter. Assign a letter of the alphabet to each student, repeating letters and omitting less commonly used letters as appropriate. On a sheet of drawing paper, have him use the format shown to write about something that begins with his letter and is associated with the past school year. After each student illustrates his work, sequence the resulting pages alphabetically. Bind the pages into a class book titled "The ABCs of Grade [number]." Ask a student volunteer to decorate the front cover as desired. Add the book to your classroom library to keep students' memories rolling!

Cathy Belcher—Gr. 1, Ripley Elementary, Ripley, WV

## Memory Web

This class activity is bound to get students caught up in fond memories! Obtain a ball of yarn and sit with students in a circle. As you hold the ball, share with students a memory of a chosen school experience from the past year. Then gently toss the ball to a student, keeping hold of the yarn. After the youngster tells the class about one of her favorite school memories, have her toss the ball to a classmate as she keeps hold of the yarn. Continue in this manner until each student has shared a memory. Then cut the yarn so that each youngster has a length that is several inches long. With peer assistance, have her tie the yarn around her wrist to keep as a small memento.

Dana Sanders—Gr. 2, Hamilton Crossing Elementary
Cartersville, GA

ZOO

## Time to Meet!

Turn storytime into an opportunity for students to get acquainted with their teachers for next year. During the final weeks of school, arrange for each teacher in the next grade level to visit your classroom with a picture book of her choice. After introductions are made, invite her to tell your students something about herself and her classroom. Then have her read aloud her book selection. What a simple way to help students warm up to the teachers at the next grade level!

Shelly Lanier—Gr. 1, Reeds Elementary School, Lexington, NC

## Moving On

If your students are worried about moving to a new grade or classroom, try this literature-based idea. In Eric Carle's *A House for Hermit Crab,* a timid hermit crab confronts his fear of change when he moves into a bigger shell. After reading the book aloud, remind students of the crab's realization that his move results in exciting new decorating possibilities. Suggest that similarly, moving to a different classroom presents exciting new opportunities for students. Then, on a half sheet of paper, have each student write about what he is looking forward to in the coming school year.

To showcase his writing, the student adds desired crayon details to a white construction paper seashell that is approximately 5" x 5". He fashions several crab legs from red construction paper and glues them to his shell to resemble a crab that is entering its home. (See the illustration.) He glues the seashell on the top half of a vertically positioned 9" x 12" sheet of construction paper. After he embellishes the shell with glitter, sequins, or other decorating materials, he staples his writing below it. Then he presents his work for you to add to a display titled "Bright New Beginnings."

Thomas

I can't wait for third grade! I'm going to learn cursive. I will be on the same hallway as my big brother. I'll be able to join the soccer team too. Third grade will be great!

## Student Resumés

This confidence-boosting activity shows students that they make the grade! Comment that not only have students learned a lot this year, but they also have unique skills and interests that prospective teachers would undoubtedly like to know about. Suggest that a resumé would be a perfect tool for sharing the information since resumés tell about people's school and work experiences. Next, have each youngster use her best penmanship to fill out a copy of a grade-appropriate resumé form similar to the one shown. Post students' completed resumés on a hallway wall where each teacher in the next grade will see them. Title the display "Students for Hire" and encourage teachers to check out your youngsters' qualifications!

Ena Brunet—Gr. 1
Galliano Elementary, Galliano, LA

Name: _____

Goals for Second Grade: I want to learn _____
_____

**EDUCATION**
First-Grade Teacher: _____
Favorite Subject: _____
Skills: I'm good at _____

**ACTIVITIES**
Things I Like to Do: _____
_____
_____

**REFERENCE**
Someone Who Knows Me Well: _____

## Classy Books

No doubt your students are eager to tell youngsters in the previous grade what to expect next year. After all, they know the scoop! So why not have them share the information with this pride-boosting project? To begin, have your students brainstorm categories of information that they would like to share with students in the next lower grade. For example, have third graders brainstorm what they think second graders would appreciate knowing about third grade. List students' ideas on the board.

Next, divide students so that there is one group for each classroom in the previous grade. In each group, each student writes about a different listed topic and then illustrates her work. The group members compile their work and staple it between construction paper covers. Then they title and decorate the front cover of the resulting book. If desired, they mount a class photograph onto the inside back cover and write the caption "[Ordinal number] grade is a lot of fun!" before presenting the book to a designated class.

Alyssa Weller, South School, Glencoe, IL

## Recommended Reading

Use student-recommended book titles to spark interest in summer reading. Have each student submit to you the title of a book he thinks his classmates would enjoy. Then prepare a checklist that includes each different title and who recommended it. On the back of the paper, provide space for a student's name and reading goal. Also provide writing lines for additional titles and comments about a favorite book. Give each student a two-sided copy of the resulting reading contract and a stamped envelope addressed to you.

During the summer, a youngster reads books from the list or of his own choosing. He checks off or writes the title of each book that he reads. When he reaches his reading goal, he writes about his favorite selection. Then he mails his reading contract in the provided envelope and awaits a congratulatory note from you!

adapted from an idea by Carol Smith—Gr. 2
St. Paul School, Highland, IL

## A Happy Ending

With this gift idea, summer reading is in the bag! Enlist parents' help in collecting a class supply of gently used books. Purchase an inexpensive pair of sunglasses (reading glasses) for each student, and use tagboard strips and die-cuts or stickers to make bookmarks. For each student, place a book, a bookmark, and a pair of glasses in a large, bow-adorned, resealable plastic bag. As you present each youngster's gift, encourage her to have a "sun-sational" time reading this summer.

Julie Lewis—Gr. 2, J. O. Davis Elementary, Irving, TX

# Answer Keys

## Page 107

| | | | |
|---|---|---|---|
| 1 | 6 : 00 A.M.<br>Wake up. | 5 | 9 : 00 A.M.<br>Get dressed. |
| 4 | 8 : 30 A.M.<br>Listen to the<br>weather report. | 3 | 7 : 30 A.M.<br>Brush teeth. |
| 2 | 7 : 00 A.M.<br>Eat breakfast. | 8 | 11 : 30 A.M.<br>Look for a<br>shadow. |
| 6 | 9 : 30 A.M.<br>Comb fur. | 7 | 11 : 00 A.M.<br>Check the<br>calendar. |

Bonus Box: Responses will vary.

## Page 110

The following words should be circled.
1. pickles
2. crackers
3. salad
4. bread
5. grapes
6. banana
7. hamburger
8. table
9. play
10. food
11. cherries
12. cheese

## Page 122

The order of contractions may vary.
1. can't
2. aren't
3. they're
4. shouldn't
5. you're
6. it's
7. isn't
8. where's

a. it's
b. can't
c. They'll
d. Don't
e. won't
f. Let's
g. You'll
h. We're
i. shouldn't
j. we'll

Bonus Box: Answers will vary. Accept any reasonable responses.

## Page 128

Birds: girl, shirt, stir
Turtles: curl, fur, turn
Porcupines: corn, morning, storm
Sharks: barn, far, park
Otters: her, mother, reader

## Page 129

1. No Parking
2. Birdhouses
3. See the newborn bear cubs!
4. Trail starts here.
5. More Animals
6. Postcards sold here.
7. T-shirts for sale!
8. Zoo Store
9. Do not touch the bars of the cage.
10. Rain Forest

Bonus Box: *card* or *curd, dirt, short*

## Page 135

-an: can, pan, ran, tan
-ap: cap, lap, map, nap
-at: bat, hat, mat, sat

Bonus Box: Responses will vary.

## Page 143

Students should have marked the corrections shown. (The way in which they marked the corrections may vary according to the teacher's instructions.)
1. where does Mr. Beaver live?
2. Mr. Beaver and his wife, Betty, live in lakeville.
3. they live with their kids, Ben and bob.
4. Mr. Beaver is building a new house on river Road.
5. Are Ben and bob happy about moving?
6. ben helps Mr. Beaver every saturday.
7. He bought the wood from Mrs. forest in april.
8. Mr. Beaver wants to move in july.

## Page 153

A. 3, 1, 4, 2
B. 2, 4, 3, 1
C. 1, 4, 3, 2
D. 4, 2, 1, 3

Bonus Box: Leave the cabin. Walk on Raccoon Road to Pines Way. Turn onto Pines Way. Walk on Pines Way to the dining hall.

## Page 163

Answers will vary, but each student should have written one story detail for each part of María Isabel's name. Possible responses include the following:
María—This name is for her grandmother María. María Isabel's father cherishes a picture of her.
Isabel—This name is for María Isabel's sweet, smiling grandmother Chabela who lives in Puerto Rico. She saves money for María Isabel so that she can study one day.
Salazar—This name is for María Isabel's father and her grandfather Antonio.
López—This name is for her mother and for her grandfather Manuel, who told stories.

## Page 164

 3 A new friend takes María Isabel to the school library.

 1 On her first day of school, María Isabel trips and falls.

 5 Mrs. Salazar gives María Isabel a key to the apartment.

 2 María Isabel's teacher calls her Mary Lopez.

 8 María Isabel sings in the pageant.

 6 The teacher does not give María Isabel a part in the pageant.

 7 The Salazars visit the old neighborhood.

4 The librarian tells María Isabel to take a book.

## Page 178

Nouns—jar, Nikki, home, neighbors
Verbs—collects, teaches, shout, carries
Adjectives—orange, brown, happy, proud

Bonus Box: Answers will vary.

## Page 179

Suggested sentences are listed below.
1. Hungry apes ate apples.
2. Both boys blew big bubbles.
3. Little lambs leap over long logs.
4. Tiny trains travel on tracks.
5. Seven silly seals sleep.
6. Five flies flew from the fields.
7. Don's dogs dig in the dirt.
8. Cute cats climb on the couch.

Bonus Box: Answers will vary.

**Page 186**

1. P
2. C
3. S
4. A
5. P
6. S
7. A
8. S
9. C
10. S

Bonus Box: Answers will vary.
Accept any reasonable responses.

**Page 187**

1. turtles
2. teakettle
3. sun
4. fish
5. bucket
6. whale
7. dogs
8. feathers
9. fireflies
10. crows

**Page 193**

| | | |
|---|---|---|
| 1. The mouse makes a soft nest. | 2. The mice scurry under the clock. | 3. A lonely boy hears the mouse talk. |
| 4. During the winter, the mouse lives indoors. | 5. The noise scares away the mouse. | 6. A mouse learns how to talk by watching TV. |
| 7. The mouse wears a crash helmet. | 8. All of the mice want to ride the motorcycle. | 9. The hungry mouse nibbles its food. |
| 10. The mouse fixes its motorcycle. | 11. Several mice live in the hotel. | 12. When it is warm, some mice go outside. |

(circled numbers: 1, 2, 4, 5, 9, 11, 12)

Bonus Box: Responses will vary.

**Page 194**

Answers will vary. Possible responses are provided.

1. Yes. Ryan puts Ralph in his pocket when the mouse is scared. He doesn't let his teacher put Ralph in a cage. He doesn't let Ralph ride his motorcycle at the school because he doesn't want the mouse to become lost or get in trouble.
2. Ryan and Brad are lonely, and they are both interested in cars and motorcycles. Unlike most people, they can hear Ralph.
3. Ralph learns that people should speak one at a time and take turns.
4. Possible examples include the following: Ralph leaves the inn because he thinks he might cause Matt to lose his job. Matt protects Ralph by not telling the manager about him. Ryan tries to keep Ralph safe. Brad gives a toy car to Ralph.

**Page 199**

Estimates will vary. Actual lengths are listed below.

a. 3
b. 2
c. 4
d. 3

1. Curly
2. Penny
3. 7
4. 8

Bonus Box: Answers will vary. Accept reasonable responses.

**Page 200**

1. 3 + 4 + 3 + 4 = 14 cm
2. 4 + 9 + 4 + 9 = 26 cm
3. 5 + 5 + 5 + 5 = 20 cm
4. 3 + 6 + 3 + 6 = 18 cm
5. 3 + 7 + 3 + 7 = 20 cm
6. 2 + 5 + 2 + 5 = 14 cm

Bonus Box: The drawing should be 4 x 6 centimeters.
Perimeter = 20 centimeters

312

**Page 203**

1–4. Colors will vary, but patterns should match those provided.

a. 1, 2, 1, 2, 1, 2, 1, 2, 1, 2
b. 3, 5, 7, 3, 5, 7, 3, 5, 7, 3, 5, 7
c. 4, 4, 6, 4, 4, 6, 4, 4, 6, 4, 4, 6
d. 2, 4, 4, 2, 4, 4, 2, 4, 4, 2, 4, 4
e. 3, 5, 3, 3, 5, 3, 3, 5, 3, 3, 5, 3
f. 1, 2, 2, 3, 1, 2, 2, 3, 1, 2, 2, 3, 1, 2, 2, 3

Bonus Box: The student should have illustrated a sock that has stripes in an ABCC pattern.

**Page 206**

1. $30 + $10 = $40; $44
2. $20 + $60 = $80; $79
3. $70 + $20 = $90; $94
4. $20 + $50 = $70; $67
5. $10 + $40 = $50; $51
6. $10 + $50 = $60; $59

Bonus Box: $50 + $10 = $60

**Page 217**

a. 3 groups of 4 = 12; 3 x 4 = 12
b. 1 group of 6 = 6; 1 x 6 = 6
c. 5 groups of 5 = 25; 5 x 5 = 25
d. 3 groups of 8 = 24; 3 x 8 = 24
e. 6 groups of 3 = 18; 6 x 3 = 18
f. 3 groups of 7 = 21; 3 x 7 = 21
g. 2 x 2 = 4
h. 4 x 2 = 8
i. 3 x 3 = 9

Bonus Box: Responses will vary. Each student should have drawn another candy bar and written a multiplication sentence for the array.

**Page 224**

A. 2 x 6 = 12
   12 ÷ 2 = 6
B. 10 x 3 = 30
   30 ÷ 10 = 3
C. 5 x 3 = 15
   15 ÷ 5 = 3
D. 5 x 9 = 45
   45 ÷ 5 = 9
E. 6 x 4 = 24
   24 ÷ 6 = 4
F. 4 x 9 = 36
   36 ÷ 4 = 9

G. 6 x 7 = 42
   42 ÷ 6 = 7
H. 7 x 8 = 56
   56 ÷ 7 = 8
I. 3 x 9 = 27
   27 ÷ 3 = 9
J. 5 x 6 = 30
   30 ÷ 5 = 6
K. 8 x 9 = 72
   72 ÷ 9 = 8

Bonus Box: Responses will vary.

**Page 229**

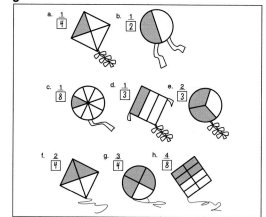

## Page 245

1. B
2. B
3. M
4. B
5. C
6. C
7. B
8. B
9. M
10. C
   a. Answers will vary. Accept any reasonable responses.
   b. Answers will vary. Accept any reasonable responses.

## Page 246

A. polar
B. black
C. grizzly

## Page 253

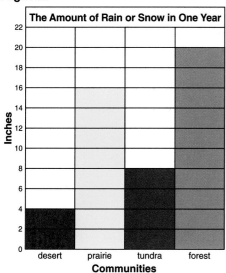

The Amount of Rain or Snow in One Year

1. desert, tundra
2. prairie, forest
3. desert
4. forest

## Page 254

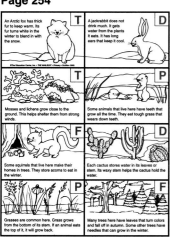

## Page 261

1. stem
2. leaf
3. roots
4. pistil
5. stamens
6. petals

These boxes should be outlined as indicated:
• pistil (green)
• stamens (yellow)

## Page 276

Answers will vary. Possible answers are shown.

1. angry (red)
2. happy (pink)
3. jealous (green)
4. sad (blue)
5. happy (pink)
6. jealous (green)
7. sad (blue)
8. angry (red)

Bonus Box: Answers will vary. Accept any reasonable responses.

## Page 277

A. $2 + 7 = 9$, $7 + 2 = 9$, $9 - 2 = 7$, $9 - 7 = 2$
B. $4 + 5 = 9$, $5 + 4 = 9$, $9 - 4 = 5$, $9 - 5 = 4$
C. $3 + 8 = 11$, $8 + 3 = 11$, $11 - 3 = 8$, $11 - 8 = 3$
D. $4 + 6 = 10$, $6 + 4 = 10$, $10 - 4 = 6$, $10 - 6 = 4$
E. $4 + 7 = 11$, $7 + 4 = 11$, $11 - 4 = 7$, $11 - 7 = 4$
F. $3 + 9 = 12$, $9 + 3 = 12$, $12 - 3 = 9$, $12 - 9 = 3$

Bonus Box: $6 + 9 = 15$, $9 + 6 = 15$, $15 - 6 = 9$, $15 - 9 = 6$; or $3 + 6 = 9$, $6 + 3 = 9$, $9 - 3 = 6$, $9 - 6 = 3$

## Page 279

(Answers are based on a 2004 calendar.)

1. Sunday
2. Thursday
3. February 16
4. one quarter, two pennies
5. two quarters, one penny
6. three quarters
7. one quarter, three pennies
8. two quarters, three pennies

## Page 280

Possible pattern block combinations are shown below.

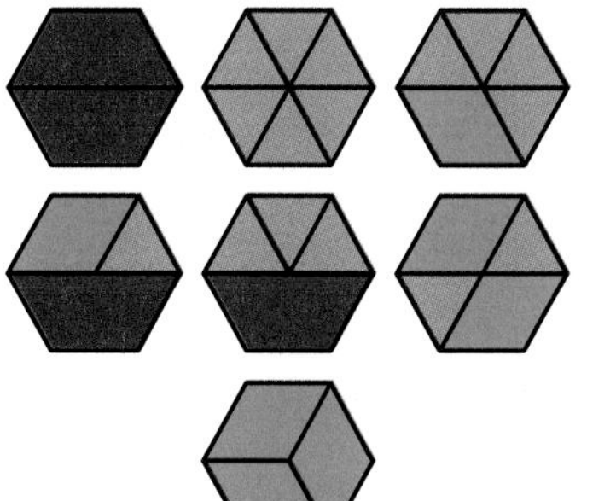

## Page 281

1. barn
2. field
3. orchard
4. field
5. south
6. north
7. north
8. west

## Page 282

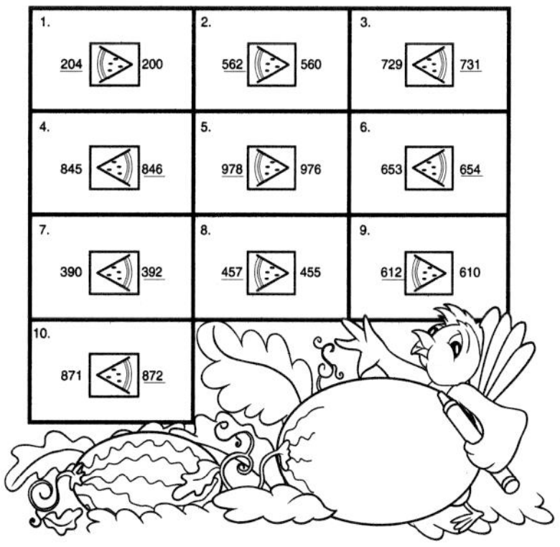

1. 204 200
2. 562 560
3. 729 731
4. 845 846
5. 978 976
6. 653 654
7. 390 392
8. 457 455
9. 612 610
10. 871 872

## Page 300

A. Dome Mountain
B. Fold Mountain
C. Block Mountain
D. Volcanic Mountain

# Index